THE BEST OF STILLMEADOW:

A Treasury of Country Living

Gladys Taber

Edited and with an introduction by
CONSTANCE TABER COLBY

Drawings by
EDWARD SHENTON

G.K.HALL &CO.

 Boston, Massachusetts

1977

Library of Congress Cataloging in Publication Data

Taber, Gladys Bagg, 1899-
The best of Stillmeadow.

Selections from the author's Harvest at Stillmeadow,
The book of Stillmeadow, Stillmeadow seasons, Stillmeadow
daybook, Stillmeadow sampler, Stillmeadow road, and
Stillmeadow calender.
Large print ed.
1. Country life—Connecticut. 2. Taber, Gladys Bagg,
1899- —Homes and haunts—Connecticut. 3. Authors,
American—20th century—Biography. 4. Sight-saving
books. I. Title. II. Title: Stillmeadow.
[S521.5.C8T28 1977] 974.6 76-55760
ISBN 0-8161-6449-5

Published in Large Print by arrangement with J.B.
Lippincott Company, Philadelphia and New York

Set in Compugraphic 18 pt English Times

THE BEST OF
STILLMEADOW

Introduction

Years ago, when bittersweet still grew along the roadsides in our part of Connecticut and the quiet hills had not yet been slashed by the expressway, an aged car slowly made its way through a February sleet storm. In the back seat, walled in by suitcases, grocery cartons and shopping bags, three chilly, fretful children alternately sulked and complained.

The oldest was myself, aged ten. The other two were Barbara, who was eight, and her brother, David, who was, as he said, five years and four and a half months.

In the front seat, the two mothers maintained a tight-lipped silence. Tucked into various corners of the car, four cocker spaniels dozed peacefully. Only one thing mattered to them — they had not been left behind in New York.

Ordinarily the trip from the city should have taken about four hours (nowadays we make it in less than two), but we had already been on the road for seven. My stomach was aching and I felt like throwing up. Barbara, who was the dramatic one, had developed a sore throat that clearly meant a fatal case of flu. We would all catch it too, she reminded us. David had been sitting on the butter — a large chunk wrapped only in paper — for the entire trip and had just found this out.

As we turned down Jeremy Swamp Road, the grey sleet was like a curtain. A large brown oak leaf blew against the side window and stuck.

"Dead man's hand," I told David, and he began to whimper.

"Mother!" said Barbara. "Connie's upsetting David!"

"Now, that's enough!" said my own mother in a tone she didn't use very often.

The three of us subsided and stared grimly into space. Nobody cared about us, that was plain.

We were not actually related, but we were, as we got tired of explaining to our friends, *practically* cousins. Or at least our mothers were practically sisters, having grown up together. And now we too were destined to grow up together, it seemed, for our mothers had combined forces to buy an old farmhouse in a forsaken corner of wilderness, where we three would have to spend all our weekends and vacations for the rest of our lives.

In New York, we went to different schools and, since we were of different ages, saw very little of one another outside of school. But this country-home business would change all that.

"It will be ideal for the children," we had heard the grown-ups saying. "Fresh

3

air. Plenty of room for running. Sunshine."

Sunshine! The countryside looked absolutely drowned. And as for running, who cared about that? The cockers, maybe, but certainly not the three of us. The air was fresh all right. It smelled of fresh mud and fresh drifts of sodden leaves.

"Well," said Jill, "here we are."

"Everybody out," said my mother.

The cockers obeyed instantly.

"Catch them!" screamed my mother. "They don't know where they are!"

"David! What in Heaven's name has happened to your pants?" Jill said in dismay.

The rest of the weekend lived up to the beginning. The old house was musty and cold, and Jill never could get the stove working properly. Barbara, David and I didn't like any of the food my mother had brought along, except for the peanut butter. And since in those days children did not go outside in rainy weather, unless it was for something inescapable such as school or the dentist, we sat around indoors and quarreled.

The two mothers, however, were radiant. Bundled up in paint-stained sweaters and old corduroy pants, they flung themselves with passionate energy into the job of reclaiming and restoring the old farmhouse. There was more than enough to keep them busy, too — the place had been abandoned for years and even we children could see that it was in terrible shape. Looking back on it now. I wonder why we weren't dragooned into doing at least a few useful chores. Perhaps that seemed more bother than it was worth.

The cockers had a marvelous weekend. This place was quite unlike the city apartments they had known before. There were stairs to dash up and down and windows low enough to peer out of. And the walls were full of field mice, which a clever spaniel surely ought to be able to catch, with a little patience. Best of all, every so often you could go out (on a leash, but never mind) and investigate all that glorious mud.

As we were loading the car for the return trek to the city, the clouds suddenly broke and the sun came out.

"If only we didn't have to leave!" said my mother.

And that was how it all began.

Now that we are grown, Barbara and David and I sometimes talk about the old days. The good old days, we now realize. And as our own children have explored the same woods and fallen happily in the brook and brought home lovely bouquets of daisies and ragweed, we know how lucky we all are to have Stillmeadow.

"I took Jimmy up in the woods this morning." says David, who is now six feet tall and a doctor, "to show him where you girls had your secret places. So many brambles, we couldn't get to your ledge, Barbara, but we saw a red squirrel on that little knoll of yours, Connie. It looks just the same."

The secret places! Which were secret only from parents, though we children kept up the pretense of not knowing where they were either. We loved them despite the fact that even in those days they were full of thistles and thorn bushes and you often brought home a case of poison ivy.

6

Last winter, when my oldest daughter Alice developed those unmistakable blisters on Christmas morning, having apparently brushed against a twig in the snow while she was sledding, I felt that she was right in the family tradition. The druggist was stunned, however. Not many people ask for poison-ivy lotion in December.

Then there was the secret mailbox in the hollow of the ancient apple tree, where Barbara and I used to leave messages for each other. Recently Alice discovered some of these in the attic — tiny folded squares written in a minuscule hand. "Meet me at the usyooal place !!! 6 oclock sharp! DO NOT TELL DAVID."

And the attic itself, which was, and is, everything an attic should be, with trunks of funny old clothes and packets of faded letters. ("Dearest Girl, I miss you so much." Who in the world could Dearest Girl be? Impossible to believe that it might be my own mother.) And, of course, wasps.

Then there were the bloodstains on the floor of the back bedroom. Someone had been killed in that room, long ago. We shivered at the thought and hoped for ghosts. But the only figure to haunt the room was David, who tiptoed in every night, just in case. I notice that the magic is still there. Last Halloween my youngest daughter, Anne, invited some school friends for the weekend. And even though these worldly thirteen-year-olds laughed at the very idea of ghosts, they planned to spend the night on sleeping bags in the back bedroom and see if anything happened.

"Kind of a scientific experiment," Anne explained.

In the morning my husband found them strewn about on the floor of living room.

"Couldn't get to sleep up there," they reported. "The room was too hot."

In fact, I had forgotten to turn on the radiator and the windowpane was iced — on the *inside*.

Those early years at Stillmeadow had other benefits. Often, when Barbara, David and I get together, we reminisce about the food we used to have when we were children. Nothing since has ever tasted quite as good as those early peas or the tiny new potatoes or my mother's strawberry shortcake. Still, there was another side to the picture. As far as we were concerned, the garden was a mixed blessing. It seemed to us that the adults spent most of their waking hours either working in it or coping with its products. (Come to think of it, this was undoubtedly true at certain times of the year.) They talked about it a lot, too. When neighbors came for dinner, the conversation seemed to center entirely on whether the corn was up yet or how the weather was affecting the beans. People even called each other up to compare notes on how the squash was getting along.

And speaking of squash, Barbara, David and I were somewhat less than enthusiastic about many of the prizes that Jill and my mother so proudly gathered. For in addition to all that horrible squash, we had turnips and rutabagas and huge onions and all sorts of unfamiliar salad greens with bitter-tasting leaves.

What is more, when any vegetable came in (as the saying went), it came in with a vengeance. You might be able to survive a single turnip, once or even twice a year, but a bushel basket of them, all needing to be eaten or canned immediately, before they got one day older, was a dismaying prospect. It was a basketful loaded with vitamins, no doubt, and was the result of many hours of hard work (some of them our own), but even so. . . .

Of course, if the choice had been up to us, we would have raised nothing but sweet corn and watermelon, with perhaps a few pumpkins for Halloween.

The last time we talked about all this, Barbara, who is a specialist in adult education and given to speculating about such matters, commented that one thing our childhood gave us was plenty of social living. Nowadays when we hear so much about the importance of young people's having what is called a group experience, we can reflect that we ourselves certainly had it at Stillmeadow. At one point there were as many as thirty-five strong-willed, bouncing cockers in the group, to say nothing of two highly emotional Irish setters and a couple of opinionated cats.

Nobody could ask for a better chance to practice interpersonal relationships!

During the early years, to be sure, the household at Stillmeadow was not so large. In the beginning, it consisted of two women, three children and only four dogs.

Jill's husband was a busy New York doctor who could seldom get away from his practice. Besides, he was a city man at heart, with little interest in the country. He approved of it for his family, however, and every so often came up himself to see how things were going and to shake his head in amazement at the sight of his wife scraping woodwork or kneeling among the tomato plants.

My own father, on the other hand, loved the place. He was a teacher in New York, dedicated and devoted but so underpaid that he usually had to have at least two jobs simultaneously. But he spent as much time in Connecticut as he could. His great loves were growing flowers and restoring antiques. He has been gone for many years now, but the spindly rose bushes that he nursed so tenderly have taken over the border, and in the house every room is graced with a chair or clock or sea chest which he brought back to life. He appears very little in the written record of Stillmeadow because he was a very private man who did not like to see himself in print.

For many years, we came to Stillmeadow only on weekends and holidays. But after both husbands died and the children went off to college, Jill and Gladys moved to the country for good. Here the four original cockers were joined by a succession of spaniel puppies, as well as the Irish setters and the cats.

The human family grew too. Barbara was the first to get married, and it was a great relief to the rest of us when, after a series of stormy romances, she ended up with Val, who was then in law school. I remember clearly his first visit to Stillmeadow. With his old pipe, and a corduroy jacket almost as comfortably weathered as Jill's, he settled down in front of the fire as if he were coming home. Before he left, the broken leg on the little milking stool was repaired, the carving knife was sharpened and our long-forgotten chess set was once again established on a corner table.

Their two children, Ellen and Davy (so called to distinguish him from his Uncle David), also delighted everyone. Even as babies they were gentle with the dogs and never broke anything. Later, they figured out for themselves how to work the old-fashioned door latches and asked long, complicated questions that were as challenging as crossword puzzles. Now they are both in college, where I daresay they are still asking that sort of question.

David was next. He met Anne at college, and when he first brought her home — a tall, slender girl with long hair and grey-blue eyes — she said very little and seemed withdrawn, or perhaps only shy. But when David found an unusual turtle down by the pond, Anne changed completely.

"That's a painted turtle," she said at once. "And it's a male — you can see how the plastrum is shaped." She turned him gently in her hands. "But it's too early for him to be wandering around like this. Wonder why he isn't still hibernating.

Maybe he should stay indoors for a few weeks until it gets warmer." She sounded just like Jill talking about some problem with one of the dogs: calm, quiet, professional but concerned.

The turtle went back with them in a basket, thus becoming the first in a long line of orphaned or injured reptiles, birds, woodchucks and other creatures which have found temporary refuge with David and Anne in their big house in Princeton. They also have an extraordinary collection of house pets. But when they come to Stillmeadow, they arrange for an animal sitter and bring only their three children: Jimmy, now a leggy teenager with his father's sense of humor and his mother's interest in wildlife; Betsy, brilliantly intense about everything she does, from riding her bicycle to studying algebra; and little Amy, who is, according to my mother, an elf child.

Then my turn came. When Curtis and I met, he was working at a publishing company, and the very first time he came to Stillmeadow he and my mother sat up half the night discussing the latest fiction.

I think they polished off music as well. When Jill and I weakly said goodnight to them at one thirty or thereabouts, they scarcely even noticed. But the next morning Curt was the first one up and had already started pancakes when the rest of us crept forth. Later in the day Jill discovered that he had backpacked through the Sierras several times and could not only split a log but also broil a steak. And when Linda, the small black cocker who viewed all strangers with profound distrust, suddenly took it into her head to climb into Curt's lap, there was no question but that the entire family had been won over.

We were married in the white church in the village and afterwards our friends came back to Stillmeadow for turkey and ham in front of the fire. Then we left for a few days on Cape Cod before returning to New York.

Our own two children, Alice (called Muffin by her grandma) and Anne, completed the family circle. Like their older cousins — well, not cousins but practically — they moved quietly in the old house, played gently with the dogs and cats and mourned when they had to leave for the city.

Now, at sixteen and thirteen, they spend a good deal of time browsing through the books their grandmother has written about Stillmeadow. "Aren't we lucky," says Anne, "that Gram likes to write."

Over the years my mother had always kept a sort of diary, a day-by-day account of the weather, ideas and people that made up life at Stillmeadow. Tucked inside was a bulging assortment of recipes and garden lists and reminders about dog shows. Finally, when the collection became unmanageable, it occurred to her to try using some of it for an article about country living. She had been writing fiction for some time — whenever she wasn't busy with meals and children and puppies — but this was her first attempt at an article. To her surprise, it was accepted immediately. She tried a second and it was taken by the same magazine. Before long she was writing a monthly column, with all the news about birds, dogs, visitors and the changing seasons. Jill clipped the columns as they appeared and pasted them into a rapidly thickening scrapbook. So did a lot of people, according to the letters that began to come in. "You know, Gladys," Jill said one evening, "you really ought to make a book out of all this." And so the first Stillmeadow book came into being.

That first book has been followed by many others, recording the changes that have taken place over the years. There was the time when most of the apple trees were flattened by a hurricane. Then one winter the old barn burned down. Puppies came and went and so did people. Of course, someone who had read only the latest book would not know about all this. In time it became clear that a collection of excerpts from the early books (now very hard to find) was needed. Since Gladys herself was busy working on a new book, I offered to look through the first seven in the series, select the high points and put them together in a single volume.

This book is the result.

— Constance Taber Colby

This collection has been taken from:

Harvest at Stillmeadow, Little, Brown and
  Company, 1940
The Book of Stillmeadow, Macrae Smith
  Company, 1948
Stillmeadow Seasons, Macrae Smith
  Company, 1950
Stillmeadow Daybook, J. B. Lippincott
  Company, 1955
Stillmeadow Sampler, J. B. Lippincott
  Company, 1959
Stillmeadow Road, J. B. Lippincott
  Company, 1962
Stillmeadow Calendar, J. B. Lippincott
  Company, 1967

Foreword

And so we bought Stillmeadow.

Although Jill always said Stillmeadow bought us.

We lived in New York City. I was raising my daughter in a sixth-floor apartment about the size of a station wagon. It had what I called a sometime elevator, for it did run sometimes. The windows looked out on an air shaft, and people kept throwing bottles from adjacent apartments. They all, I thought, lived on cabbage. I didn't smell it so much in my own kitchen because the gas stove leaked and I smelled gas.

I was working for my Ph.D. at Columbia and at the same time trying to learn how to write. My husband had two teaching jobs and also, since our budget was very shaky, did tutoring on the side.

Then, since life was insupportable for me without a dog, I got Dark Star, a small, temperamental black cocker. She had to be "taken out" four times a day and she was terrified of traffic, policemen and all the dogs in the neighborhood. She also hated elevators and would never put paw on the stairs but expected to be carried. I also had two wild kittens who were born free at the animal shelter and kept swooping through the air.

Jill had no cat. She lived around the corner on a nice wide avenue jammed with trucks and buses. I considered that she lived in the traditional lap of luxury, for she had daylight in her apartment all day. She had a small son and a daughter and two black-and-white cockers. Sister was all a cocker should be, gay and loving and adorable, but she had a minor fault. When left alone, she ate pieces of the kitchen linoleum and the arms of the best dining-room chairs. In those days of our innocence, we had bought her a lovely wicker dog bed, which she also ate. Blue Waters Ripplemark was almost too good to be real. He was, at four months, already a gentleman and stuffed with virtue.

Jill had a full-time career as an administrator in one of the city departments and a husband who was a distinguished and very busy doctor. There were many weekends when he practically lived at the hospital. Since my own husband also had very little free time, Jill and I took to combining children and cockers for weekend outings.

We had been doing things together ever since we could remember. In fact, I think many people simply assumed that we were sisters. We had grown up as next-door neighbors, lived in the same cabin at summer camp, and spent four magic years as roommates at college. When, after we married, we both wound up in New York, it was only natural that we would settle in the same neighborhood. My own apartment was on a different street, though, and that put it in a very different world. But at least it was easy for the two families to get together.

It was a busy life, or so we thought then. There were times later on when we felt the old life was sheer idleness.

During this era we went to our first dog show, just to see what a dog show was like. We also bought another parti-colored cocker, Sweet Clover, because she insisted on it.

"After all, four dogs are as easy as three," said Jill.

The kittens had been turned over to someone else because I had to have the windows open now and then, and flying cats are no help. So it wasn't very crowded. The main problem was that Star never did get leash-trained and wound me up like a Maypole when we went out, leaving Clover off at an angle where people kept running into her.

On Saturdays we used to take the children and cockers to City Island, then a lonely dirty piece of shore lapped by doubtful water. Jill acted as a sheep dog herding the flock while I sat on a rock.

"What we need," said Jill one day as we breasted the traffic back to the brawling, roaring, fume-ridden city, "what we need is a place in the country. Fresh air," she added, coughing as a truck ground past. "We could put up tents and spend lovely summer weekends."

"And the children could play in the brook," I said. "And think of all the money we would save."

This was a remarkable statement to which we referred often in subsequent times.

"I could raise fresh vegetables and fruit," said Jill, avoiding one of those freight cars on wheels that abound in the city.

We felt very sensible at the moment. All we needed was a small piece of land with apple trees and a brook. It was as good as done, I thought, lugging Star up the stairs and hoisting Connie while Clover toiled along behind. "Tenting on the old campground," I hummed.

We were on our way.

But after some weeks we discovered that land cost more money than we dreamed of ever having. And the price of tents and camping equipment seemed to put them in the class for millionaires, who wouldn't need them anyway. We also figured out, belatedly, that we would have to have water and some sanitation even while tenting. We must dig a well, have a septic tank.

"We'll have to go farther out," said

Jill, "and look for an old beat-up house, an abandoned farm. Or just a barn. I could do it over, weekends."

I consulted all the magazines and found out that for ten thousand dollars we could do over a barn and make a charming home of it. All we would have to do would be to add plumbing, floors, windows, a new roof, fireplaces, etc., etc., etc. And dig a well. Put in septic tank. Afterward you furnished such a home with priceless antiques from your aunt's attic. We had neither aunts with attics nor any attics at all.

At this point, when sensible women would have given the whole thing up, we started hunting for an old house. We looked at houses in which you had to be wary or you fell into the cellar. Houses with plaster falling in chunks. A house with a dead pig on the parlor sofa. It had no front steps, so you went in through the woodshed, bothering the rats no end.

Also at houses which were very cheap at thirty or at forty thousand dollars, which in those days were staggering sums. Frank and I had no extra money at all, and even at Jill's house most of the family income was already budgeted for private schools and rent and so on.

I gave up. But Jill never stopped cutting out ads from the Sunday paper for more places to look at. There was very little of New Jersey and Connecticut we did not traverse. We got to know that a country road meant a teeth-knocking challenge. And Jill developed an aversion to hard-boiled eggs and sandwiches which she never fully overcame.

I saw that we would be aging in subways forever, and the children would grow up with never a breath of cool country air. A museum full of dead things or a zoo full of caged animals, I said morosely, was their destiny.

It was February, I think, after we had hunted hopelessly for over two years, that we decided to take Rip to the Eastern States dog show.

"May as well see how good he is," observed Jill's husband.

We drove off in a blizzard in my worn-out car with no heater. We had Rip tucked up in blankets and with a hot-water bottle. We ourselves just got numb.

"We're early," said Jill. "Let's stop and look at this place listed in last Sunday's *Times*." She added, "We can warm up at the agent's house."

The agent had not expected anyone so foolhardy as to look at houses in such weather. In fact, he got stuck and spent his time shoveling out while we waded through snow and ice to see the house.

There it stood, half-buried in snow: a small white farmhouse tucked under huge maples. Built in 1690 or a bit earlier, it had withstood the years. It even had plumbing, and how were we to know it was all cracked? It had floors pegged with square hand-cut nails. It had fireplaces. Twelve-by-eight windows, some with the old bubbly glass panes.

It had some furniture — tables with broken legs, chests that sagged sadly, an old iron cookstove. It had, also, a well house. And a frozen brook. And forty acres of land.

So we came home. We paid a deposit that made our bank balances sigh into oblivion.

We hardly noticed the sleet storm as we drove back to the city that day. Rip had not won — he was too carsick to show well — but we didn't mind at all.

The windshield wiper gave out and Jill hopped in and out scraping the sleet from the windshield. The hot-water bottle was cold and Rip melted down my neck as I snuggled him. But we were so busy wallpapering the house (won't take any time at all, said Jill) that we hardly noticed we were the only car on the road. We were in a tranced state, no doubt of it.

For the house was a wonderful bargain. It was not only on a dead-end road (which for years never got plowed in winter) but had to be sold to settle an estate. The previous owner had shot his wife and killed himself.

"But they were such nice people," said the agent. "It isn't as if they were just ordinary people who murdered; they were just lovely."

The ghosts have never bothered us. I used to listen for their voices on still summer nights. They had loved our house, that I knew. And I felt they were happy because we were giving it life again.

In any case, nothing could have discouraged us.

"Think of Christmas in the country," I said. "Yule log burning in the great fireplace, cutting our own tree, the children sliding downhill in clean fresh snow. We can have winter weekends, since there is a furnace."

The furnace was broken but we didn't know it. It had kind of rusted away, we were told afterward.

We also did not know how hard it is to manage a Yule log with a dull ax. In fact, there were many things we did not know. Even if we had, I think we would have gone ahead just as recklessly.

Because we heard the house say, "I've been waiting for you. What took you so long?"

Our basic equipment for this venture consisted of a staggering fortitude and no common sense. But we didn't know it then. We came out the next weekend and paid some more money. By then most of the furniture had vanished, except three carders and five spinning wheels, and one rope bed which had been too big for moving out quickly.

High-hearted, we advanced. We bought tons of wallpaper, and it turned out to be tons, since we had never papered before and so were uncertain about quantities. For years we gave away wallpaper. I sent for some furniture stored in Virginia, and three weeks later a disturbed Kentucky racehorse arrived while the furniture rode along to some racetrack. It takes time to swap a horse for your furniture. But by then we had discovered the fatal truth about every sink, toilet and tub in the house.

"Well, one could not expect a man to drain the pipes before shooting his wife," said Jill. "He didn't think of it."

We had to borrow money. But once we got in shape, we said, we would really save money. This day has yet to come, but it might. *Good, Did well*

We took ten days of vacation, so-called, in which we cleaned and scoured and got a back door built, and wallpapered and found a mason to repair the chimney and a neighbor who would help scrub the woodwork.

The front bedroom leaked. The pump didn't pump water. Just air.

We found that wallpapering was quite a job for women who had no manual skills. Wallpaper has a fiendish way of falling on you and winding you up in paste. The paint did not dry on the upstairs hall either.

But at the end of ten days of hard labor we had accomplished a good deal. We had also gone further in debt to get the pump pumping and the furnace going. We put a pan under the leak in the front bedroom. And went in to bring the children out to the dream house. Also the four cockers and some more furnishings. It was, we felt, a triumphal tour.

And the fact that it was still winter we hardly noticed. Most people, we afterward learned, buy country houses when the lilacs are in bloom and not when they are up to their knees in snow.

That was a highly unsuccessful weekend. There were not enough blankets and the stove kept going out. However, Jill and I were undaunted. This was a house in the country and never mind if we scraped snow from the windowsills every morning. We were finally under our own roof, though of course it was leaking. And the furnace was working. Jill went down every hour to throw on more coal. It was very warm in the middle of the house, but around the edges it was pretty chilly.

After the children had gone to bed, we sat by the fire and had one of the few moments of relaxation we were to know for years.

"Isn't it wonderful?" Jill poked the fire.

"You are sure the furnace won't blow up in the night?" I asked.

"No, it won't," she said.

"And once we pay the mason and the furnace man and the man who is going to fix the roof," I said, "we can really begin to save money."

"I'm going to put in a garden in May," Jill said.

"Do you know anything about growing vegetables?"

"I can learn," said Jill.

So this was the way it began.

This much has been told to friends as we sat by the fire popping corn and eating

31

wine-sweet apples. And every now and then, one of the children says, "Tell how we got Stillmeadow."

And I do.

On later weekends we worked twelve to sixteen hours a day. We scrubbed and hammered and scraped. As Jill remarked, college had not prepared us to do any of these things. But we learned.

And we loved it. The sense of achievement I had when I painted my first floor, and painted myself into a corner and hopped out on a board, was terrific. And the first old highboy we scraped and sanded and waxed and polished was a better thing to us than any mink coat. For we had earned it by our own hard labor.

Jill had wonderful ideas about supplementing our income with everything from asparagus to goats, but nothing ever came of these schemes. For instance, the old orchards with their sweet apples. We found that the cost of spraying them six times a year was prohibitive. So we gathered the windfalls and made applesauce.

Marketing seasonal crops is a big business too, we found when we had too much asparagus.

We read bulletins about everything from goats to geese, honeybees to hens. But our subsistence farming, in the end, extended only to raising enough vegetables to feed the family, including canning and freezing enough for all winter. For fruit we have had wild raspberries and strawberries, currants and a few blueberries, wild cranberries and the windfall apples. We tried hens, and gave them up as being a luxury. It cost us more to feed the hens and take care of them than we could realize from them.

In moments of real desperation, we called the neighbors across the road. There were three boys, Frank, George and William. And sometimes now we wonder whether we could have managed our project at all except for them. Frank plowed, mowed, chopped logs, fixed wiring, moved the immovable rocks until he married and moved away. Then William took over, and when he went away to school, George stayed home to run the family farm and to help us in his off hours to keep Stillmeadow from falling apart.

Now, when people ask me what I consider absolutely essential to country subsistence living, I say, "Somebody across the road like George and William."

When the "electric" goes off, I move to the fence and begin to yell, "George! George!" When the grass catches fire after Jill has been burning weeds, we say, "Run for George." When the sink is frozen, I say, "Better find George."

When the car won't run, we just wait for William, who now has his own house, just down the road.

When the lawn-mower motor dies, we wheel the giant over to wait for William to come home.

And when we are snowed in, George digs us out.

Of course, we didn't have forethought enough to investigate the neighbors ahead of time. We just moved in and there they were.

We had a really good barn, large enough to become a kennel for the increasing bevy of cockers. Rip and Sister and Star and Clover were happy in the house, and then we thought puppies would be wonderful. Puppies are. Sometime later we counted thirty-five cockers on our place. We bred and raised many, and always kept the ones we just couldn't part with. The idea was that the cockers would help with that last payment on the mortgage, but it didn't work out quite that way. It turned out that we worked harder to support the ones we just had to keep because we loved them so much. As a commercial kennel we were an absolute flop.

Of course we couldn't sell Linda or Snow In Summer or Saxon, although once, when we were at our lowest financial ebb, someone offered us any sum at all for Saxon — anything. I simply retired to my bedroom and shut the door. There was not, I felt, money enough in the world to buy Saxon, no matter what.

This is not the ideal temperament for a kennel owner.

It is possible to make money on dogs, but not if you are the way we are.

We finally compromised by having one or two litters a year and keeping only one puppy from a litter. And we remodeled the barn for a kennel, with an oil heater in winter so that whatever dogs were not in the house could stay comfortably in their own habitation. The house dogs began to take turns by the time we had not only our original four, but also the second generation: Saxon, Linda, Snow, Windy, and my beloved golden Honey. And the younger ones, Melody, Hildegarde and Silver.

Then we completed the household with Tigger, the black and rugged Connecticut Manx cat, and Esmé, the royal Siamese princess.

For a very brief period, until he went off exploring in the woods one day and never came back, we had an Abyssinian kitten whose name was Aladdin. And finally we decided that we had to have an Irish setter, so we got Maeve and later Holly.

Over the years, many friends have sat beside the hearth at Stillmeadow. The three children have married and come home with husbands and now with our grandchildren. The house has seen many bright days and peaceful nights.

It has also seen storms, of course. There have been times of sorrow and death. But in spite of everything, I have always thought that the little farmhouse was a firm shelter.

For as the children grew up and went away to their various schools and colleges, they had a home to come back to, instead of a series of transient city apartments.

And when we lost our husbands, the farm was a refuge and a haven, something to hold fast to. And something we had to work for, which was a blessing.

The name. We tried to settle on just the one that was right. We grew tired of being referred to as "the ladies who wear trousers." (Slacks were a rare sight in those days.) Or as "the place they have all those dogs." Or as "the old Oxford pheasant farm, where the man shot his wife." Neither were we pleased to be addressed as "the house across from the Phillipses."

At first glance, Stillmeadow might seem doubtful as a name for a place where a couple of dozen dogs and three children lived. But we thought that the name might have a tranquilizing effect. We weren't too sure, though. Spaniels are one of the quiet breeds, but when a cow passes their line of vision, or a car comes down the road, they out-terrier the terriers.

Connie, of course, at eleven years old had retired into a great silence. But her feet hadn't. David was a constitutional faller. Down the stairs, over the rake, off the bed at night — he fell wherever he went. Barbara was a dropper. Milk bottles, glasses, dinner plates. Her progress was always traceable by the sound of something crashing.

But in spite of all this, we liked the name Stillmeadow.

When you look out in the moonlight across the meadow, the soft silvery mist lies like a quiet sea. Fireflies lantern the lawn. The air smells of summer — warm, sweet, drowsy. And the maples are shadowy against the stars. It really is Stillmeadow then.

One

In our New England valley we begin the year with the big snow. We have an appointment with winter, and we are ready. The woodshed is stacked with seasoned apple wood and maple; the snow shovel leans at the back door; the shelves are jammed with supplies. When the first innocent flakes drift down, we put out more suet and fill the bird feeders. (The grocer says he can't keep enough suet because everyone simply snatches it.)

When the snow begins to come in all directions at once and the wind takes on a peculiar lonely cry, we pile more wood on the fire and hang the old iron soup kettle over it, browning the pot roast in diced salt pork and onions. As the blizzard increases, the old house seems to steady herself like a ship against a gale wind. She has weathered too many winter storms to bother about a new one! Snow piles up against the windowpanes, sifts in under the ancient sills, makes heaps of powdered pearl on the ancient oak floors. But the house is sung in the twilight of the snow and we sit by the fire and toast our toes, feeling there is much to be said for winter after all.

"Now we can read all those good books," says Jill, "those we were going to read last summer."

"And I'll do the jigsaw that Faith sent me, the really impossible one."

Jigsaws bore Jill. My partner in the sport is Faith Baldwin, and when she comes to visit we work for hours at a particularly sadistic one. But as suppertime approaches, Jill drifts by, picks up a piece and fits it in a critical hole. This can be maddening after we have hunted an hour for the right piece, but it expedites supper. It is also frustrating when Holly, the Irish, puts her paws in the middle of the table and breathes away a whole section.

A blizzard is a beautiful thing. As the drifts pile up, topping the picket fence, I can see from my window the meadow brimmed with silver. The pines in the backyard stand black-green in the veiling snow. The sugar maples seem to reach the pewter sky. Inside, the Christmas greens still make the house festive, the bayberry candles are ready to burn to the socket and the house is spicy with pine. The pot roast and all the fixings are ready, and the problem is whether the snow will be be too deep for the neighbors to get down the road.

There is something comfortable about a pot roast, for it will not be ruined if a few guests have to stop and shovel out the cars. Stillmeadow is on a narrow country road that dips down a hill. Where the brook crosses it, there is a ditch on each side. If the snow is bad, the village plow does not get around until the main roads are plowed. And few sounds in the world are more wonderful than the sound of a snowplow coming *swoosh-swoosh* down the road. But even if they have to hike down the road, people always seem to make it to the house. And there is nothing like a brisk tramp in the snow to put you in the mood for dinner.

New England cooking is the thing for deep winter. The kind of food our forefathers invented out of the simple fare the rockbound coast afforded was hearty and comforting. It still is.

Take beans, for instance, and molasses and salt pork, and you get those big brown crocks bubbling over with crusty brown goodness for Saturday night.

The Indians taught the early settlers the uses of maize, but it took the pioneer women to make Indian pudding, corncake, muffins, crackling bread and my favorite, Spider Corn Bread. Nowadays we make this the easy way with corn-bread mix in the old iron frying pan, popped into the oven. A sprinkle of crisp bacon bits is good.

When my husband, Frank, was alive, New Year's always meant a steaming cup of mulled wine, for that was a specialty of his. And although he usually drank nothing stronger than tea — except for that single holiday cup — he once made George Washington's favorite, hot buttered rum, but without the flaming poker. Frank was an adventurous cook. He tried shish kebab long before most people in this country had even heard of it, and one year he experimented with Syrian stuffed grape leaves. The stuffing was delicious but our wild Connecticut grape leaves were like leather. No amount of simmering helped. Still, as Frank said, the flavor was unusual.

Seeing the new year in seems to involve much noise, night-clubbing and hangovers, at least for some people. This is not my idea at all — never was. I wish to start my new year with a few people I dearly love, and in front of an apple-wood fire. And playing some good music, and reading aloud some choice bits. And feeling so secure in the fact that beginning a new year is a beginning with the same old friends.

Usually, Barbara and Val and their two children come to spend New Year's with us, arriving just in time to wave good-bye to Connie and Curt, who are heading back to New York after having spent Christmas here. Barbara always brings a carton of groceries — all sorts of special cheeses and meats which we can't get here in the country. Val mixes his traditional clam dip, and everyone, dogs and cats included, helps supervise the baking of the cranberry-glazed ham.

After dinner, the children toast marshmallows and pop corn over the open fire. The cockers like marshmallows and popcorn too, and Holly hangs around the kitchen waiting for more ham. After the children climb the ladder stairs and go to bed, the four adults settle down for a warm and comfortable talk. Jill once said, "There is one thing about us — we are a verbal family." So we are!

Midnight comes all too soon, and Barbara brings in a tray with freshly baked sourdough bread with cheese and salami and thin slices of ham and pickles. When the chimes ring out (over television, to be sure), we hold hands and say our private prayers for the year to come. I couldn't wish for a better way to begin than this.

Making New Year's resolutions used to be serious business when I was growing up. I made a list of mine, and tacked it over my dresser. If I had faithfully followed all of it, no doubt I should have died young. But by February I went right back to reading in the bathtub (forbidden), writing verse in church under the cover of the hymnal, and turning the clocks back an hour before I went out on a date.

Now, as the earth turns toward another year, I sit quietly and begin to make a new set of resolutions. My first is to be better organized. There is really no reason why Holly's rabies certificate turned up in last year's Christmas cards. And an unpaid bill in a box of carbon paper. I always put things away, but my problem is that I never remember where.

My other New Year's resolutions are simple. I resolve to be more patient, less selfish, cherish my friends and in my small way help whoever needs help. I cannot conceivably influence the world's destiny, but I can make my own life more worthwhile. I can give some help to some people; that is not vital to all the world's problems and yet I think if everyone did just that, we might see quite a world in our time!

So, as a new year begins, we make new resolutions and also take out the resolutions we made last year and didn't keep, polish them up and try again. But after all, the only resolution we really need is to work for peace among all the nations. And no one is too obscure to help, for it is really the sum of the people that moves the government. And if every voice in America says, "There shall be no war," the volume of sound will become thunder in the ears.

On a January night in our snowy valley, it is easy to have faith. It is so still and the snow is falling so quietly. The village church spire lifts a silvery tip, and the little white houses glow with the warm supper lights. The lights of Stillmeadow shine on our own drifts.

And Honey moves like a pale gold shadow on the terrace, sniffing with delight the fresh pure air of a new year!

One of the best New Year's resolutions we ever made was to get a cat. Of course, we eventually wound up with four, but at first we thought in terms of a single Siamese kitten. We hesitated for some time, though. Partly it was because we read such a good cat book first.

"Mercy," said Jill, "cats are delicate! Probably we can't manage to raise Esmé after we get her."

But that was long ago. Royal Siamese Queen Merrimac turned out to be a good strong kitten and an even stronger adult, well able to cope with a dozen cockers and the human family she took on. The first week, I remember well, she spoke a great deal of Siamese; in fact, all day and all night she spoke lustily. Nothing made her quiet except being carried in the curve of someone's neck. When we began to understand a little Siamese ourselves, she felt better. But after all, we had never spoken anything but cocker here, and it takes a little time to pick up one of these Oriental languages.

A few months later, Tigger, the black Manx — what the cat lady called a domestic shorthair — turned up on the doorstep. He speaks a Connecticut dialect which is quite simple. When he wants to go out, he lies down by the door of his choice and rolls over and over, keeping large glass-green eyes fixed on the nearest person. If he is ignored, he rolls faster. No one can resist it. Then when he wants to get in, he mounts a windowsill and utters a firm sentence.

The main difficulty is that his hours are like a night shift at a factory. About ten P.M. he takes his lunch box under one paw and rolls out, and then toward five in the morning he wants his breakfast. He knows where I sleep, and he climbs the window screen nimbly and wails and wails until I admit him. "It's about time," he says firmly. As I sleepily scold him, he rushes at me and purrs like a motorboat. He lifts his funny black face and eyes me blandly with those amazing green eyes. I give in and stagger out for milk.

Tigger is Jill's cat, but Esmé belongs to me. She brought with her a beautiful pedigree full of royal Oriental names, and Jill at once decided that what my cat had, hers should have also. So we composed a lovely pedigree for Tigger. We put in Salmon Sam and Broken Jinx, Sentimental Tom and Catnip Girl, Red Herring and Black Narcissus, back five generations. We wrote it on one of the cocker pedigree blanks, so it is just as impressive as Esmé's.

Esmé has names behind her like Moonglow, Minaret's Tamarind, Siam's Won Lon Son and Imported Champion Siamese Star Prince Favo, which is a mouthful in any language. But perhaps Siam's Sapphire of Khyber is the most romantic name.

Esmé seems quite aware of her lineage and is always regally poised. Tigger is not impressed. But he is fond of her and always saves his best mouse just for her.

It is time to put up the new calendars, and as the old ones come down I wonder where the past year went. Some of it is now what Emily Dickinson would call "an amethyst remembrance." Perhaps some of it is better forgotten, but there is so much to remember and treasure. And as I open the calendar to January, I think that soon lilacs will be in bloom (just four pages away), and then the Spartan roses (two more pages); I remember that the children will be coming for visits and the grandchildren will be celebrating their birthdays.

But right now winter at Stillmeadow walks down the low hills and brims the meadows with her tides of snow. Some years winter does more than arrive; she invades the valley. Then snow tops the picket fence; drifts are five feet deep. The whole landscape changes as the dune-shaped wind-rippled snow lies under a dark sky. There is a coldness, a purity, such as we seldom see, and landmarks vanish.

With waves of snow cresting around the old house, Jill and I feel like mariners. But we are fortunate, for we do not have to stand outside and mark a course. Instead, we sit by the open fire and have tea and cookies. I like to look out across the fields and see the pre-Revolutionary houses, anchored steadfastly. Summertime lights are not so lovely as winter lights on snow.

Now when we walk down the snowy road, we often cut some evergreen branches for the house. A beautiful arrangement can be made in an old white ironstone tureen — mixed evergreens and three scarlet geraniums from the window box. I make mine with the branches for the height and a focal point of the geraniums in a triangle near the base of the container. It is dramatic and beautiful, and lasts a long time.

Begonia cuttings make nice bouquets too, and if you leave them in water long enough, they usually root, and there you have a new set for another window box or row of pots. The begonia is an amazing plant, anyway; it just keeps going along and blooming, and when cut back, it starts up again.

The summer flowers are a memory now, but the house still looks loved with the green arrangements in ironstone or shining copper bowl.

A pre-Revolutionary house has great charm but also drawbacks. I thought of this when we had our January thaw, for suddenly in the night the house seemed boiling hot. I got up and turned the thermostat down, but the furnace paid no attention. I hardly expected it would, since that thermostat has been leading its own life all winter, no matter what the service men did. So I decided to open a window and get a breath of air. Connie was spending the weekend, and I remembered how the heat rises in our house and felt she must be suffering in her bedroom upstairs. I did not worry about Jill, for her room never is really warm — something to do with the eccentricity of the pipes.

I opened the inner door to the back kitchen, and propped the storm door open with a piece of kindling. All the dogs, of course, rushed out. After they came in again, I put the kindling back and shooed them into the living room. I shushed them as best I could, for Connie is supersensitive to noise. Then I crept quietly again to the back kitchen, found the toolbox, got out the hammer, went to the woodshed for a block of wood and returned to my bedroom. I put the block of wood against the edge of the sash, laid some tissues over it and gave a soft tap with the hammer. The theory is that the window goes up and you hastily insert an out-of-date World Atlas. Then you reach out and force the storm window to swing enough so the metal pieces unlock. It is really quite simple. But this time the dampness had affected the window. I tapped harder. By now an inquisitive Irish nose got in the way. I shushed her. I banged. Finally I raised the hammer and leaned back and really let the window have it.

Suddenly Connie and Jill materialized, wild-eyed and screaming, "What's wrong? What is it?"

"Everything is fine," I said quietly. "I

am merely opening a window."

As I got back to bed, I reflected that modern windows must be incredible. Just imagine opening a window by hand! I was, of course, too wide awake to sleep, but the smell of the air coming in was worth it. Melting snow, the curious winter scent of the swamp and a small whiff of apple-wood smoke from the fireplace made a heavenly blend. I lay sniffing happily. Then there was a buttermilk sky around four in the morning as a thin moon rode down the horizon. At the same time, the temperature dropped, a cold wind swung in and the house was colder than a mackerel. (I wonder why a mackerel is so cold?)

"Oh, never mind," I said crossly to Holly, and I stuffed a bath towel in the open window. I would hammer it shut in the morning. I could not, I felt, face Connie and Jill again.

January is a bitter month for the birds. There is a mystery about birds which I have never understood. A bird is a delicate creature. I have occasionally held a damaged bird in my hand and was always reminded of Shakespeare's "Oh, so light a foot, can ne'er wear out the everlasting flint." You feel as if you are holding air when you hold a chickadee. The delicate feet seem too small to support anything. Under the softness of feathers the body is too small.

So how in our below-zero January weather can these small birds fly? And sing? And why don't their feet freeze on the branch? My friend Hal Borland says a few birds have feathered feet, such as the snowy owl. But the small winter birds that eat all day long at our feeders have no insulation. There they are — juncos, towhees, evening grosbeaks, bluejays and chickadees. And the small sparrows, always so busy. They must sleep in the pines, for in early morning the branches quiver as they come out to eat.

I think it is a miracle when I see these small people hopping over ice and through snow. I also was amazed the first time I saw a chickadee and a fox sparrow sitting down in the window feeder. The way they did it was to tuck up those delicate legs and stick their tail feathers out flat behind them. And then they whacked away at the suet, *sitting down.*

This I never read in a book. I saw it. And although the chickadee is no bigger than a butternut, the sound of pecking was tremendous. I have spent a good deal of time at the window by my desk watching the hammering of tiny beaks at frozen suet. This energy harnessed by man would undoubtedly run a lot of power stations.

When we came to the country neither Jill nor I knew any birds except robins. And the best bird books present the same problem as dictionaries. To look things up you have to know what you are looking up, at least in a general sort of way. Otherwise you read madly, from bitterns right through to the index, and you get absolutely nowhere.

"It's not in the illustrations," Jill said often. "It has to be an accidental."

I think we had more accidental birds than anyone ever had. But when we did find out that one accidental was an evening grosbeak, triumph intoxicated us.

And this week when I tracked down the strange and lovely birds at the feeder — birds I had never seen — I hopped up and down with excitement.

"Meadow larks, meadow larks." And I shut the book and remarked, "Why are they here now? What are they doing?" In over twenty years we had never seen a meadow lark. We heard them in the meadow, loud, clear, beautiful, but we never saw them. So here they were, at the ground feeder with the regular members of the gang.

We have a number of bird books, but the small compact Hausman and Peterson are the favorites. We pencil in the date and location of new birds as we see them. The cerulean warbler has a note: May 20, Dump. Why he was at the town dump, he didn't say, but there he was like a flying piece of azure sky.

There is one thing we have never been able to do and that is to identify birds by their songs. We have to see them first. The truth is that it is not possible, at least for us, to know who utters "a smooth series of husky-sweet notes." Or "a high,

rather nasal yap, yap-yap. Kent, kent."
Or "a loud harshly metallic or wooden
rattle." An easy one is the yellowthroat,
for he definitely does say, "Wichity,
wichity, wichity."

An old diary of Connie's turned up
yesterday as we were doing some January
cleaning. It really wasn't a diary, exactly,
but a weekly journal. A typical issue read
like this:

1: Nothing queer happined.
2: A girl from 6 grade came in our
room today for an hour.
3: We had a little treat today in school
it was.
4: Turtle getting along all right in
basement.

Tucked in the back was a letter to Santa
Claus.

Dear Santa Claus,
I want a baby doll with a little pink
bonnet and coat and a little white
dress on. And I want some new paints

and a new paintbook. I want a game of Oz if you have any.

P.S. I have tried to be a good girl.
With lots of love . . .

P.S. I will leave it to you to bring me anything else you think I would like.

I'm sorry the days of attics are gone. We are so lucky to have one. Finding old letters, diaries, papers, faded valentines brings the past to life again as nothing else does. I was reminded of Connie, in a smocked dress, sitting demurely and relating a long story about some episode in her life.

"Is this true, Connie?" asked the guest who was listening.

Connie's round blue eyes widened. She looked up. "Well," she said firmly, "that's the story as I tell it."

We have done a good deal of talking this winter about training the puppies, Melody and Hildegarde and Silver. We saw the Obedience Trials at the Spaniel Specialty Show and our consciences were smitten by the idea that our own darlings were growing up like hoodlums. Rip and Sister are the only perfectly trained cockers we have ever raised. There was nothing Rip could not have learned except to cook roast beef. He would have had to taste the roast. He would retrieve over an obstacle, heel and even sit motionless while Jill walked away, and he would hold his pose until she called. But he learned all this more or less on his own, without going to special classes, and he never went to an Obedience Trial. It might be fun, we thought, for the younger dogs to have a bit of formal training.

So now every week we drive over to Newtown with dogs, leashes, dumbbells and of course a thermos of coffee. Then for two hours the trainer puts us through our paces — Great Danes, dachshunds, cockers and just plain house pets — with an equally varied assortment of owners — auto mechanic, farmer's wife, lawyer, sixth-grader. Most of the dogs catch on very quickly and the tails never stop wagging for a minute. It is the owners who get the real training. "Move more slowly. Don't jerk the lead. Call clearly but don't screech. Be patient — take one small thing at a time. Remember to praise your dog at the end of each exercise."

During the week we do our daily homework. Short but frequent practice sessions are best. We work in the backyard if we can, otherwise in the living room. The school dogs go through their routine smugly, while the others watch jealously from the sidelines.

All the things we work on are important; there are no tricks-for-tricks-sake in obedience training. The aim is to teach yur dog to come promptly when he is called, to walk along close to you even without a leash, instead of dashing off tally-ho if he is unattached, or yanking and bucking if he is on lead. He also learns to drop to the ground on command, which might save his life someday if he starts to run across the road and you suddenly see a car approaching. Besides all this, he is supposed to sit and stay and also lie and stay. In more advanced classes he learns to jump different kinds of hurdles, find the keys that you drop on the ground as you walk across the dog ring and also to follow gesture commands as well as voice commands. But in our group we are all still beginners. Some of us are glad if our darlings just learn to move among other dogs without either growling and bristling or trying to lure them off for a romp.

The hardest thing to teach a cocker is to stay while you walk away. Heeling is fine because you do that together, but when you get about two paces away from your future champion, there is a mad scramble, and she flings herself at you, saying wildly, "You didn't really mean you were going to leave me *alone?*" Most cockers train very quickly to the leash. Even Melody leads very well now that she has gotten over the habit of lying down on her back and waving her paws helplessly in the air the minute the collar goes on.

Now and then in January we get what I call a dividend day. The sun is clear and warm and the sky soft as lake water. The tree trunks seem to glow in the light, and a hundred misty colors appear in the swamp. The birds are very gay — they seem to fly with a lighter wing somehow — and the dogs sit by the well house and dream quite as if it were spring. Squirrels whip around in the maples, always so busy and so important. I think a squirrel would make a good bank president: he saves, he is thrifty, he feels important and he must have a very sound head on him.

The Quiet Garden on such a day is lucid with sun, and it looks as if we might even eat there. I toy with the idea, but, Jill says firmly, the benches will be cold as glaciers. And I realize they will.

So we settle for trays by the fire. But it is incredibly exciting to get such a day in January. It is not even the January thaw; it is just a small jewel of a day set in the silver band of winter.

"Let's take a ride," I say suddenly.

So we drive along the wintry country roads looking at the snug farmhouses, the tidy barns. Light falls on the greystone fences, here and there glinting with a sheath of ice. As the sun goes lower, it intensifies the colors: the white church steeple is whiter; the red barns are set on fire. All the browns of the thickets and meadows are touched with a rosy tinge. The snow, where it lies in the hollows, has blue shadows on it.

Mittened and furred children go past carrying their ice skates slung over their shoulders; the steel catches the light and flashes like white fire. A hitchhiker waves a red thumb, but we dare not stop.

Time was we picked up everybody on the road. In those innocent days, I picked up a wayfaring tramp with a guitar, incredibly smelly and dirty, but very nice. He sang "Red River Valley" to me for some miles, and then a few others, and I loved it, although I had to run the car window down to be able to breathe.

To me, one of the saddest things about the terrible increase of crime in the country is that the kindliness of the road must be forgone.

Now that Jill and I no longer have to commute to the city, I often think back to those days and wonder how we survived. The trip was slow, especially in winter, and the car was always overloaded. It was also crowded, for the dogs took turns coming in with us. Two or three would be chosen every week, while the rest stayed in the country, with George to keep an eye on them. Some actually preferred to stay and so were no problem, but we always had a few who insisted that they would die if they were separated from us for even a minute. No matter where we were, they wanted to be there too.

Often it was Sister and Honey who came to town with us, and a very odd pair they made. Sister was such a stable, self-reliant little piece and she loved town life. In the back of her mind was the smug satisfaction that she was in New York and Star was in the country because she, Sister, did not bite strangers.

Sister floated along on the leash, light as a butterfly, so I kept peering around to be sure she was still there. Honey walked with her head over her shoulder, looking backward, as if something would get her from behind if she relaxed a moment. She started nervously when a truck roared by, bucked suddenly at a dragon bus.

I remember trying to explain this to Jill. I had been down a side street which was mainly residential and, as New York streets go, very quiet.

Jill said, reasonably, "But there isn't any traffic there."

"No, but the houses look funny," I said. "You know there's always something funny."

You wouldn't think a cocker spaniel would be sensitive to architecture, would you? Well, Honey peered distrustfully at the old brownstone houses, the dark, peeling stone steps, the odd embrasures. It wasn't, she averred, natural. It made a dog uneasy; no knowing what you might find next. Once we came to a cleaning outfit, a machine blasting a stone front. Honey flew through the air — without a flying trapeze, too — her eyes starting from her head. Then she saw Sister quietly heeling along, looking dreamy and content, and suddenly Honey rushed wildly to her and kissed her face and fell into line beside her. Sister was a lifeboat in a stormy sea. Sister gave me a look from a wise bright eye, as one should say, "Well, after all, she's related to Star, and you know how difficult *she* is!"

But all that is past now. I go into this New Year without the companionship of my small black-and-white cocker. Sister was never any trouble and she died with as little trouble as possible, her tired heart just beating into silence. She was a funny little thing, shy and retiring, unlike the rest of the cockers, who are leap-into-lap-at-once people. When strangers came, she retired under the sofa and just poked a small black rubber nose out. If they were very quiet, nonjingling people, she would eventually emerge and casually enter the social group. If they made advances too soon, she got under the radiator and squeezed flat.

She sat under my desk when I typed, with her head on one of my feet. Whenever I looked down, one bright dark eye was looking up at me. When I went in the yard, she heeled beside my left foot, steady as my own shadow. She did not bark at the laundryman. She was neat and tidy and drank her water without spilling it all over the floor as some did. She ate as if she were dining out on Spode china. Her son, Tiki, always spreads half of his meal on the floor and skates around in it. Her daughter, Little Sister, always wades in hers.

She had little sense of humor, whereas some of the others felt they had a career as comics. She worked soberly at whatever she did, but even when she won silver trophies in dog shows, she had no feeling of superiority, whereas the Irish is a born trouper. The only time Sister moved fast was when I started to go away without her. Then no door, no gate, shut quickly enough. She was mule-stubborn about ever being away from me, even when I went to the dentist. Many a time I had to lug her small plump form back from the car and plop her in the yard, and no matter how I explained, she looked betrayed. Then she would take up a vigil on the terrace and just look down the road. In her later years I got so upset over this that I would have some member of the family take her to the back kitchen and offer her a piece of chicken while I stole out the front door. It never worked. She knew.

She was beautiful only to me, for she

was a small old-fashioned cocker, nicely put together but no glamour girl. Most visitors exclaimed over the rest of the cockers, but only the discerning noticed Sister peering thoughtfully from under the couch. Non-dog-lovers who came never knew there was a dog in the house, for we simply put the rest in the kennel and let Sister alone.

Possibly I could sum it up by saying Sister was a gentlewoman. But who can ever sum up one small cocker who inhabits one's heart? I can only be grateful that I was privileged to have her for her lifetime, and quite sure she is no farther away than the floor under my desk as I write this.

My other special companion, Honey, the quiet golden one, still comes for a walk with me almost every evening. We seldom go very far — halfway up the hill, above the pond, is just right.

The color of winter is pure and lovely: the long, darkly blue shadows, the purple stalks of the briery bushes, the glistening white of clean snow, the pale amber of shell ice where the little brooks walk in summer. The meadow is latticed now with the pattern of dark branches, and the great timeless trees lift intricate patterns against a still sky.

As I look up at the pearl-clear light over the snowy valley, I think that surely all we need for the new year is peace over the world so men can lift their eyes to the sky and know that death will not hover over.

Honey pads along with her own thoughts, which have rabbits in them, and all her yesterdays, and being loved, and the memory of tonight's snack, and maybe an idea as to tomorrow's leftover waffle with a smidgen of wildflower honey on it. For she has reached the age when she can have just about anything she wants and no nonsense about it.

As I turn back toward the little white house, I wish with all my heart that the serenity of woods and hills and valleys could be shared with the whole restless and uneasy world.

Two

February cannot be called a restful month in New England. Even before we get the bacon sizzling for breakfast, the wild birds have to be fed. As Jill says, "They are not what I call wild. If they were any tamer, they'd all live in the house."

We keep a new, clean garbage can at the back door, filled with chick scratch feed. Jill stirs in sunflower seed and some regular wild-bird food. A worn-out dog-food can acts as a scoop and in bad weather we fill it several times a day. We also use stale bread and cake and keep suet in the suet cages on the sugar maple in the backyard.

Our birds do not care for raisins, thank you, and none of them eat the rape seeds which abound in the packaged bird food. They love doughnuts hung in the lilac outside my window. We experimented with lettuce leaves and so on, but the dogs ate them up — the birds did not touch them. But they all love sunflower seeds, which are the most expensive. The ground feeders eat the scratch feed (so do the squirrels) and we try to keep the ground birds busy so my window tray is left for the chickadees, tufted titmice, fox sparrows and of course squirrels.

We used to make a fantastic mix of melted fat with seeds and crumbs and (innocently) raisins which we molded in juice cans and hung from branches. We gave it up, not because it was such a job to prepare but because as soon as the birds ate off the top layer the squirrels took the rest. We tried the prepared suet cakes and they vanished overnight.

"Too easy for the squirrels," said Jill.

As far as the packaged food is concerned, I figure we cannot afford to spend so much for a few sunflower seeds along with all the rest our birds won't eat. We get tired of sweeping the rape seed out of a clogged feeder and fearing it will sprout in the lawn, it makes me wonder why the manufacturers do not put up regional packages. There must be some birds somewhere who will eat rape seed, but not around Stillmeadow. Would it not be a good idea to do a New England package, substituting plain old chick scratch with the sunflower seeds and the little black things that our birds will eat?

Another blizzard last Sunday — sleet mixed with snow. The windowpanes were pebbled over with ice and I could not see out. Mainly it troubled Holly, who loves looking out of windows. She kept breathing against the panes, so the inside steamed up. In the midst of the lashing storm, Connie's voice came from the back kitchen.

"Anybody home?" she called.

Curt built up the fire, and my little granddaughter Muffin was hauled out of various layers of sweaters, snow suit, mittens (two pairs), hoods (two). I turned up the thermostat, for I notice city dwellers like a tropical temperature. But I find city apartments chilly and drafty. I think we all adjust to one temperature and like whatever it might be.

In the morning the world was a drift of pearl and the sun shone from an intensely blue sky. Muffin, at a year and a half, had her first experience with pure country snow. In her blue bunny suit she looked like an indigo bunting as she went out. Her boots had been forgotten, but Connie devised boots from a plastic bowl cover and a plastic bag and tied them on with some leftover Christmas ribbon.

At first Muffin just stood and stared. Then she sat down in a soft drift, ate some. Then she made miniature brooms of her arms and swept. All the time she said, "Whoo — whoo — whoo," like a tiny blue owl. By the time she had gotten both mittens off and her hands were snow-cold, Connie brought her in.

"Whoo — whoo," Muffin said.

When I thought of the world opening up for my granddaughter, the immeasurable experiences and the things to learn, I felt awed. She was like the first human being in the first snow. Somewhere along the line we lose the sense of wonder. We look out, and sigh, and say, "It's snowing again."

For adults in the country it means shoveling, stalled cars, more wood lugging, being housebound until the road crews finally get through. It means empty bird feeders until we make a path. It means an added load. But to Muffin it meant a strange new wonder. Her hands were full of sparkles and then they were gone.

As I watched her being peeled off like an onion, I wished we might all keep the sense of wonder she now has when all life is a mystery.

We have a little trouble with the cockers these days, for a whole kennel of house dogs complicates the snow-and-mud problem. We are always resolving to alternate them, two by two, but Melody will look so sad when she goes to the kennel that Jill lets her in, and I am always sneaking out to rescue Little Sister, so that by the time we are ready for bed, Jill says all of a sudden, "I didn't realize we had seven in tonight."

"We didn't have at the beginning," I say. "But honestly, they are so good!"

If I ever built a house, which I am sure is highly unlikely, I would attach the kennel right to it with a nice arched passageway between. Jill says why not just build the kennel large enough for the family to move in there too?

Some of the houses in the valley are closed now, while their people are in Florida. They have a lonely look, shuttered and still, and wearing the State Police signs on their doors. Icicles hang from the eaves in long silver needles, and around the unshoveled walks the small prints of stay-at-home rabbits make fascinating patterns.

It is a fine thing to follow the warmth to the South, I always think, but I am always sorry for the house left lonely.

Those of us who stay in the valley make out very well. We build up the fires, light the candles, and the soup kettle over the hearth makes a pleasant simmering sound. No mangoes or hearts of palm here but, on the other hand, corned beef and cabbage and flaky potatoes cooked in the rich liquid make a handsome meal for anybody. The corned beef (good done at home too) slices in tender rosy slices; the cabbage is in delicate ivory wedges; the carrots from our own garden are honey-sweet. Open a well-done potato and spoon over some of the long-simmered juices, and there you have a dish fit for anybody. Not Bahamian mustard on the corned beef, as it is too rich, but a mild musty Bavarian mustard.

In lieu of roaming a moonlit tropical beach, we play Scrabble by the fire, later on pop big fluffy popcorn and get out the red apples. And then, perhaps, play a few records. César Franck's symphony or some old Caruso, thrilling and rich over the thin reedy sound of the early accompaniments.

Or folk songs. From "Lord Randal" to the "Eddystone Light," I love them all.

Or if we do not feel like changing records, we read. And stretched out by the fire with a really good book to read and popcorn at hand is not a very dire fate to wish on anyone.

Now, in the deep heart of winter, I settle down every evening with a stack of favorite books. In between letting cats in and dogs out, I mean to reread *Walden* and the letters of Keats, and *Wuthering Heights,* and all of Katherine Mansfield — I can't read her often enough.

Sometimes I play a game with myself on these snow-deep nights. I choose an imaginary companion, and how real and close they come. My friends range from John Keats to Charlotte Brontë. I'd love to have Emily, but she wouldn't come. Charlotte is easier, though shy and retiring. Keats goes right down to the fruit cellar to see the "lucent syrops tinct with cinnamon," the jams and jellies. Keats had such a zest for life, a rich and deep perception of beauty.

I don't feel so much at home with Shelley. Any minute he might turn that dazzling gaze on me and say, "Let's try the great adventure now," and set the house on fire. He was slightly notional. Byron I admit I would rather meet at someone else's house. But Byron would be horribly bored with me. Not being dark or slim or beautiful, never being able to "walk in beauty like the night," I wouldn't get any attention from Byron and I wouldn't have the kind of small talk to carry it off.

The February thaw is a miracle. It is the curtain going down after Act I in New England, for we shall have more winter up to April. But now snow melts; icicles drop from the well house; the air is suddenly silken soft. Out we go without our mittens and wearing our summer jackets. A kind of intoxication sets in.

True, we may catch pneumonia, but never mind. We race around with cockers and the Irish and keep thinking the snowdrops will be up any day. Perhaps nature herself is pausing to look toward spring. The snow melts fast, the dogs bring in bones long buried and the lost tennis shoe is retrieved, via Holly. Jonquil drags in a bathing towel. What's left of the pink rabbit Jill's grandson discarded is now in the house, on the sofa. The only thing I mind is Holly's collection of old dog-food cans. I do not like them tucked in my bed.

This last item has nothing to do with our housecleaning. It has to do with Holly's agility. She can snatch a dog-food can while you are stirring up the dog meal for the day, and then ask to go out. Only as she whisks out do you see that can in her mouth.

It happens with a head of lettuce or cabbage too, but they wilt down in time and are not observed by guests.

Here our decision about values enters. Is it better to have empty cans in the yard and a happy, happy dog, or to have a dog that gets spanked for lugging them out? We settle for the dog. As Jill says, "We'll get the cans back in the spring."

So far as possible, we have raised all of our dogs with what we felt was enough discipline but not too much. We always ask ourselves what is vital and stick to it. For the rest, if it makes Holly radiant to carry a can around the yard for days — well, why not?

February is the time we think most about heat and heating problems in the country. After a bad storm, when everyone meets at the village store, the first and constant question is, "Did your pipes freeze?"

We learned how to cope with just plain below-zero weather. Jill got a huge trouble lamp and hooked it in under the sink. It has a wire cage around it and yards and yards of heavy cord which we coil here and there and then try not to trip on. We got an electric panel for the back kitchen, under which there is no cellar and possibly a bit of unmelted glacier lurking. We got several electric heaters to plug in here and there.

And, naturally, blew the fuses out the first time they were all working.

"It would have been all right," Jill said, "if we hadn't had the waffle maker on too."

The next time it was ten below we did a merry-go-round pushing in and pulling out plugs, alternating.

And of course once the current goes off, all of these aids are lifeless. We go right back to wood fires and kerosene lamps, and hope for the best.

Winter storms are not such a problem, of course, if you have an old-fashioned wood-burning range. Even in summer, an old range is a blessing, but in a month like February it really comes into its own. I wish we had kept the Indian way of calling a time the Moon of Hunting, the Moon of Corn (if there was a moon of corn). I would call February the Moon of Stoves.

Stillmeadow didn't have a range when we first came, although we could see where a chimney pipe had been. But one icy February night, after a particularly long seige without electricity, my husband said, dreamily, "If only we had one of those old cast-iron ranges. We used to have one when I was growing up and it almost seemed like a member of the family."

"It certainly would be nice," I said, "to have something that would work even when the wires blow down."

"It certainly would," said Jill, who was crouched on the hearth stirring the soup that was just beginning to simmer in the kettle suspended over the fire. "After a while this open-hearth cookery gets awfully hard on your back."

We had to put it off, however. Our budget simply could not accommodate any extra items. So it was mid-June before we finally started off in search of a stove.

It was a typical family excursion. I got lost, we almost got arrested and we came home with not only a stove but a crate of green grapes.

Our first problem was to find our way in Waterbury, a city apparently laid out along rabbit trails.

As we went from store to store we never found a street that went where we wanted to go. Frank would drive madly around the block, using up our rationed gas in a horrible way, while Jill and I dived from basement to basement. All dealers keep their stoves in the basement.

Finally I ran ahead, leaving Jill to inspect one place and Frank to park. I had a large flashlight because our neighbor George had told me earnestly that I must look inside at the firebrick. As I loped down the crowded street, intent on the chase, I wondered why everybody seemed to fall back in surprise and then turn and look after me. Heads were craned from stores. Drivers leaned from passing cars.

"I must have aged terribly in three days," I thought sadly. "Or maybe it's this red shirt that used to be David's. Maybe it looks funny on me, somehow." After about six blocks, the truth came to me. There I was, dashing down a blazing hot street, in dazzling sunshine, holding a mammoth flashlight in my lifted right hand. I had too much else in my arms to hide it, but I did turn it backward.

We found the range. Frank parked the car.

A policeman materialized instantly.

"It's going to cost you six dollars to park here," he said happily, getting out his pad.

I was buying an antique flatiron at the moment, having just gotten a bargain in grapes, as well as a loaf of Italian bread at the next shop, and I saw him.

"Run, Jill, run!" I screamed. "Frank's arrested!"

She ran, carrying a length of stovepipe in her arms. The secondhand man ran after her with the legs of the stove, muttering that his heart wasn't so good any more.

The policeman gave in. And when he saw the pieces of our range lying on the walk, he said warmly, "Stay as long as you need to," and went on.

So the stove came home. I had a feeling that it was happy to be set up in a home again, polished and come to life. I wondered what other home it had lived in, how many little children had warmed their hands by it. George came over and set it up, Jill got out the stove polish, and I couldn't wait to stir up onions and peppers and olive oil and get them

85

simmering on it.

The old stove settled down in the back kitchen as comfortably as if it had always been there. And we wondered how in the world we had ever managed without it.

I don't mean to sound critical of modern equipment. We have a fine electric stove in the middle kitchen, and it has its own elegant, streamlined personality. It is a modern invention, better than emeralds to own. Turning a switch and getting the immaculate, hot cooking power is a fine thing. I say my best for it.

But also give me an old-fashioned range. The kitchen is as warm as new-buttered toast. The chunky stove wood sends a good smell out when you lift the lid, almost like burning leaves on an autumn hill. The soup pot simmers gently in the back corner. You can eat at the table right near the stove and bask in its warmth.

I like the way you can get any gradation of heat by just pushing your pan an inch to the right or an inch to the left. And the way the oven cooks so slowly — the rich meat juices just seal themselves in the roast.

We have two kitchens, and we call one the back kitchen and one the middle kitchen. This often confuses guests. I shout from upstairs, "You'll find it in the middle kitchen!" and if they are not used to our peculiar, unlogical family vocabulary, they may be found later in the taproom, and nobody knows why that room is called the taproom, either! We have tried to call it the family room but we never remember.

But when we had our range, the back kitchen belonged especially to the Moon of Stoves. The popcorn in the evening! The stuffed spareribs on a blizzardy noon! Honey by the oven, lifting a golden nose to smell what Mama had inside the stove this time. Esmé climbing happily into the oven when the fire died down. I am sure few people keep cats in the oven, but Stillmeadow had them there. It was highly unsanitary, and only people who also belong to Siamese cats could possibly understand.

Besides Esmé, there would be Melody, the smallest puppy, poking a black satin head from under the range. And that's another thing! In the middle kitchen there is no waste space under the electric stove. It has drawers and warming ovens and tray racks. But there was no waste space under the range either, really. It was always packed solidly with cockers. They felt that a stove equipped with a full quota of spaniels really completed the furnishing.

It was an old-timer when we bought it, but it lasted a good many years before it finally gave out. We still miss it, and I'm sure that someday we will have another. In the meantime, I am glad to see that so many people are buying wood-burning stoves these days. For they really do seem like members of the family.

Jill says this is the time of year to reorganize everything in terms of what is oftenest used and where it is kept. She is certainly right, and if I were an organizing person I should instantly wrestle with the jammed-up china cupboards and put away all those dishes never picked up except to dust. Also, sorting out old letters and bills, and straightening the sewing basket — Yes, this is the month to review the whole inside of the house at Stillmeadow.

Building additional shelves here and there, and then filling them up, is a February job. Though Jill often lays down the hammer to say despondently, "It isn't much good if you stand right behind me with armloads more of junk to park on them before I even get 'em painted."

The trouble is that as I pick up a cracked ironstone plate, I get to admiring the glaze and the way the edge is scalloped and I think it is nice to look at with the candlelight glimmering on the soft finish — and back goes the plate in the same old spot.

"Have you used this in five years?" Jill says in an executive tone.

"No," I admit feebly, "but you know I might put peanuts or something in it."

"Peanuts?" says Jill.

Very often, after one of these reorganizing bouts, I will be able to pack away two chipped butter plates, one broken fork and ten of the fifty meat skewers from the silver drawer. Then I relax with some old book that ought to be thrown out for scrap, and say happily,

"Isn't it nice to get all organized before the outside work begins?"

Jill usually does not answer. She is reading seed catalogues. So I suggest brightly that she throw away all the old ones.

"I need them to refer to," she says haughtily, "to know what we planted in past years. I write in the margins."

The seed catalogues bloom like the fabled Rose of Sharon. And here the difference between Jill and me becomes apparent. I am for ordering a few packets from everybody who sends us a catalogue, as a kind of thank-you and to encourage them in their work. Jill is for consolidation, getting all we can from just one place. She says it is better to have one order that is a good one than to spread around.

"What difference would it make to Mr. Burpee," says she, "to send three packets of Crosby beets?"

So she makes out a firm order for everything from just one seed company and dispatches it.

Then it turns out that this is not the

firm that handles Bibb letuce. So we order a packet of that.

Then we check our list and find edible-podded peas are not on it, so an order goes to somebody else for that.

It is true that every one of the top companies has some varieties others do not have, and a cross section gives the ardent gardener complete choice.

Ah, never blooms so red the rose
As in the garden pages glows,
Never crops so free from pest
As on P.20 and the rest.
And all the beauties we'll be
    growing
Blossom in catalogues without
    our hoeing!

When we first came to Stillmeadow, both Jill and I were complete innocents. We ordered everything that looked lovely in the catalogues. It took us a number of years to learn the facts of gardening. Some things will grow for you; some will not. Climate is not something to ignore; nor is consistency of soil, nor location.

Most of our shrubs were perambulatory, as Jill moved them from shade to sun from rocky soil to loam, from sheltered to exposed spots.

"I am going to move the mock orange one more time," she would say, "and put the primroses on the south side of the border."

We have given up on the forsythia, because all they do is leaf out. Jill planted our bushes long ago, and they grew with the vigor of ragweed. When they put forth only one pale blossom, she consulted a garden authority. He advised moving them to a different location. She did. Those bushes are especially well traveled, having been all over the yard. In due time, another adviser inspected the single weak blossom each plant usually produced and advocated serious pruning. They were pruned. Nothing has ever stopped their fierce growth, but nothing has made them the golden shower they should be in spring. Across the road, untended bushes bear dazzling blooms.

But in spite of the disappointments, we keep trying new things. This year we are tempted to order just a few more berry bushes, fruit trees and roses; it isn't too late. Jill reads dreamily, "The fruit is sweet and juicy enough to eat when it is only half ripe. The catalogue says so. In the golden stage. Continue to eat and enjoy it until September, when the skin is rich maroon red and the flesh is tempting gold."

"What is it?" I ask.

"Kind of a peach and plum and apricot all mixed up," she says. "It is delightful canned."

"Get one," I say. I never resist the lure of anything that may be canned.

Jill reads on: "The originator removes one third to one half the crop every year to keep trees from breaking down under the load of fruit. When properly thinned, the fruit becomes so large it must be canned in halves."

Just once I should like to see one tree on our land that had enough fruit to break down a branch. Or even to shatter a small twig. But I am always as hopeful as Jill. You never know when the seed catalogue's dream may come true. After all, we had three plums this year.

Of course, the catalogues never take into account such things as we have to cope with. All their trees and berries grow in some Elysian field, where age does not wither them, nor scale nor blight nor curculio enter in. No rabbits eat their apricot trees just as they get their feet firm in the ground. No cows get in and step largely among the tender berry shoots. No horse — certainly no horse — ever dances back and forth on their strawberry patch, eating all the mulch and bashing all the berries. The roses and lilies bloom in serenity, also. There are no puppies scrambling back and forth through the iris beds, no cats tiptoeing through the tulips.

No, in the catalogues there is only flowering perfection and there are only flawless fruits. So we read all the catalogues eagerly, and plant once more, which is an annual experiment, an annual thrill. In the end we have marvelous vegetables and plenty of lovely flowers, a handful or two of berries and one pear. So we should feel satisfied.

Valentine the saint was a Christian martyr who died about 270 A.D. in Rome. I wonder whether he leans over "the gold bars of heaven" like Rossetti's "Blessed Damozel" and watches while on his day heavily ribboned boxes of candy and bouquets of roses in green waxen armor go merrily from one to another!

Perfume seems so appropriate to Valentine's Day as a token to "the object of one's affection," as the dictionary says with such reserve. Possibly perfume is more romantic than most things, for a whiff can transport us to the sandalwood groves or the land of far Araby.

Flowers certainly, for flowers breathe of young love. Roses especially. But when I was turning sixteen, my beau brought violets, a rare luxury. The cool dark purple was beautiful as a dream, the glossy pointed leaves framed the flowers, and the stems were wound with silver foil. The air on Olympus could not smell sweeter than those violets. I laid them on my pillow at night. It did not matter that by the time the violets had been carted in on the old sweating Northwestern train to our little Wisconsin town, they were half dead; nor that by the next day the leaves rusted, the flowers crimped with death. Those violets were immortal, for I can smell them yet.

I sprinkled them with cool water. I laid them in the icebox — too near the cake of river ice Mr. Lutz had just tonged in, as it turned out. But never mind — I had my violets. The whole world was a blossoming garden to me!

Years later, after my mother died, I found a small box tied with pink ribbon in her big walnut dresser. In it were all the valentines I ever had made for her, from the first wavering "I love yu Mama" to the erudite "Sugar is sweet and so are YOU." From blue and pink crayon on oatmeal paper to a fancy deckle-edged pale-blue paper with an original poem by the rising young writer aged fifteen.

So Mama was sentimental too! Who would have guessed it? As Papa and I emoted around like rockets, she was so quiet and serene and so sensible. And all the time she was saving those valentines!

This was a holiday for her to give

parties, and, oh, the table frilly with rose-colored ribbons and shining with newly polished silver. Oh, the little heart-shaped cakes, a bite apiece and cloud-pink with icing. The maple-nut parfaits and the candied rose leaves. I remember these better than the main part of the dinner, naturally being young and dessert-minded. I can recall thin slices of rosy sugar-cured country ham, glazed with brown sugar and deep with clove. The vegetables I cannot remember at all. Sweet-potato soufflé was there. And thimble-sized light rolls.

This would be a faculty party, when History and Latin and Geology and Mathematics would forget their differences and have a merry time. Followed by charades with a sedate professor stamping around in an old bear rug being, naturally, a *bear*.

The valentine tea would be more quiet, ladies only, and the clink of silver tongs on fair china cups as I passed and passed wee rolled and open sandwiches, eating several every time I turned around.

Followed a party for my gang. We just swarmed all over everything and ate like mastodons. Rolled up the Orientals and danced. Finished off with hot chocolate beaten with Mama's Mexican beater and with cinnamon spicing it, and dollops of heavy sweet whipped cream — plus the rest of the tiny heart cakes.

And finally, when Valentine's Day was really over, a whole half week of it, a moonlight walk with my beau along the snow-deep streets of the little town.

Dreams spinning silver pathways over the snow. We always began with a million dollars — that was all accounted for and settled. But the yacht was a problem. I held out for a rose-covered cottage. I said quite frankly that life on a yacht was not for me because I got seasick even in a canoe.

Every four years February strikes another romantic note — when Leap Year adds an extra day to the calendar. According to the Encyclopaedia Britannica the origin of the custom of allowing the so-called gentle sex to do the courting is a mystery. However, it goes back as far as 1288, when Scotland passed a law to the effect that "for ilke year known as lepe year, ilk mayden ladye of bothe highe and lowe estait shall hae the liberte to bespeke ye man she likes, albeit he refuses to taik hir to be his lawful wife, he shall be mulcted in ye sum ane pundis or less, as his estait may be." A few years later France adopted the same law, and in the fifteenth century Genoa and Florence followed suit.

What is especially interesting to me is that in this one respect all "maydens" were equal. The right to woo in Leap Year was given princess and peasant. I like to imagine a lady's maid and her mistress sallying forth to court the pageboy and the lord simultaneously. Well, after all, love knows no class distinctions!

I have never seen a groundhog in February. Sometimes George brings me the news that we shall have six more weeks of winter or that spring is to be early. I am a firm believer in the truth underlying country legends, but I do not know why this one started. Who first saw a groundhog coming out and seeing his shadow and then counted the weeks just on a hunch? One theory is that groundhogs come out early if they get too hungry, not having been stuffed before hibernating. But there is a balance in nature, and perhaps spring is earlier when harvest time has been poor.

At twilight the sun leaves a pink glow on the snowy meadow. Then night comes sudden and soon. It is not possible to mark the moment when it is no longer day. I have tried to but cannot. It is like the swooping of ebony wings over the sky. The brief warmth of the sun is gone and the air crackles with cold. As night takes over the valley, a star stands clear and pure above the chimney. A cold moon slips above the apple trees, a moon all pearl. Jill clears the trestle table of the negatives she has been filing and is cross because the one of Holly carrying a sofa pillow is still missing. I have learned that the best negatives mysteriously vanish no matter how carefully they are filed.

Down by the pond the ice cracks. I hear it as I let the snow-feathered cockers and

Irish back in to melt on the hearth and on my bed. I sleep damply in February. But snow is cleaner than the mud which March brings.

The housebound days of winter have been good, giving us time to contemplate the meaning of life. But now we look toward spring.

When we let the dogs out for a last run in the deep powdery snow, we see dark stains on the trunks of the giant sugar maples. This means the sap is running and soon every tree along the road will have a sap bucket hanging on it. The buckets look like top hats upside down and the "spills" gleam like silver and are, I think, tin. This is the first promise of spring to come, this running of the sap. For it means that life is waking in the trees, the cycle of growth is beginning which will lead to green leaves and to blossom, fruit, harvest in autumn. Hal Borland says that without winter the year would lack a dimension. But now with the sugaring-off at hand, we are thankful.

The first-run syrup is the best, of course. The last gathering will make the darker syrup, which is the only kind city people ever get. The pale translucent first-run syrup is usually reserved for the family table, where it enhances lacy buttermilk pancakes or crisp golden waffles.

One winter we tried making our own. Sat up all night supervising the pans and kettles on the stove, because you must keep sap boiling. You can never go to bed and leave it for a while. Later we had to repaint the kitchen ceiling. All that constant steaming simply dissolved the paint. In the end we had four small jars of perfect syrup. Of course, the process is easier if you have an outdoor fire or a sugaring-off shed, but it's still a lot of work. When people complain to me about the cost of pure maple syrup, I suggest they try making it.

There are still people who ask us if we aren't lonely in winter, way off in the country. Jill says that it would be a real trick to be lonely with dogs and cats swarming around, birds whipping in and out of the feeders, neighbors popping in for a snack, and the woodwork to repaint in the maple bedroom.

People scatter so in summer, but in winter we are closely knit as a community. We can have eighteen people for a buffet supper without even adding them up. And even if a sudden blizzard whirls in as a last gesture from winter, most will arrive, snowy and triumphant. Only those who live at the top of some place like George's Hill can't make it.

My theory of entertaining is simple: have a lot to eat and let everybody help themselves. We used to cook up fabulous and difficult dishes when we entertained, trying to emulate some mental Waldorf-Astoria. Now we have a couple of hot casseroles, something with burgundy savoring it, and a roast of beef, perhaps, with juices following the knife down as it cuts. A salad in the big wooden bowl with everything in it, and a cheese board furnished well with various cheeses.

It is a good theory, but last year we decided on an innovation. After much thought, we decided to have a come-and-go party, serving a buffet from five thirty to eight thirty.

Jill said, "But they'll come at once and stay the whole night."

I felt optimistic about the ones with young children to get to bed. "We ought to make it plain it is a special kind of supper," I said. "Why don't we call it a hunt supper?"

"What are we hunting for?" asked Jill, in astonishment.

"Well, we'll just call it open house," I said, giving up my flight of fancy.

"If they all come at once, it will be open house all right," prophesied Jill. "The walls will fall outward."

We finally called it a winter picnic. Out of respect for the February weather, we held it indoors.

We used a checked cloth, paper plates, cups, napkins. We had fires in both fireplaces burned down to good coals. And we had hamburgers and frankfurters and coleslaw, with pineapple chunks and celery seed and toasted buns and all the mustards and relishes in the category of such.

We had picnic ice buckets with cold drinks and big jugs of hot coffee and ice-cream sticks in an iced Thermos pail.

We had more fun than ever in our lives and Jill says it is just as well, for we shall never have the energy to do it again. Jill said, "A five course dinner with turkey would have been easier."

For one thing, I spent half a day on the mustards and relishes and pickles and such, and putting up picnic tables. Jill spent hours on the fires, getting them right for grilling. What is so simple outdoors in summer proved to be a lot of work inside in winter. All the little heated units we set up under the casseroles were a bother too.

Then there were the dogs, who are not accusomed to platters of meat being set on the floor without its meaning something to them.

We were madly splitting buns when the guests came, so we turned over the cooking of the hamburgers and franks to two neighbors, Phil Thomson and Steve Stephenson, who are experts at barbecuing. They hardly had anything to eat because they cooked so much.

Afterward we played word-guessing games until around one, and everyone said a winter picnic was a fine idea. But as we cleared up the next day Jill said, "After this, in winter, we eat a regular meal."

It was fun, though. I even thought so as I screwed the caps back on fifteen different mustard jars.

It is time not to bring in the branches to force into flowering. I am told that even pear branches will come to bloom, but we have never tried them. Apple and quince and forsythia are favorites; the delicate sprays in an old glass battery jar bring spring in ahead of schedule. We have never had much luck with bulbs in the house but I lay that partly to the restless life they lead. The wide windowsills all over the house are perfect lookouts for cockers. And Holly, by standing on tiptoe, spans the little love seat entirely and leans a large half of herself against my study windowpane.

The sound of a crash usually means we forgot and put something on a windowsill to get sun. And we find that narcissi and hyacinths don't like to be tossed to the floor, even if they are gathered up and put back in the bowl.

I keep my beloved African violets in a quiet and secluded corner in an east window behind a fairly staunch couch and with a good stout Windsor antique armchair deployed in front. This works very well, as a rule, but one day this week there was an unusual commotion as two strange dogs, speaking a strange dialect, came down the road and leaned against our fence and made insulting statements.

And I found Jonquil sitting in my violet garden, right on top of one of the best Blue Heiresses. The small blue violet, Snow Girl, was flat on her side and the wine-colored Red King leaned dangerously. As I gathered little Jonquil up, she had a sort of wreath of African violet leaves in her hair.

But I reflected that Jonquil is irreplaceable, and much as I love my violets, I can take a leaf and put it in vermiculite and start again on Blue Heiress. And I further reflected that living with dogs gives you a very sound sense of values. For you extend your belief in the importance of love and loyalty and a gay heart into the rest of the world. So if a friend does something that seems quite dreadful, you are already conditioned to think, ah, but what a heart he has!

We set our values very early in our life with dogs and cats. We never knew why Silver chewed the middle out of my one and only American Beauty down-and-silk puff, but she did. She was just a lonesome puppy, because we had gone away and left her briefly. And when she died, suddenly and terribly a short time later, that patched puff was incredibly dearer with the patch.

From then on, whenever a gay Irish tail has "sculled" across a coffee table, as Ed Shenton would say, and a bit of milk glass goes down, I only say, "Better move the milk glass."

Our newest puppy, Stillmeadow Jeremy, celebrated his sixth-week birthday by lugging a whole walnut across the room. It was a large walnut with a crinkled shell, and it looked as big as he did. Staggering with effort, falling and starting over, he made his triumphant way. Then he dropped it, withdrew and attacked fiercely. His growl is about as large as the sound of a small egg beater. He eats baby food, scraped beef, milk and egg, Pablum, and has a dropperful of tomato juice and of cod-liver oil for tea.

Esmé and Tigger think very little of him, but if he lunges into their orbit they withdraw to a shelf and peer down. They seem to know he is a chewer and a pouncer and lacks stability. Esmé shows her Siamese possessiveness by leaping on my lap and rubbing her head on my hand to indicate that the new little black thing is of no consequence.

Tigger, being a Yankee Manx, has a different idea. He is one of the most secure beings we have ever known. Jealousy is not for him, nor doubt of our feelings about him. He does not yearn over us; he takes whatever loving he needs and then goes about his own affairs. He is never rushing up to say, "Do you still love me?" the way Esmé and the cockers do. He is a comfortable cat. We all admire his rugged individualism and so does Esmé.

Meanwhile, Jeremy beams at them both

and wonders why they won't play with him. Then he goes off to try his luck with Holly.

The days are getting warmer, and before long we will be able to put away our heavy coats and scarves. But it occurs to me that I do not really mind the cold. In fact, I think that we need winter, even February, which can be the worst month of all in New England, with March running a close second. We need to tighten our belts and shovel the paths, thaw the pipes in the back kitchen, pile the logs on the fire. Subconsciously, I think, we need the discipline of the long dark cold. And then too we have an awareness of spring to come, and summer, and autumn. We are at home in the changing seasons; they are an integral part of us.

Now, toward the end of February, the white horses of winter still pound down the valley, but the end of the course is in sight. For example, I wade through melting snow to the pond and find the tips of skunk cabbage poking up where the brook runs in. I don't know why, but they remind me of medieval hooded monks. Later, they look absurdly tropical with their rank green growth. Now I can imagine that if I lifted a hood I would see bright eyes looking at me. "See," they would say, "winter is never the end."

Names are curious. The skunk cabbage is elegant, but its name is not. I like names that bring out the best attribute of a plant. A New Jersey friend writes that they have always called lady's slippers "whippoor-will's-shoes," and I find that charming. It's just *better* than lady's slippers.

In any case, everything will be coming up soon. For we are turning toward spring, no doubt about it.

Three

Now great winds roar down the canyons of the sky. Branches crash, brooks race, snow scud along grey-stone walls. The world is incredibly clean as the strong vibrant energy of March pounds in the pulses and invades the chilled lungs of winter.

As for the wind, despite the scientists, I feel that nobody knows whence it comes or whither it goes. The dark of north woods is in it, the white breath of polar ice, and underlying this is just a whisper of melting warmth as it passes some sun-warmed hollows where the secret little flowers of spring woods are already stirring.

How it blows away the settled feelings of snug hearth and flickering candlelight! Now I think suddenly, with Edna St. Vincent Millay:

It's little I care what path I take
And where it leads it's little I care;
But out of this house, lest my
    heart break,
I must go, and off somewhere.

I can fancy taking sixpence in my pocket, a loaf of crusty long bread and a wedge of sweet fine Cheddar and setting off for the world's end to see where the wind comes from.

I have always loved those English stories about men who took to the road, eating under leafy hedges, sharing their bread and wine with fellow wayfarers. It is all mixed up with hawthorn blossoming and nightingales singing and the silvery rattle of a tinker's pans as a cart jolts down the road.

I think, in spite of poverty and political troubles along the way, the strolling play companies of Shakespeare's day must have had a merry time. The pennons flying over the cobbled inn yards, the small boys scrambling about, the ladies of the villages and town peering demurely from leaded casements as the actors dismounted, the music sounding in the blue of evening, and then the play. Torches flaring, lutes being tuned, the smell of damp leather jerkins, of ale, of stables, and the voice of a young player sounding bravely:

> Was this the face that launched a
>   thousand ships
> And burned the topless towers
>   of Ilium?

Possibly Kit Marlowe was there himself and thought he had excellently turned a line. And indeed that description of the fatal beauty of Helen of Troy would have been enough to make him memorable if he had never written anything else.

Well, I am not wandering the byways of merrie old England, I remind myself. I am hanging blankets on the line in Connecticut. I have been standing with a clothespin in my mouth for some time, bending against the wind and wandering far away.

But as I hang up one blanket I begin to think of Will Shakespeare himself. It is just not possible that this man's plays, written three hundred and fifty years ago — and count that time, three hundred and fifty — have never, but never, stopped being played. And read, and studied. He survives all fashion. And the miracle is, he cannot be dulled or diminished.

Here in this bright March wind I think of all the travelers of time. And I suddenly know just why my forefathers in 1672 left the secure little English village and went on the wild seas to the new land. Of course they were brave, as I am not.

My favorite ancestor was the Reverend Richard Mather, who crossed the sea in 1635. He left Warrington in England and made the journey to "Bristoll" to board ship, "dispaching 119 or 120 miles in seven days," which he felt was a profitable trip. But when the passengers were assembled in "Bristoll, they had to wait a month and two days, for the ship was not ready. It was the twenty-third of May before they went on board, and on August fifteenth they were still at sea in a "most terrible storme of raine and easterly wind whereby wee were in as much danger as I think people ever were." The cables and anchors were lost; "the sayles were rent in sunder and split in pieces as if they had beene but rotten ragges."

At this point, the Reverend braced himself on the tilting deck and firmly addressed God. The storm, he says, was quelled. I can see him, short, stocky, lifting his long Mather nose, his beard drenched with spray, his voice rolling out over the crashing of timbers. I have an engraving of him at a calmer time, wearing a full robe and a white collar with tassels under his indomitable chin. His curly hair was covered by a ministerial cap (velvet, by the looks). Except for the costume, it could be a portrait of my grandfather, and the resemblance to my father is astounding. So I feel I know him well, and I can easily imagine him facing God as an equal and praying the ship to safety. The ship came to port in twelve weeks and two days. I would give a good deal to know whether the Reverend spent the rest of his life bing unbearable around the house because he had saved the ship! I pity his wife if ever the venison was not cooked to his liking!

Along with the Mather nose and imperative chin and bright eyes, the feeling of partnership with God was passed down. My father had a strong sense that God was always on his side, and that it was up to God to cooperate with him in everything from the stock market to the national elections. When he prayed, there was not a hint of submission in Father's voice — far from it. When I was very small, I used to hope God would manage not to upset Father.

I don't remember exactly how old I was when I first discovered Shakespeare but

I must have been very young. I was immediately swept off into another world, which must have been rather hard on the rest of the family. But I was a very fortunate child when I was growing up, for nobody ever laughed at me when I was serious. When I was being an Indian in the backyard, attired in Papa's heavy Navajo blankets, nobody whistled as I played the Bridge of the Gods and declaimed, "The Bridge of the Gods has *fallen!*"

And when Shakespeare came into my life and I began staying home from church to memorize *Romeo and Juliet,* I was allowed to do so. It was the only time in the week I was alone in the house, and the house reverberated with "No, 'tis not so deep as a well, nor so wide as a church door; but 'tis enough, 'twill serve: ask for me tomorrow, and you shall find me a grave man," as brave gallant Mercutio dies.

I always thought Shakespeare had to kill off Mercutio or he would have stolen the show from Romeo in the next act.

In any case, the excitement of saying the

play aloud always uplifted me so that when Mama and Papa came home, I could only eat a few helpings of fricaseed chicken with dumplings and a couple of pieces of deep-dish apple pie.

Came the time when I felt I ought to impart the beauty of this to the town. I had discovered Shakespeare, and I was fevered with it. Somehow all my family's friends were persuaded to come to a neighbor's house while I did *Romeo and Juliet,* all alone, by myself. The neighbor was chosen because he had a stairway with a sort of balcony effect. By hanging an Oriental rug over the banister, it gave a really fine, I thought, imitation of Juliet's balcony.

The only remarkable thing about this is that I was a very timid child, a mouselike person. I never talked in gatherings; I just passed the sandwiches. But borne on the wings of Mr. Shakespeare, I did the whole play for a quietly respectful audience of adults who must have been amused but were indubitably polite.

In my later years I have made a good many public appearances, but nothing could ever compare in any way with leaning over that Oriental rug and saying with passion, "Farewell, farewell, one kiss and I'll descend."

Naturally descending would have meant landing on the grand piano in the parlor below, but that was nothing.

I can only think that Master Will Shakespeare had given me a kind of madness at that time — I just had to let everybody know how wonderful every word was. And after this remarkable exhibition, I went right back to school in my navy-blue middy suit, my hair in neat braids with a barrette on each end, and did not dare recite unless called upon.

In spite of the winds and the March storms, the house is secure and quiet under the great maple trees.

> He who loves an old house
> Will never love in vain —
> For how can any old house
> Used to sun and rain,
> To lilac and to larkspur,
> To arching trees above,

Fail to give its answer
To the heart that gives its love?

A friend sent me these lines, which were found on a wall panel in an old house built before the Revolution in Concord, Massachusetts. Apparently the author did not sign his name or give the date. I should like to have known him. The lines sound strangely modern — I suspect they belong to a later period than the house. And also the house must have been already old to have inspired the verse.

In any case, I wish I'd written them, for they are lovely.

There is a special relationship between an old house and its owner. An old house has endured so many storms, sheltered so many people, kept steadfast against time. It speaks of love and happiness and grief, of babies rocked by the great hearth, of young lovers on the settle, of men and women growing old serenely. It speaks of death, for there is the coffin door at the bottom of the steep stairs. Our coffin door gives on two stone steps by the well house. The steps are pleasant to sit on in the spring, for we have violets on either side, big dark purple and the pale ivory Confederate violets lined with blue. The steps themselves are hand-hewn stone, and what a task that must have been, bringing them in and shaping them.

The borning room is sometimes called the birthing room. It is a small room and has no fireplace. I suppose enough heat was thought to come in from the great fireplace in the family room. But it must have been chilly on winter nights, even with a feather bed. We found the old wooden cradle in the attic. It may not have been the first one, but we like to think it was. It has a sort of wooden hood, and the sides are plain slabs of wood. It rocks on hand-carved rockers which are badly worn. Plenty of babies have been rocked in this cradle.

The borning room is now Jill's bedroom and has room for her desk, a pine chest of drawers, a bed, a chair and the bookshelves which line two walls. It is rather small for Jill, who is so tall, broad-shouldered and long of limb. But she says it is cozy and she loves it. When puppies are born, the room goes back to its original use, which is rather interesting. It is the borning room and then the nursery. The small ones stay in a playpen by the radiator with a wooden box at one end lined with shredded newspapers. They sleep in this in a pile of softness and tumble out to learn the business of walking in the rest of the pen. Jill nailed a double layer of muslin around the pen to prevent drafts. The mother gets in and out when she wishes to and naps on Jill's bed, which is covered with an old quilt. From this vantage point, she can view her offspring but not be nagged by them!

When the puppies are able to swim in a pan of Pablum, we promote them to the back kitchen, pen and all. And Jill has her own room back. She does not like to sleep in an upstairs bedroom.

"I can't hear what's going on," she says. "Can't hear if the furnace goes off or the pump starts pumping for nothing or the puppies get in trouble or anything."

By the time they are galloping around, climbing the playpen and leading their own lives with vigor, we move them to the kennel to finish housebreaking.

Some people think this is all a silly process. Why not just pop the mother and her babies in the kennel the minute they are born? There are several reasons. In any litter there will be strong puppies and others that need special attention. Even more important, both Jill and I believe that almost any dog is as good as the care and attention he or she gets during the first ten weeks. Kennel-raised puppies seldom have the sunny, secure dispositions that house-raised ones have.

And finally, of course, we just love every minute with the puppies, and it is better to have them at hand than in the kennel at the end of the yard. The development of a puppy is a miracle, from the blind squeaking morsel that fits in your palm to the bouncy ball of fur that struggles to get paws coordinated. The day the first puppy has a slit of blue for an eye is a great excitement. The day the two strongest begin to bat at each other is delightful. They wave their raspberry paws; they fall down; they growl fiercely (in a sort of purr). In the end they are both victors and collapse one on top of the other and fall asleep, often with paws outspread. They are "tard out," as George says.

The easiest part of raising new puppies, I think, is discovering what sort of temperament each newborn arrival has. Jill says it is not true that I can predict what a puppy will become when it is only two days old, but I can. There are always the quick ones, the placid ones, the adventurous ones (who will later dig a hole under the fence and *get out).* There are what I call genius types and what I call steady comfortable ones.

As they grow, they tend to fulfill my predictions. When Jeremy was born, I predicted great things for him and in no time at all he was riding around on the vacuum cleaner. I predicted Especially Me would be placid and easygoing but someone to depend on. (He chases away the woodchucks that demolish the garden.) I predicted that Honey and I would never be separated a minute, and she turned out to be the best typewriter help I ever had. And I predicted that Linda would have sheer charm than any puppy we ever had but would be flighty. She was.

Choosing names is a different matter. Long before new puppies are due, we begin considering names. Of course, the fascinating thing about a cocker litter is that you can't forecast the color. We pick out a sweet golden name like Crocus, and are apt to get four solid blacks.

So we make a list covering all colors, and then when the babies arrive, they almost name themselves. We picked out the name Nightwatch for a lovely little black girl, who is always Linda. Quicksilver slid into Sister pretty neatly. Sweet Clover was called Clove until a young neighbor, who wasn't used to poetry in names, hailed her as Rover. She answers equally well to all three. Snow In Summer is always Snow.

Stillmeadow Especially Me ("People love puppies and especially me") looked so much like a small golden teddy bear when he was a puppy that he quickly became Teddy. We use both names, but there is never any problem, since he comes running happily no matter what name is called. He answers to everything.

One of the best names we ever thought of, Stout Cortez, belonged to a vigorous fat boy who rolled into everything. He was renamed, by his purchaser, Paddy or some such name. And Stillmeadow Faun became Mike.

People often ask me how to go about choosing the right puppy and my advice is always the same. Stand quietly and watch all of the litter. If you need a strong, aggressive dog, watch for the one that pounces on the others, bowls them over, gets to the feed pan first and at once observes *you*. If you wish a gentle, easy puppy, choose the one that sits quietly. A non-pusher and -shover. If you wish a difficult but dedicated puppy, ask for the one that stays in the corner of the run and trembles if someone slams a door. For the right owner, such a puppy will be pure delight. For the wrong owner, the puppy will be either abused or brought back to the kennel.

If possible, before you choose what will, after all, be your companion for some years, meet the mother and the sire. And watch their behavior. Most children take

127

after their parents, and so do most puppies. It is hard to think that many people spend more time choosing a rug or some draperies, which are just things, than picking out the lovable companion for the family. But often it is true.

However, it may well be that the puppy chooses you and you have nothing to say about it. If, out of a bevy, one wiggling morsel suddenly flies to you and looks up with extreme admiration and then begins to chew your shoelaces, this will be it. "You were a long time coming," he or she says.

Jill and I had this experience when we decided to get an Irish setter. You might think that with three children between us, and assorted cockers, to say nothing of the cats, we would not have needed another puppy. But ever since my high-school days, when my setter Timmie was my treasured companion, I had longed for another Irish. And Jill confessed to a secret wish for at least one animal she could pat without having to bend down.

We would name her Maeve, we decided, for the great Irish queen Mr. Yeats wrote about in his poetry. An Irish setter, even at nine weeks, needs a royal name. Especially when Milson O'Boy is in her family. I had a dim memory of Maeve "with the bright and burnished hair" and also "with the lucky eyes and the high heart." And when we saw the puppies in a driving rain, twelve rapid-motion pictures, the color of Maeve's coat was like fire in the darkness.

We told ourselves that the cockers needed a big dog to be a companion, warder and guard dog. And so, with my usual inconsistency, I chose Maeve, who was no fiercer than a baby pigeon. And when we got out of the car, her father and mother gave up chasing the hens and dashed over, waving wild flags of welcome, and at once embraced me warmly. Not exactly in the manner of a watchdog!

At nine weeks Maeve was just the size Little Sister and Linda had been at seven months. Linda was simply enchanted, and hopped around, kissing the new bright one, wagging and leaping. Little Sister took a sniff or two and went about her business. Maeve sat quietly, obviously frightened but with the grave dignity of her inheritance upon her.

In half a day the three were tearing the house to ribbons while the cockers taught her the rules of cocker ring-around-a-rosy and catch-as-catch-can and hide-me-find-me. Meanwhile, between removing my best sweater from their tug of war and saving the small rug from their chewing, I hunted in vain through my copy of Yeats for that "bright and burnished hair" and decided finally that I must have made it up myself.

In any case, Maeve was everything we had hoped. And it was fascinating to see how different she was from the cockers. She was all legs, and in play she was not nearly as quick as the sisters — she lunged and fell on her nose and got herself up and lunged again. And that tail — the only real tail around except for Esmé's — was always waving. We quickly rearranged the house to leave plenty of room for wagging. And when Maeve saw George's hens outside our fence, instead of rushing and barking, she checked at once, lifted a paw and pointed.

There were other differences too. It is possible to go outside the gate and leave the cockers behind, but an Irish setter is a different affair. The only way to go anywhere without Maeve was to let her get in the car. She would sit half a day in the car. Jill said she pretended she was driving.

It is strange how the dogs have always known instantly if we planned to go anywhere, even if it was no more than run to the village for the mail. Half a dozen cockers may be asleep around the house, and suddenly they are all galvanized into action. Little Sister and Linda leap from the sofa. Honey pokes a golden nose around the corner of the bed. Teddy rushes wildly to the wood basket and seizes a prize to bring us. He is one Indian forever bearing gifts. The cockers mill around in the doorways, but an Irish will be already lifting the latch on the front one (which is the right one, of course) and whooping out to the road.

When we are going to leave them for a whole day, we take the most elaborate precautions. We secrete purses, gloves, coats and scarves in the front room and close the door. We plug in the night-light for Honey when nobody is looking, so if it gets dark before we come in, it won't be blank dark. We shut the stairway door casually in passing by so Linda won't be able to give in to her baser instincts and chase Esmé up the stairs. Eventually we do get away, leaving a mort of absolutely broken hearts behind us. And loud in our ears echoes the banshee wail of an abandoned Irisher.

But, oh, when we return, the scurryings and swishings and skidding of rugs! The bounds and leaps and the plump loping about of Honey! Wonderful welcome, and what better place to come to than a house of cockers and cats and setter?

Maeve loved us all but she was Jill's coppery shadow. Except for the times when Maeve took Linda a-gypsying through the woods, she was never far away from Jill. If you wanted either one, you just looked for the other.

And when at last Maeve was gone, Jill kept her green leash hanging by the back door. It is still there. Our present Irish, Holly, has a leash of her own, which is usually under my bed or dropped in a corner, together with an old tennis ball and a half-chewed slipper.

Now, on a sunny day, we hear the sound of the last pond ice breaking. The singing of freed water as it pours into the brook is gay. The brook itself is almost a small river, hardly contained in its course. I would like to follow it down to Eight Mile Brook and on to the river, but much of the way is through wild terrain suitable only for a stream. All I can do is toss a short stick in and watch it sail out of sight.

Which reminds me of Christopher Robin, who tossed sticks over a bridge and was so excited when they appeared on the other side!

The return of the redwings is the true beginning of the year. They come in and fly around in great circles talking things over. Now this is curious, for in the end they always light in one particular sugar maple. Just why this maple is better than the others, I cannot decide. I keep walking around and staring at it and, to my eyes, it is just like the others. But the redwings find it superior. Why? And why do they always discuss it first? And why, when the tree is quivering with them, do they keep changing places? They are very talkative birds at midday. And early in the morning I love to hear their *o-ca-lee, o-ca-lee*. It is a pure clear liquid note, as easy to identify as the yellowthroat's.

Once in a while, we have snow in March, but it has a theatrical look, not quite real. Big feathery flakes fall with an idle grace. The road up the hill to the mailbox turns silver again, but a light, lacy silver. And when George goes out with the milk, the truck leaves dark ebony marks. The sky is pale, but not as low-hanging as a February sky. The swamp is veiled; it looks mysterious and lovely in the falling snow.

When it clears, the world has a brisk look, sky a startling dynamic blue. All the wet branches glow with color — the osiers, the alders, the young willows and the wild berry canes. The brooks rush down the hills with splendid thunder. By August they will be modest little trickles, but now they have their day as they sweep down the watershed.

During a severe snowstorm, we always defrost the refrigerator. Jill's theory has always been that if you put everything from the freezer out in the snow, you can defrost without worry. I am appalled at all the odds and ends in the refrigerator. When the children were little, we never had any. In fact, what we put in toward a casserole was never there when we looked for it. But when the children went away to school, we had a real problem with the refrigerator. We were raised never to waste food because there were hungry children in the world.

"Why is it we are always eating leftovers?" Jill asked mildly. "I would think now and then we could start fresh on something."

I pointed out we were used to feeding at least five.

"Still doesn't explain it," said Jill.

"Why don't we throw out the works and begin again?"

"But you can't waste —"

"I know, with hungry children all over the world."

So we ate leftover string beans, spinach, a potato and some leftover hamburger, plus a green salad to use up half a head of lettuce.

March is a good time for a steaming bowl of soup. And this of course can be made with those leftover vegetables and the remains of last night's chicken. But today I decided on a thick, old-fashioned lentil soup.

As I was stirring contentedly I reflected that every woman must have a favorite utensil. I am deeply devoted to a certain wooden spoon. It is worn down at the edges and has a faintly pinky glow from having stirred so many ruby jellies and jams. But I always reach for it — it fits so comfortably in my hand and stirs so well, and it feels like a companion. We have been through a lot together — crises of sticking chili sauce or carrots in a precarious state. I am very fond of the old black iron spider too.

I love the new gadgets, the shining utensils, the smooth modern efficiency, but I still like to have the old friends right there within reach.

Small things can be important anyway. A spoon, a pan, a special dish — they make one's kitchen peculiarly one's own.

Small jobs can be important too. Washing the milk glass would never go down in history as an achievement, but how good I feel after I have done it! I sit down and look at the old corner cupboard and think about the days when the milk glass was made — and all the people who cherished it, and they did cherish it or it would have been broken long ago. The swan compote has swans forever swimming on their white stream; the lacy-edge plates are lacier than ever. And the little log cabin looks as if tiny folk must be inside, snug and happy. The hens look out at the world with a fierce eye as they sit on the woven basket dishes. The little sleighs look as if they were ready to take on passengers and skim over imaginary snows. I can imagine the tiny figures, waving muffs as they glide away.

We used to set the table with milk glass on a dark-green linen cloth to bring out the translucence, but now we are growing lazy. For the milk glass has to be washed by hand — the torrid heat of the dishwasher cracks the lacy edges. After all, this is old and needs gentle warm suds.

We use milk-glass cups to hold pencils, milk-glass saucers on the bureaus and the bathroom dressing table, and milk-glass lamps on the mantel. And so even though we don't eat from our collection, we do use it. I feel strongly that a collection should be used. We keep the milk-glass candlesticks in constant use and the H-and-L bowl for fruit, and in season I do bouquets in everything from saltcellars to spoon holders.

Of course, as I say rather often, a collection is only really the memories that go in it. You cannot go in and write a check and own a collection. A collection means to collect. It means piece by piece. It means, remember the day we found this in the junk pile at the auction? Remember the dear old ladies who found the matching tiny tureens with one wee ladle? Remember that darling woman who said this piece was her grandmother's but she had only one and it should go with ours?

At its best, it also means you figure the pennies. You give up something to get that swan compote. You save and pinch and squeeze and then proudly buy the eight Gothic plates all at once, all eight.

And, oh, the excitement of having one square blue wheat-design vase and years later finding a mate in Maine or Vermont.

A friend who is a very wise woman started us on the milk glass in the beginning. We had a great deal of illness and sorrow in our families, and life had a grey visage for us.

"Collect something," said she. "There is nothing like collecting to revive your interest in life. Try milk glass."

And she helped us find our first small piece. From then on we were so busy scouring around that we got a lot of exercise and had less time to brood over our troubles.

Connie collects mugs and, just by starting with one mug which I gave her, now has a comfortable collection. Mugs are fascinating and also useful for serving hot bouillon or hot chocolate. I like those thay say, in gilt, "Love the giver" or "Remember me." The alphabet mugs are very choice and wonderfully colored. I like "G is for Gander, Goose and for Gift."

I do not think the monetary value of a collection is very important. Connie's mugs and our milk glass happen to have increased (astronomically in value because they got to be the fashion, but we had nothing to do with it. I know a woman who collects and presses ferns, which cost her only time and energy, and her fern collection is now a museum piece. We have a friend who collects African violets, and often she starts with only a single leaf from some rare variety which she is given. And her violets are like a tropical garden, incredibly rich and beautiful and a rainbow of colors.

We are all collectors at heart, I think, whether we are aware of it or not. Of course, there are many kinds of collections. Thoreau, for instance, wouldn't give a fig for our milk glass. Thoreau retreated to his hut at Walden Pond and made his great contribution to mankind in surroundings hardly suggesting a collector — a bare table, a stool or chair, a pen. In fact the one object he collected was a stone which he found on his ramblings and brought back to the hut. Perhaps it was a chunk of rosy quartz or a piece of granite with glacial scratches. I would like to know. But Thoreau shortly afterward threw it out, for it was a thing extra.

No, he would not collect even a stone. Yet he was a collector who put his life into collecting nature, from sunsets over Walden Pond to the tides on Cape Cod. When he walked the length of Cape Cod, he studied the beach grass, the terns riding the air currents, the dunes, the thickets farther inland. He observed the habits of sea clams and ate one and was quite sick. Food never bothered him except in this instance, for he stopped to eat blueberries or munched a windfall apple as he studied the breaking waves.

In other words, he collected Cape Cod. But I do not think he took a single shell back with him. He didn't need to. He was a great naturalist, a profound philosopher. He has left a priceless heritage in Walden Pond, although this collection has been devastated of late. But Walden Pond, as he wrote of it, is forever. And all the time, no matter where he was, he collected ideas.

"Time is but the stream I go a-fishing in. I drink at it; but while I drink, I see the sandy bottom and detect how shallow it is. Its thin current slides away, but eternity remains."

Shakespeare was a different kind of collector. He collected individuals with their particular characters, tossed by life, reacting to its stresses according to their pattern. His collection was actually mankind, from the trivial Rosencrantz and Guildenstern to the tragic Lear. His characters, so carefully interpreted, so fully evoked, he made immortal.

Few of us may ever be great collectors, and what we collect may not value for generations to come. Our collection may be personal — my grandmother collected bits of silk from her friends and later made a silk patchwork quilt.

"That was Emily's wedding dress," she would say, pointing to a tiny bit, "and that was your mother's first party dress."

Yes, she had her collection and, I may say, it was an exquisite quilt. It wasn't exactly useful, but it was lined with deep-blue silk and edged with wide hand-made lace, and sometimes I take it out of the cedar chest and admire the tiny stitching and wish I could remember all the stories about it.

Some people collect differently. Some collect grudges and take them out from time to time to refurbish them. Some collect self-pity and envy. Then there are the collections of jealousies. These seem to be easy to collect and come in many varieties, from the jealousy of a wife when her husband admires another woman to deadly professional jealousy, to name just two.

Like all collections, once you begin them, they grow. Once a single grudge is collected, inevitably more come. And, naturally, children are apt to inherit the parents' collection. It is well to be sure we collect the valuable intangibles which will enrich the small portion of eternity that is our time.

This morning I went out to burn the trash and found the yard as sticky as molasses. At every step I took, a strange sucking sound came from the thawing earth. Nobody could dream that this would become more or less of a lawn in another month.

There was still an edge of ice in the air; it smelled incredibly pure and fresh and the brave March wind tumbled my hair and the battle with mud seemed inconsequential. Tomorrow, I thought, we can do all the floors again and lay newspapers down in the traffic lanes.

The puppies are enchanted with the mud. They love to smoosh around in it awhile and then bounce up in my arms because they feel good and it's going to be spring. Wild licking and wagging and squirming and whoofing, as if they never could bear being so ecstatic. Too small a cocker is, to carry so much love. Linda and Snow give a couple of affectionate leaps in passing and then whirl away like blowing leaves.

Linda flashes to the front gate to see if there isn't someone coming that she can bark at and tell off in no uncertain terms. And maybe she can see Shep, the German police dog belonging to George across the road. Then she can jump up and down and carry on like a soap-box orator. What she thinks of police dogs! Shep is very polite and always rambles over to cock a thoughtful listening ear on the other side of the picket fence.

Clover greets me and tears back to the swamp side of the house where the big rabbit lives. Who knows — he might just happen to be inside and ready for fun.

Honey sits on the terrace keeping her golden feet nice and dry. Teddy doesn't care how muddy it is, and there is so much of him, and he is so blond!

Snow looks the worst, because her white is so very white, and her hair so soft a texture that the mud gives her the look of a wet mop. I try not to wash her until she can stay clean at least a day or so. She has nice long petticoats, and they make a snowy fringe after she is laundered. She stands proudly waiting to be brushed out; I suspect Snow of being on the vain side about her looks. But Snow is almost too good, as a matter of fact. She is so gentle and unselfish and reliable and anxious to make everyone happy. I always feel apologetic that she cannot go to the Red Cross and roll bandages every afternoon. And she is just the kind of girl who would peel the potatoes for the church supper, and wash the pots and pans afterward.

Before long, everybody discovers that the melting snow has uncovered all the frozen secrets of winter. Now all the lost toys emerge, the cold bones, the soggy pink plush rabbit, the torn bath towel, a bathing shoe. The dogs retrieve all the delightful things they mislaid during the first snowfall. Holly and Teddy gave a good tug-of-war with an old sweater of mine. Jonquil snips up the rabbit (which is Holly's) while Holly has her back turned. When they all pile in again, they bring the treasures plus as much thawing mud as can be accommodated.

The cats do not think much of this weather. Our sturdy Manx ignores it, but he does spend more time than usual indoors. Esmé says that March is not at all to the taste of a royal Siamese. She does not care for wind, or damp earth either. she stays in the sunniest window, looking out and keeping her fur dry. Summer nights are for Esmé and also Tigger, when it is hot and still, and they can go wild in the moonlight.

Esmé catches a mouse now and then. It is always a very small, very special mouse. She seems to feel a little doubtful about the propriety of a royal Siamese engaging in mousing. She reminds me of Marie Antoinette milking a cow in her imitation rustic village on the grounds of Versailles. But when she brings her mouse in, she comes with long, beautiful leaps in the air. She rises completely above the law of gravity, and the mouse rises with her!

A cat has so much imagination. A cat invents a whole drama around a mouse; a cat is, by and large, sophisticated and complex, and capable of creating three-act plays around any single piece of action. Also, *our* cats at least, have a drive that cockers lack. You can talk a cocker out of something but not a cat. Esmé and Tigger both feel confident that they are always right, and the best thing for their humans to do is fall in line with them and not waste energy trying to reason.

As I brace the door against the wind and let a swirl of dogs rush out into the yard, I find myself waiting for Sister, although I know that she will not come. For she was always the sweet one. Whenever I let her out, she always ran back three times and jumped against me and said thank you. Little Sister is so much like her that we often think Big Sister had something to do with sending her to comfort us for the never-failing grief of being without one who was so much the heart of the place. We seem, in a strange way, to be given Sister's baby days all over again. And when we reflect that in all these years of dog raising, this is the first time we have had a puppy exactly like another, we should not be blamed for having special feelings about it.

George came in the other morning and said, "You know what Little Sister's doing now? She's covering her dish with paper before she eats!'' Big Sister is the only dog we ever had who followed this etiquette. It was like unfolding her napkin. She always covered her dish with a layer of paper and then took it off again and began eating. If there were no bits of paper available, she would use straw from the kennel, or fallen leaves. In the house, she could find paper napkins. And now Little Sister was laying paper on her dish before eating. George said, ''She's Sister sure enough, come back.''

Life renews itself, no matter how much we may suffer. Whatever beautiful and precious we may have is always ours to keep. Losing one we love is possible only if we let it be. Death and disaster, separation and sorrow, seem sometimes so much larger than all else, but they are not. Death really prevails only when we walk with him.

This week we took Holly back to Boston to spend an afternoon with her celebrated parents and her breeder. It was the first time since she was seven weeks old that we had been there. It was quite an experience. Mother Holly skipped around getting in people's laps and paying little attention to her daughter. Father sat in his wing chair looking like a banker. Being an international champion, he naturally feels important. When Jill took out the camera, he crossed his paws, lifted his head and posed. We wanted a royal-family portrait. But big Holly (Champion Red-Log's Strawberry Blonde) wandered to the kitchen, where something good was simmering on the range. By the time we got her back, young Holly was upstairs changing the furniture around in the bedrooms. Meanwhile, Father, bored with posing, slipped out the front door and got into our car, which had one open window. He wanted a ride, he indicated. No amount of coaxing and hauling on our part budged him an inch. Paula, the breeder, was brushing big Holly and posing her for the portrait. Finally she came out and persuaded Int. Ch. Red Star of Hollywood Hills to abandon the hope of an immediate ride and go inside again. We got them arranged, and my Holly, tired from her upstairs work, hung her tongue out half a yard. I kept tucking it back in, and it slipped. We were finally ready for the important picture of three Irish, and at that point Cricket, Holly's younger sister, bounced in from the back porch and jumped around. Paula hauled her away, protesting, and I pushed Holly's tongue back in. By this time, Father was ready to go back to clipping coupons and he left the wing chair and took his briefcase to the kitchen. Big Holly got in my lap.

When things were organized again, there was a breathless moment as Jill snapped the camera shutter. It would have been better if the flashbulb had gone off, but it didn't. It was defective.

"Animal photography," murmured Jill, gritting her teeth.

We began all over, while Paula squeaked a toy poodle to keep the banker interested. It kept him interested all right, but drove my Holly into fits, for she had never seen a squeak toy like this in her life.

In the end, as the sun was setting, the royal-family portrait was taken. Then, while Jill put away all the trappings which seem inevitable with a camera, Red Star slipped out and got back in the car and clung firmly to the seat when we told him he could not have a ride *now.* He was quite fretful, in a gentlemanly way, as he was hauled out.

Like most family reunions, it was wearing. But rewarding. All afternoon, I kept noticing how like Holly is to her mother, and yet how like her father too. Every once in a while, Holly feels noble and she acts noble. (This is from Father.) She will be noble five or ten minutes, grave as a judge. The next ten she leaps from sofa to sofa and skims through the air. (Mother.) I mentioned, with hesitation, the trouble we had keeping her inside the fence.

"Oh," said Paula airily, "big Holly can take a ten-foot one with no trouble. No trouble at all. She climbs."

On the three-hour drive home, I told Jill that Holly was the best of both sides of her family. She had, I said, her father's sound sense and stability and yet her mother's elfin spirit and grace and charm.

I said she was noble but not stuffy. And I said she had her father's head and elegant chest but her mother's lively candid eyes. And her charm. After I had worked this out for fifty miles, Jill said, "So all right. Holly is perfect. You are completely besotted over this Irish."

I retired into a hurt silence. We got home and Holly indicated she wanted her supper fast.

After she had eaten and had fresh water, Holly let herself out by jumping on the door latch and thumbing it with a firm paw. We warmed up our own supper.

"You know," said Jill thoughtfully, "I do think our Holly sort of combines the best qualities of her father and mother."

I held my tongue.

This is the time of the year when the house looks shabby, and between mop-up jobs we notice the wear and tear of winter. This year we decided to get fresh pull-curtains for the taproom, a soft apple green with an antique brown pattern over it.

"But that is all we shall do," said Jill,

firmly. "We've got those insurance bills coming in. Just the curtains."

"You are absolutely right."

The curtains looked lovely. But after they were hung, the walls of the room looked worse. The open fires all winter long, plus the coal gas which our furnace affects, had ruined them. So we repainted the walls to match the green in the curtains. It really looked beautiful but the woodwork was a sight. We had to do over the woodwork, which led, inevitably, to new slipcovers for the chairs and sofa.

"Certainly dangerous to put up new curtains," said Jill.

"Well, it's all done now," I said, and added, "except we really have to paint the insides of the corner cupboards. That cherry red looks awful. We need a darker tone of the green."

"And wouldn't you like the floor sanded and redone too?"

"Well, not until the mud season is over," I said meekly.

I didn't mention the kennels, but they needed repainting too. Jill decided to do it herself. There was a little difficulty about the color, as the shade I chose was, of course, out of stock. I settled for the next shade to it, and the tiny cardboard sample looked all right. But it's a far cry from a color card to a paint can. When the paint was on, and dry, it turned out to be a flamingo. The inside of the kennels resembled one of the more lurid night clubs, and I expected to see the younger puppies doing a tango any minute.

"It's cheerful, all right," commented Jill, cleaning the brushes. "And I daresay it is unique. I'll bet there isn't another flamingo kennel in the country."

"It will fade," I said.

"Maybe in five years it will be shocking pink," she said.

Two or three cockers at once poked their noses in to investigate and came out dotted with flamingo. If there is any way of painting anything without the dogs' help, we have not found it. When we paint the picket fence, they appear striped with white. When we paint the trim dark green, Holly has a green tip to her mahogany tail. We don't mind touching spots up for a few days, but the problem of getting the paint from the dogs' coats is a difficult one. You cannot use the normal solvents, for dogs are allergic to them. Shampoos have no efect. We try to comb out as much as we can, and oil the fur and brush it.

As Jill says, it is just something to keep us from being idle!

Two years ago we bought a washer-dryer combination. It is one thing to hang wash out in the sweet sun and wind but, come January, if you venture outside you may have to chop the sheets from the line. And when the children were at home, the upstairs lines were a bother.

"And we are no longer five," Jill pointed out. "We add up to twelve when they are at home."

Children grow up, get married and have babies. You enter a world of diapers before you realize it! So we got the washer-dryer, and Ed Koch fitted it in the back kitchen by knocking out part of the sink counter. We took it pretty lightly, for we had Erma, our neighbor and friend who helps us with odd jobs and housework, to run it for us. Mechanical equipment is a challenge to Erma, and she figured out the new machine in no time. For her, it purred.

But came the weekend that Connie and Curtis, her husband, and Muffin, a lively one-and-a-half-year-old, arrived with more than the usual caravan load of luggage. Connie had brought a lot of washing.

"The dryer fluffs things up so beautifully," she observed.

"Nothing like it," I agreed, "but mechanics is not my field and Jill isn't here and Erma has gone to Bridgeport."

"Have you got a book?" asked Curt. As an editor, he believes stoutly in the written word.

While I hunted for the book, he and Connie read all the labels on the switches, of which there are many. After the usual frenzied search I found the book in with the cookbooks. Why not? It was tucked in with *The Gentleman's Companion* and *Magic with Herbs*.

Curt read the book. "It's foolproof," he said.

So we tossed the wash in and recklessly

pushed a button. Like magic, the machine began to stir into life and whiz along. So we went in and removed the light cord from Muffin, who was chewing it. We removed Muffin's pink rabbit from Holly. Teddy had eaten the teething biscuit. Jonquil was giving Muffin nice warm licks. All was serene. We sat around the fire disagreeing about politics while the washer washed. And washed. And washed. And washed. Finally we wondered about it.

"Better turn on the dryer," said Court. "I think it's washed enough."

So he manipulated a button or so with casual grace while Connie and I stood admiring his efficiency. The machine acquired a new lease on life and started filling with water again.

"Oh, Curt," said Connie, "it's beginning all over. And we've got to leave for New York in a little while."

So Curt pushed the off buttons and fished the sodden laundry out, dripping.

"Everything is blue," said Connie with surprise.

"My nonrun socks," said Curt grimly.

One of Curt's admirable qualities is calmness in times of stress. He wrung out the laundry, loaded the washbasket and went out to the line. He felt it would dry faster outdoors than upstairs.

He was just pinning the last diaper up when it began to snow.

"Oh, Mama," wailed Connie, "we ought to start right back to town!"

I then offered my first and perhaps my last advice to my child.

"Give him ten minutes to sit down," I suggested, "before you ask him to take it all in."

So they carried a soaking wash back with them and Connie borrowed a friend's washing machine and did it all over again. She did not think Muffin should wear blue diapers.

I broke the news gently to Erma the next day. What I said was, "I have bad news. We'd better call Ed Koch. The washing machine is out of order."

"It worked fine Thursday," said Erma with surprise.

She tossed in a load, pushed buttons and brought me a pile of warm fluffy towels a short time later.

"But it might have lint in the drain," she said, and got half inside the machine and found a ball of lint. "Now just let me show you," she said. "It really is foolproof."

But I was thinking what a complex world we live in.

I had just become used to the warm mud when we had another cold snap. Today Jill put a hopeful spade down in the garden and came in saying we might never be able to plant at all. I didn't ask how deep the frost was. I just told her it was pork chops baked with cabbage for supper. This made the world look better, for it is her favorite dish. She got out the seeds and arranged them in the way she planned to plant. Tomorrow she will have a different garden pattern. During this period we always eat on trays so the trestle table is available for the imaginary garden.

While the chops baked, I went out with the cockers and the Irish. The cold sky was smoky pearl; the air smelled of damp and sap. Teddy got up an obliging rabbit and the other cockers flew in to chase. Holly is at a disadvantage, for she freezes to a point at the sight of game, plumed tail level, motionless, one paw lifted, one elbow bent. She can stand thus, on three legs and with that wagging tail still, for an indefinite period. I have, at times, tried to time her point but she outstays me and I have to go and sit down. The cockers do not freeze to a point — far from it. They have a mind to bring back that rabbit as a lovely present for us. The rabbit nipped into the swamp and Holly gave me a reproachful look. Nobody, she implied, minds the rules of the game except me.

Later, we sat in front of the fire, listening as the wind beat against the house. I imagined the last snowdrifts sliding into yesterday. I knew that farmers in the low part of the valley were worrying about flooding. Those people who have built close to a stream lie uneasily, wondering whether the bank will cave in.

Branches cracked down, and often we got up to be sure the last old apple tree was still there in the back yard. The Irish didn't care; she stirred in her sleep and twitched her paws. The cockers were as close to the hearth as they could be without catching on fire from the embers. It is not true that dogs do not worry; they worry every time we leave them to go to town. They worry dreadfully when they are all shut in the back kitchen because non-dog people are in the house. But weather they do not worry about at all.

We sat for a time discussing whether to put on another log or not. We talked about what to give the children for their birthdays. We talked about modern poetry and decided we like non-modern poetry best as a rule.

"I like to understand what I read," said Jill.

"There goes the front storm door," I said.

"I'll fix it tomorrow," said Jill, finishing her coffee.

We are at such a time an island of peace. It doesn't matter if a few shingles fall off in the hurrying wind. It isn't important that the yard is going to be an inland lake for some time. It doesn't matter too much if a falling branch cuts off "the electric."

Spring is on the way and the time of snowdrops is at hand!

Four

April in New England is like first love.
There is the tender excitement of gathering
the first snowdrops, the only symbol of
life in the deserted garden. They are the
lyric expression of music to come — as the
symphony of lilacs will surely come —
because I am picking the cool delicate
bells of this first flower. When I brought
the first tiny bouquet in and put it in an

antique pill bottle, the greenish glass was the color of the center of the snowdrops. I often wonder what pills went in the bottles, for they are only half an inch to an inch high and pencil-slim. My own pill bottles look gigantic in comparison! And when I swallow my vitamins, I feel as if I were choking down acorns.

But like first love, April has bitter days. This morning we woke to a sky as dark as the inside of a snowboot. Leftover wind from March tore down branches that had withstood all of the winter blizzards. The pond iced over in the night again, and as I made pancakes for breakfast I had a silly fancy that winter had flung her last scarf across the water because she did not need it any longer. The confused robins tipped around in a wormless world, and the winter birds made almost as much noise as a social hour after a Garden Club meeting. The red-winged blackbirds swooped down from the sugar maples, and it seemed to me they were quarreling.

I could imagine the wives saying crossly to their mates that it was all their fault that they had come north too soon. So I went out after breakfast to set up the birds' buffet. Jill says that we spend half the day on the dogs and half on the birds and what's left she doesn't know.

For a time we shall have both the winter birds that companioned us during the long cold, and the migratory ones coming from strange southern lands. The air is filled with the excitement of wings. However, much as I welcome the wanderers, I love most the chickadees, nuthatches and woodpeckers, for they have shared the bitter season with us, and never a blizzard too fierce for them to chatter away at the window feeder. I suspect we always love best those who share the hard things with us. Spring and summer friends are delightful, but give me winter friends for my dearest.

Last year we turned the furnace off the last week in April. Some years we can do it earlier; sometimes May is the first possibility. Even when there was plenty of fuel, we used to turn it off the first moment possible. I like the house warmed by the great open fire in the stone fireplace, and by the little fire in my Franklin stove in the bedroom. And when we had the comfortable old cookstove in the back kitchen, we could heat both of the kitchens nicely. Upstairs you can run for your money, but who cares? It is fun to go to bed and watch the Franklin glow, and mine has little doors opening in two places so you can see the crackling flames and the garnet embers.

It is fine that the habit of saving has become part of our lives. Maybe some people still waste, but I don't personally know a soul, either country dweller or city, who has not a strong conscience about my kind of waste.

At Stillmeadow we never throw away anything. Literally. Except used tin cans, which I always wish we could convert somehow to something. Of course, Holly collects them.

Jill is already planning the garden, happily sorting seeds. Early seeds can go in any day now: lettuce, radishes, those nice crisp first things. Peas, too. In our valley you either have early peas or no peas at all. They must mature in the cool fresh days before the aphids rear their ugly heads and dry warm weather sets in.

Easter always comes as a surprise to me, even though the date is clearly marked on my calendar. In our family we have never bothered with flowery Easter bonnets or new spring clothes in fashionable pastels. And we don't have the traditional pot of white lilies, which I dislike because they look so stiff in their formal satin and because their perfume is overpowering. But we do have snowdrops and a few early violets on the table, and the house smells of vinegar after the children have been dyeing eggs and also of chocolate when the hidden baskets are found early in the morning. By midday there there is also the rich fragrance of roast lamb or a rosy virginia ham.

For me, Easter is a shining day. Here in New England it is also apt to be a day of chill winds and mud and grey skies, if not actual downpour. Every so often it snows on Easter and the children wear mittens when they go outside to hunt for eggs under the lilac bushes. But still it is the brightest day of the year for me, and many people must share my view because the little white church in the village is always full.

After the service we come home and change back into our country corduroys. I put the roast in the oven and then there is time for a short walk up the hill to the old orchard. The hazel bushes are budding and I see that the first green tips of Jill's daffodils are showing on the bank above the pond.

The seasons change but new life is always coming, and in the country one never looks backward. As soon as the crops are harvested, we begin to plan next year's garden. When the rose is faded, there is pruning to do for another lovelier rose. Moments of sadness when the delicate amethyst and ivory lace of the lilacs die may shake the heart, but the next morning we go out to the border and see the rosy red peony, like an English country maid in a lyric, spreading a full skirt.

As I sit for a moment on my favorite granite boulder, I think back over the past year and all the things that have happened, all the days that have made up life here at Stillmeadow. And not only life, for in my heart, too, is a goodly portion of death.

The death of those dear to me, and the death of the loved companions who looked at life from the eyes of a dog or cat.

I remember my mother, who never walked across the lawn here, and is always here.

And somehow I remember all the dead who lie under white crosses in alien lands, and their death is also in my heart, and I am at once their mother and sister and lover.

And not being a wise woman, I do not know why I am alive up here on the hill smelling the faint sweet tang of apple leaves and the soft damp odor of the ferns.

But this I know. There is something in the world of new beauty, of loveliness and of grace. There is the meaning of Stillmeadow, deep under the external, and a meaning that will go on down the deep ways of time.

There is the moment of immortality, and this moment is tangible in the first cool crocus sturdy over a froth of snow, in the dark purple of the first glossy globe of the eggplant, and in the slow fall of the first red leaf against the breast of the autumn wind.

And after a little while, alone in the upper orchard, I know that there is actually a God, and that we, his smallest creatures, do have a meaning somehow, even if we do not know why, and that love is the real and the tangible, but the rest may be a shadow in the sun, and cannot endure.

So I go down to my world again, walking through sweet fern.

We always look ahead in the Farmer's Almanac to be sure of the weather.

"Temperature drop might kill apple crop," says the almanac, and we watch the thermometer anxiously.

"Now it clears, let's give three cheers," is a signal for the inevitable window washing.

The old bubbly small panes of glass in the windows are part of the charm of the old house, but they are simply maddening to wash. Half the time we finish one window and go for fresh water and Holly jumps up and leaves a goodly layer of spring mud right on the clean window.

The only time there isn't a setter looking in the window, I thought yesterday, is when we are all inside and she is on the sofa.

Only one of the cockers, Especially Me, is tall enough to reach the windowsills, and his blond velvet muzzle is pressed into every clean pane too, his large amber eyes regard me eagerly, his golden paws smudge the white clapboards under the sill.

We have, at the moment, only nine dogs — eight cockers and one Irish, Hollyberry Red. And the house reflects it.

However, I feel a clean window is fine but isn't a precious memory to store away particularly, whereas the sight of a shining Irish setter and a small sturdy cocker both trying to crowd on one deep windowsill — well, there is something I can remember with pleasure. We can always wash the windows again another day.

An immaculate house is a wonderful and elegant thing, but it can also seem empty and cold. I'll take mine with flying paws and whisking tails and eager loving looks from dark earnest eyes. When the children go away to school and get married and move away, there are so many little quiet corners in a house. A couple of cats and a bevy of cockers and an Irish liven things up considerably. It is hard to be melancholy with somebody playing leapfrog around the room.

Paw marks on the windowsill are a small price to pay for joy.

April and spring cleaning have always gone together. But I doubt whether many homemakers "turn things out" as they used to. In my childhood, fathers had a way of disappearing during this time because the confusion was too much for them. At our house, Father did consent to beat carpets on the line, but his beating was so vigorous that Mama feared he could wear the nap off. Eventually she replaced him with a college boy who beat idly and carelessly.

It was a time when meals were sketchy and I was asked not to bring my gang home but to play outside. Mama went bustling around, very rosy, her soft dark hair tied up in a kerchief. She never looked prettier than when she was battling the winter's dirt. And this was strange, for Mama was an excellent housekeeper any time of year, and a most efficient one. The house was always sparkling, but somehow she never seemed too busy to sit a while over tea and cinnamon toast with a troubled neighbor. Or to have Father bring home unexpectedly a few of his special students or somebody he happened to meet on campus. Or to read my latest composition.

But spring housecleaning was traditional in our town, and we spring-housecleaned when everybody else did. And this was pretty complicated, for the time had to be just right. Before the weather turned really warm but after there was no danger of an April storm.

Came the day when nature was cooperative and all along the street, banners of carpets and blankets hung out. Mattresses sunned on porches. Lace curtains on stretchers decorated the greening lawns. Wash lines were heavy with drapes, damask, satin, chintz. And husbands and fathers, when they could be caught, painted the porch furniture.

This was no mean job, for most of the furniture was wooden and had spindle backs to it. Porch swings were canvas set on an iron frame which always rusted. The wooden tables were decorated with fretwork. The truth is, most of the porch furniture was simply retired house furniture and not designed for porch or yard. A few families had wrought-iron settees and chairs, admired greatly except by the unfortunate painter.

I think now that this was the beginning of America moving outdoors. Daring souls, like Mama, even served meals on the porch on hot days. But when we went to the family doctor's we could, indeed, sit on the big cool screened-in porch but not to eat. When we ate we went inside to the steaming dining room and ate privately, out of view of passersby.

Later came the era of eating in the yard, picnicking, and now we are in the barbecue age, and I fear it is getting pretty civilized. We are overrun with electric gadgets, automatic rotisseries, built-in refrigerator units. This will, I fear, move everyone back into the house eventually. Where the sink is!

I remember spring cleaning as a time of high drama. For one thing, Father did not want his study disturbed. "You leave my papers alone," he warned.

"I just want to dust the books."

"I want them just where they are. Don't touch them. And leave my fossils alone too."

Mama chose a time when Father had examinations and was not apt to bolt home for one reason or another. Then she and Mrs. Novak, who always came to help out when there were major household chores, advanced to the sanctum.

"It has to look as if nobody had been in here," said Mama.

In view of the speed necessary, I was enlisted. Usually I was excused from such work: as a household help, I was a good writer of poetry. I dusted, being careful not to disarrange a single volume. Mrs. Novak did the rug and floor; Mama did the windows and the minerals and fossils. The Indian artifacts got a hasty wipe-off.

But the blowfish was a problem. It hung on the wall and was Father's pet. It looked like a very plump porcupine, and every spine or quill or whatever caught the dust from our hot-air furnace heat. Cleaning the blowfish was a crisis. And usually just as the job was going on, we would hear Father gunning the motor of the Keeton as he swept into the driveway.

Unfortunately Father had the nose of a bloodhound and as he went into his study he would say, "Somebody's been in here."

"I had to answer the telephone," I would say.

The only telephone in the house was on Father's desk, which enabled him to hear every conversation that went on over it.

"Did that boy call up again?" he would demand.

Now I never lied to Father, but I sometimes evaded. The phone had rung while we were madly cleaning, and I was thankful it was not that boy.

"Something about the church," I said.

Mama and Mrs. Novak were scrubbing the kitchen.

"Why don't you stop this infernal

fussing?" he asked. "Get out and get some fresh air and exercise." Then he gathered up some books and spend back to his next class.

His final words floated back: "Whole confounded house smells of wax."

So, all in all, spring cleaning was not the most tranquil period in our family life.

During the spring cleaning, Mama also had her annual battle with Father over the storm windows. There were seventy-two, and she hated them. I have inherited this, for I also hate them with a deadly hatred. I do not like to look through two layers, usually clouded, in order to see the outdoors.

But Father was a restless man, to put it gently, and he usually decided to put the storm windows on in September, just to get it over with. This was a fierce job because the house was built at the very edge of a steep hill and it took double extension ladders to get to the upper windows. Father would not hire the job done.

"Can't trust these college boys," he said. And since college boys were *the* help for everything in our small college town, that left it up to Father.

But in April, Father had decided that the storm windows might as well stay on because it would be winter again any minute. He conceded the smaller ones because he himself suffocated if the temperature in the house was over sixty. But we had two enormous windows overlooking the swift-flowing Fox River. They were Mama's idea and she had never heard of picture windows but that was what they were. They did not open. They did bring the beautiful drop of the wooded hill and the shining river and the stars and moon practically into the house.

"Now, Rufus, you may as well take the storm windows off the big windows," Mama would begin.

"No use," he would say. "I'm going to leave them on this year. Just have to put them back up before you know it."

"But, Rufus, nobody leaves storm windows on in summer," Mama would answer.

"I don't care what anybody else does," said Father, and in this he was so right.

He never did.

"I don't want to look through two sets of plate glass," Mama pointed out. "Besides, I want to wash them."

"I'll hose off the outside," Father offered.

"I want to wash the insides." Mama was firm.

She seldom crossed Father in anything, but these storm windows were to her like Custer's last stand.

"You can't get any air there anyway," said Father. "They won't open."

"I told you when we built they should open," said Mama.

"We have enough windows that do open." Father's face was always red at this point.

"I know it's an awful job," Mama would say sweetly, "and I fear it is too much for you. I'll get two of the college boys. It's a two-man job, anyway."

At that, with a furious snort, Father would rush down-cellar and get out the extension ladders. Fortunately a neighbor always happened by (did Mama call him?) and held the huge windows as Father slid them perilously down.

"I hope you're satisfied," he said savagely to Mama.

By September, Mama began to suggest that these storm windows be left off. The windows didn't open anyway.

"You want to waste all that heat?" Father would say furiously. And back the windows would go.

Now that I am in charge of my own house, I must confess that I find housework very tiresome in spring. So much suddenly seems to need doing. The light is brighter now, and lasts longer, and it shows up everything! You can't do it all at once — curtains, rugs, woodwork, attic and cellar. It is Jill's theory that things put in the cellar just grow. As for the attic, what can we do with the Bridge of Sighs, Venice, the Colosseum by Moonlight, and the High School diplomas of our children? They all add up to a firetrap and happy haven for wasps. And if we really get in a ruthless mood, because it is spring, Jill says wistfully that she is sorry she burned up all the letters with the Pony Express stamps which were in the attic after her grandfather died.

An attic is a state of mind, I tell her. I myself have a small chest with love letters tied in ribbon, some moth-eaten football letters from my first beau, dance programs. (Oh, what a wonderful time that was when I stayed to the very end and Father put me on house rules for two weeks. Worth it.) Everyone has a mental attic too. Old thoughts, faded dreams, hopes laid away in lavender. But a mental attic is just there and you rarely spring-clean it. A real attic is something else. I suspect that even apartments and modern ranch houses have a closet or a pantry or back shelf loaded with old cartons that collects things just the way an attic does.

One year I crept up the ladder to our own attic and threw almost everything out of the window, and a passing neighbor thought the house was on fire. The house wasn't, but I was, at the moment. I regretted it later.

Both Jill and I give away anything and everything that can be of any use to anyone who needs anything. This has caused considerable difficulty in times past when we gave away the children's things. ("I do wish I had the old crib for my baby now," says Jill's daughter.) But I know the Bridge of Sighs framed in three inches of gilt is not going to do anyone any good.

And no child would be caught dead nowadays wearing my daughter's first smocked dark-blue silk frock (size 3). Then there are those booties. The children are grown, married and with children of their own. Their children do not wear booties. Nobody does. They wave chilly little feet in the air even in winter. But the booties do bring back the memory of the baby feet, and somehow we can't throw them away. So the attic upsets me no end. It has more memories than wasps, which is saying a good deal.

I often wonder who does the cleaning in the houses you see in magazines. They always look so perfect — never a thing out of place, and the people, if any, sitting perfectly groomed and smiling on an immaculate terrace. The interior views are even more amazing. How fresh and shining every single object, how uncluttered the tables.

Sometimes I am irritated by the decoration experts. The last article I read was about a woman whose house was full of whimsey, said the writer. It was. It was simply bursting with whimsey, if by whimsey she meant down with gilt and red velvet and dark green. When I reached the room where "the dresser had been whimseyed up with white and gold," I uttered a frightful sound and rushed away. Passing rapidly through the living room, which has no whimsey at all, I entered the kitchen and proceeded to whimsey up the stove by cooking perfectly plain golden wax beans and a panful of beets with no humor in them. I afterward scrambled eggs with chicken livers, and whimseyed up the table by putting on the knives, forks and plates.

Of course, I love the beautiful table settings shown in my favorite magazines. If I ever envied anything — and I often do — I would envy the fortunate housekeepers who can set an entirely new table every time. Imagine having so many sets of china that every meal you can use a different color scheme!

With us, if the Bennets come to dinner, they find themselves eating from the very same set of dishes they had the last time they were with us. They undoubtedly recognize the tablecloth, too. Furthermore, as I look with the eye of a critic on our table, I admit to Honey and Esmé that all is not according to Hoyle, anyway. The dinner plates are modern, a pale soft glaze. Because we haven't enough antique ones. But the glasses are old thumbprint, some of them chipped. And the platter is my Wedgwood with the soft grey-blue pattern, so beautiful. The vegetables are probably served in French earthenware casseroles, which keep things piping. It's authentic Stillmeadow, and not whimseyed up.

At this season of the year, I think often of Thoreau living his solitary life in the hut by Walden Pond. I too, in spring, feel impatient with the busy-ness of life. Thoreau knew what he was about. ''I went to the woods because I wished to live deliberately, to front only the essential facts of life, and see if I could not learn what it had to teach, and not, when I came to die, discover that I had not lived.''

Sometimes, I think, we rush so, we finish a schedule only to make a newer and busier one. We do not, ever, live deliberately and fully, for we haven't time. I know few people who go outdoors now and sit quietly for a couple of hours just looking at the miracle of spring. Sometimes as we drive along the country roads, I see occasional figures stretched out in lawn chairs. But they aren't observing May; they are reading the newspaper or a magazine. They are like the people I have seen on the great beach at Nauset on Cape Cod who never hear the music of the tide because they have portable radios playing hot music!

I hate to think what Thoreau would have said to that!

A spring snow is somehow unconvincing. The old well house has an extra peaked roof of pearl. The yard is drifted. The branches of the lilacs are outlined in silver and have a Japanese look. But even as we shovel out to the gate, we take a casual attitude. For it is spring, and snow cannot last. The farmer's Almanac says, "Nothing wrong here, except the last big snow of the year." And the neighbor down the road says the peepers have to be frozen in three times, and I should not worry about them. This is only twice.

We pile the apple logs on the hearth, and say this is the last snow. I am reminded of my friends who always put on the upper left-hand corner of the envelope when they write: N.W.H. — nothing wrong here. This originated with Beverly Nichols, the English writer, and is a very comforting thing. So often people write only to tell bad news. But if you see that N.W.H. before you open the envelope with the French kitchen knife, you feel happy. Nothing wrong here, I murmur.

I am frightened of the telephone, for so often it brings news of illness or trouble. A telegram numbs me. I think it would be nice if friends wired saying, "Everything is wonderful!" Or phoned long distance to say, "I have a pair of bluebirds in my yard." But usually we tend to communicate only the dire events, and the good times go by without comment. Perhaps we feel that bad news cannot wait, but good news can be postponed.

Yesterday, though, we had a long-distance phone call that brought wonderful news, for it announced that Stillmeadow Hollyberry Red C.D was now a champion.

The C.D. itself is pretty special, of course. It stands for the Companion Dog degree which is won in the Obedience Trial. But this call brought news from the breed ring.

"You have yourself a champion," said Art Baines, his voice muffled by the sounds of the dog show. I dropped the receiver and sat down and cried. Jill finished the call.

"So what are you crying about now?" she asked. And took off her glasses and cried quarts.

We didn't give a fig for Holly getting

her championship in the beginning. We liked her right at home, and we knew she was perfect. But since she was a descendant of champions and her father was an international champion and obedience dog to boot and her mother a champion and a field dog too, Paula, the breeder, begged us to put her through as a tribute to her sire, Rusty, who had died.

For regular accustomed dog people, it is quite simple. You just pick the best of the litter, get a handler and pay no more attention. But we sat up all night wondering whether we could part with Holly even for one weekend. We couldn't show her ourselves, for you have to run like a racehorse in the ring, and kneel, and stand on your head, and spend weeks traveling from show to show, none of which we could do.

Finally we took Holly to one show and sat with her all day so nobody could pat her and give her a germ. Then Art Baines came over to meet her. He is a small, quiet man, brown and smiling. He sat down by her and said, "Hello, Holly," and she got in his lap. "You look like your mother," he said.

Holly kissed him, and he kissed her back.

This got us in for a lot trouble. For one thing, it got us into commuting late at night to the parkway to pick her up or deliver her, so she did not have to be away from home much.

Once it also led to a phone call, when Art's light comfortable voice said cheerily, "Meet me with Holly at Route 128 Station near Boston at eight tomorrow morning. Do you girls good to get up early for once."

This led, of course, to our getting off at four in the morning, running out of gas in a town forty miles from Route 128, finally getting refueled, only to get started on the throughway in the wrong direction. My tearful voice and Jill's explanation changed the whole course of traffic as the tollmen flew about taking down barriers and putting up barriers, and the traffic piled up for half a mile. In the end, we went backward the wrong way and got Holly delivered, tail wagging.

Finally, with two points to go, he took

her to Virginia and we moped around, deciding we would simply give this up. We would write him tactfully and say we just didn't feel, etc., etc.

Then came the phone call, and back came Holly (this time we only had to go to Mahopac, New York, to get her). Holly was glad to be home, but had a regal air. Naturally winning a four-point show and her championship could not register with her. But she felt she had made Art happy, and somehow had done what she was supposed to do. Her whole being radiated success.

It made me wonder whether it is imperative for everyone, human or canine, to fulfill the destiny one was born for. Holly's main interest in the rosettes is to snatch them and race around and play tag with them with Especially Me. But there is something, nevertheless, that she has acquired. For one thing the constant admiration of so many people gave her a sense of being even more important than all the spoiling we have done. Her very walk indicates a sense of royalty. √

I guess it was worth it, although when

when we look at the mass of ribbons and rosettes, I sometimes say that I think we won them, too. I would not wish again to go through with such a schedule or have my Irish away from me, even briefly.

But the championship certificate hangs right over the picture of Holly and her royal parents, and I like to see it there. "Irish setter Stillmeadow Hollyberry Red, C.D.," it says and goes on, "has been officially recorded a CHAMPION. By the American Kennel Club."

Now she races around, untrimmed, and getting burs in her long feathers. No longer does she get rubbed nightly with vitamin-A oil from a famous beauty salon. She can stay out in a downpour and just get dried with her towel when she comes in, and who worries about how much damage it has done to her coat? She may look like a country dog, dusty and bewhiskered, but the certificate is framed and even if she gets in the briers and loses part of her petticoats, who cares? Her life is very busy, what with pointing quail and pheasants, chasing rabbits, helping the service men by removing their tools whenever they lay them down, and so on. I wonder whether she ever thinks back to the days when, brushed and satiny and with no feather blowing back, she pranced in the ring? Perhaps not, but I know that when we go to visit Art, she will climb in his lap and melt as only an Irish can melt.

She really liked living up to her parents, I think.

Weekending begins in spring. City folk feel the ancient urge of mankind to be close to nature again. Besides, the roads are open. There is no danger of sliding into a snowbank or skidding on ice. Jill's daughter, Barbara, and family come early in April. The grandchildren are now five (Davy) and seven (Ellen). Davy is a thoughtful dark-eyed thin boy who has a most endearing way of happening to lean against you when he is telling you something about spaceships. This makes it easy to slide your arm around him without its being a public affair. He wants to know the *why* of everything, from why the daffodils have different roots from "other things," to why we have a bootjack on the antique pine cabinet. He also wants to know how everything works, and upon being introduced to a folding yardstick spent an hour measuring everything in the house.

Ellen has dark hair but very blue eyes. She thinks like an adult. When her father came home from a business trip she said gravely, "The family isn't complete without you. *no* And when she was describing a cottage the family had rented the summer before, she said, "Now it has no dining room, but the dining area is related to the kitchen."

Most of the time they spend going up and down the stairs.

"Let's climb this mountain," says Davy.

When resting, Davy turns the big hearth brush into a horse.

"Look how the world goes up and down for this cowboy," he says.

Ellen watches Jill baste the roast.

"On thinking it over, Grandma," she observes thoughtfully, "I find there is only one thing in the world I do not like, and that happens to be spinach."

Somehow I feel it is a tradition with

children not to like spinach, and I wonder when it started. The dislike seems to go from one generation to the next, spurred no doubt by parents who say it is *so good for you*. I think if parents would say, "You are not old enough to eat this," the story might be different. And the truth is, spinach is not what it used to be in most parents' childhood. It is crisp, delicate, savory. I have always liked it, but I can remember when you had to cut it with a knife, the leaves were so tough.

Ellen and Davy manage to gobble up everything in sight, and once, when Ellen was very small, I caught her solemnly helping herself to a puppy biscuit from Teddy's bowl. She ate it all, too. I imagine it was good for her — dog food is loaded with vitamins.

In the evening, after the small ones are tucked in bed with various stuffed toys, the adults sit up and talk, and around midnight Val puts on another log, and Barbara brings in a snack — paper-thin cold ham, Port Salut cheese and crusty bread (she baked it herself).

"And what is your opinion of Katherine

Anne Porter?'' she asks as she sets down the tray.

Which is good for a long conversation!

The weekend after Barbara's and Val's last visit, Jill's son, David, and his family were here. Young Jimmy, who has been taking swimming lessons all winter in the city, confided to me that he can do the dead man's float now. Looking up at me through long, dark lashes, he reminds me of his father, and I recall the time he learned to swim at camp. David had never embraced water in any form, and even with two pairs of water wings he idled at the edge of the swimming hole, not wetting one toe. But the first weekend we visited him at camp, he came flying across the sand saying, ''I can swim! Watch me!'' And swim he did, going through the water like a slim silvery fish.

''Our counselor says there are some people who can't sink,'' he said as he dripped out, ''and I just happen to be one of them!''

Now six feet two, David has taken up skin diving while his son learns to float.

Tall man, small boy, and the pattern repeats itself. It made me think, as I watched Jimmy in his father's lap, that perhaps the real secret of success in life is faith that we cannot sink! When we are faced with a problem, if we believe we can solve it, we are likely to. So, as you embark on a new course, why not assume you cannot fail because you just happen to be one of those who cannot sink!

I wonder how Jimmy will feel about letter writing, though. That was a challenge his father never seemed able to meet. I remember that when he came home from camp the first summer and we unpacked his suitcase, we found two dozen postcards addressed to us, each one saying, "Hi, I am fine. Love, David." He admitted sheepishly that he had written them all before he left home and it just happened that he forgot to mail them!

Even today, he prefers making long-distance telephone calls to writing even a few lines.

For me, April is a time of remembering. It may partly be because this is my birthday month. Or perhaps it is that the long winter is over and done with, and spring walks down the hill over the dogtooth violets. Or possibly it is just that when the air blows softly over the melting snows, and the crocus is established, one naturally has a tendency to take stock of other times, other springs.

I remember the birthday parties Mama used to give me when I was a leggy teenager. I don't know how she stood it. Mama let me ask anybody I wanted, and the house bulged. There was always a lot of breakage, but Mama said it didn't matter. The gang consumed tons of food and gallons of hot chocolate. We danced, rolling up all the rugs. Butter from the popped corn dribbled all over the floors. But in those days, nobody went out to sit in parked cars and of course nobody got intoxicated on hot chocolate.

Father retired from the scene and holed up in his study. But if the party went on too long and he wished to go to bed, he appeared and cleared his throat and asked what time it was. This was always effective.

I remember birthdays when I was away at college, where I learned that birthdays weren't important at all. Classes went on, exams came, themes were due, and I was just about as unimportant as a body could be.

This was painful, but salutary. Growing up is never easy. I still had the security of the box from home, however, with date bars and cake and fondant dipped in bitter chocolate, and a fancy nightgown. And from Father a book of Shakespeare or Byron or Keats. From my beau, a box of candy which had always melted and came out as a sticky mass.

Now I no longer look on my birthday as something special. All through the year there come days which seem to have the radiance of the early birthdays. It may be an unexpected kindness or a special letter from a dear friend. It may be the sun shining on the lilacs when they are newly budded. It may be the Irish bringing me a knuckle bone, which she cherishes and offers to me as if it were invaluable. It may be a phone call from a faraway loved one who says, "I just thought I'd say hello." Or it may be seeing a neighbor's lights shining across the field. I can see them now, through the green mist of young leaves. I like to think there are neighbors all over the world, despite wars and poverty and oppressions. The human heart does not vary much, although we may speak in different tongues.

Today I noticed that the ugly scorched place in the backyard is beginning to green over. It was only last winter that the barn burned down. Hal Borland says that in the country a barn is not a building but a way of life, and so indeed it is. Our barn was around two hundred years old, with the grace and dignity of hand-hewn chestnut beams, hand-forged hinges and latches, and a lovely slope to the ancient roof. Wrought-iron railings marked the horse stalls. Some of the windowpanes still had the greenish glass from the early days.

When we came to Stillmeadow, the old carriage house had fallen to pieces, a crumbling sleigh still under the mossy fallen roof. But the main barn was staunch, and it did become a way of life.

We took out the small pen that still smelled faintly of pigs and built a good workbench for Jill, for when you buy an old house, you buy a lot of minor carpentry and general repairing. The iron railings we used on stairs to the haymow as guardrails. We cleared the hay dust from the mow and moved in a desk and chair, a Boston rocker, a maple settee and a coffee table which was really a butchering block. I loved to work there and in the course of time a number of books emerged from the old haymow, as well as countless short stories. The stillness, the drowsy air and the smell of newly cut hay from the meadow made a very special world for me. In May I could look out through the open door almost as if I were a mariner looking from a ship's deck. How green and deep the meadows looked from that height as the new grasses invaded the earth. Apricots, peaches, nectarines and Seckel pears made a flowering lane this side of the fields. They never bore any fruit, but the blossoms were beautiful.

Often in summer we took tea there, for

it was cool and shadowy even in August. Watercress or cucumber sandwiches and iced tea with fresh mint leaves made a pleasant break in the day's jobs.

Downstairs there was room for four kennel units, each opening on a grassy run. There was room enough for a car, too, but we used that space for the Ping-Pong table for the children to use on rainy days. There was space for croquet and archery sets, fishing tackle, lawn mowers, snow shovels, rakes and hoes, bags of cement and peat moss. In fact, whenever we looked for anything, someone would say, "Oh, it's in the barn." Usually there was a piece of furniture there, half refinished, such as the old butternut chest, the maple highboy or the spinning wheel bought at an auction.

The night the barn burned down was the coldest of the winter. We sat by the applewood fire eating popcorn and reading. Jill was, I think, rereading *The Nine Tailors* by Dorothy Sayers. (She reads it every year.) I was rereading *Romeo and Juliet*. This was partly because in the novel I was working on, the secondary character kept taking over and I wanted to consider Shakespeare's problem with Mercutio. Nowadays one cannot kill off a man in a duel just because he is more interesting than the hero, but I felt I might get some help, duel or no.

Suddenly an explosion shook the house. "A jet plane in the swamp," I cried. For some reason I am always expecting one to crash in the swamp. Jill shot up and looked out of the window. "The barn's burning!" She flew to the door, flinging back the words, "Call the fire department!" The whole building was already a wall of flame. The roof wore a fringe of fire. Jill was racing across the yard with a fire extinguisher, in what was probably the greatest peak of optimism ever recorded. The yard lights lasted until she got to the kennel gate, then they went out. But when she called, miraculously the cockers poured out, Hildegarde coming last, being elderly and somewhat stunned from being flung from her bed by the blast. Jill's problems were added to by a dogfight, for we had two jealous females who fell on each other with fury.

I had my problems too. Even normally I am no good at all on the telephone, and in a crisis I cannot even dial. I dropped the phone four times and finally got it braced against a shelf. Naturally I dialed incorrectly four times. I have not much idea of who answered except that once it must have been a nightwatchman in the Medical Center in Waterbury. Finally I dialed Long Distance and screamed, "We are burning up!" I managed to tell where we lived, and she rang back to the fire department in Southbury. So the report about our fire was relayed via Waterbury which is fourteen or fifteen miles away!

The local volunteer fire department was attending a Lions Club dinner, and the speaker of the evening had just begun a talk on first aid for ambulance cases, when the siren shrieked. To a man, the audience jumped and ran. Five minutes later the first truck rolled up and men in their best clothes, topped by helmets, began hauling the hoses out. Fortunately, our pond was not frozen, and as our young neighbor dashed across the yard, he said, "Get the hoses down this way."

Without the the pond, the house would have gone too.

Luckily for us, Phil Thomson, the neighbor, had stayed home from the Lions dinner because he was coming down with something. He had on slacks, a sweat shirt and moccasins. When he heard the siren, he grabbed a jacket and said to his wife, "I don't know where it is, but I'm off." By the time he backed his car out, he could see half the sky flaming. No doubt where this fire was. Minutes later he was at our gate. Since he knew the place so well, he took over at once. By this time, Jill had stuffed the separated cockers in different rooms and put the rest in the back kitchen. And as the hose snaked out, Phil paused to say to me, "Now just don't worry. Everything will be all right."

Three hours later the fire was dying down. The firemen came in, sheeted with ice, their best suits ruined. They had climbed to the inferno of the haymow to play extra streams of water down on that tank of kerosene stored below. They saved it. They had chopped at burning timbers, and one of them had rescued a single lawn chair which stood on the ice in the yard. Meanwhile about thirty neighbors came to stand in the dreadful cold, waiting. They offered to take some of the dogs home, to put us up overnight and so on if the house caught. To do anything at all.

The fire inspector came in and said gently, "I am sorry. It is a total loss. There is nothing left." We thanked him. Then he put away his notes and remarked, "I would say there must have been a fault in the kennel heater."

Then they all went home. The men would be up and at work in the morning — farmers, storekeepers, young executives commuting to the city. The women would be up fixing lunches, getting children off to school. And around two thirty, when I began to cry, and I really cried, it was only partly over the loss of that cherished barn, but chiefly because I was overwhelmed at the goodness of people. Our volunteer firemen get no pay. They raise money by an annual clambake and a chicken barbecue and such projects as selling brooms or whatever. Rural distances are far, yet they are on call day and night.

Whatever they are doing, they hear that siren and run. And then I cried about the neighborhood women who stood those hours in that killing cold, some of them shivering until they positively rattled. They were just there, in case.

Now, in April, as I walk around the yard, I can see that the roses we planted where the barn once stood are going to live. The pine trees that had one side scorched are beginning to show signs of life. Nature herself has great possibilities for recovery. In time, the site of the barn will not prick my eyelids with tears. The barn will be a memory, a precious bit of life past. We were fortunate to have had it during the years when the children were little.

But every now and then Jill hunts for a level or a scuffle hoe. And suddenly stops and says, in disbelief, "Why, it must have been in the barn!"

Five

It is difficult not to be sentimental about May. I always think of Edna St. Vincent Millay's "I am waylaid by beauty." After a thunderstorm, it is an opalescent world. Lucent drops fall from the lilacs; the young leaves of the maples look polished. The wet grass smells sweet. The cockers and Holly race through fallen apple blossoms, and the cocker ears are feathered with pink-white petals. Apple blossoms have so short a stay, and a thunderstorm is hard on them.

I have a few friends who enjoy thunderstorms; I myself am not addicted to them. In our valley, they are savage. We had the giant maples cabled as soon as we could afford it after we came to Stillmeadow. But lightning brought down a maple in the farmhouse yard across the road, and the tree fell on the house, smashing the upstairs. During that same storm, I was answering the phone when what looked like a ball of fire ran up the curtains two feet from me and somehow seemed to explode on the stone hearth. To say I was electrified is an understatement. I dropped the phone and ran to the kitchen, although why I thought the kitchen was a refuge, I do not know. A kitchen is so full of wires and pots and pans.

When we went out, after the thunder rolled on over the hills, the yard was deep with fallen branches and part of one apple tree had crashed on the garden fence. I know a thunderstorm shows the magnificence of nature. My father used to go out and admire the lightning. He was what I call a storm buff. But I prefer to pull out the floor plugs, shut the windows and lock the doors and sit quietly on the couch. I try to be sensible and trust in God and the lightning rods and the copper cables, and I would not go so far as one friend of ours who has glass casters under the posts of her bed and just gets in bed when the lightning flashes in splendor.

A regular rain in May is something else. You can see everything grow, and after a good rain there will be a fresh crop of asparagus. But if we have, as happens, two days of it, I have had enough. Not the farmers, however, who always say, "Need more rain." The only time a farmer will admit we have rain enough is when there is a flood and the lowland is covered with water.

When the lilacs bloom, I look for my unicorn. Yes, I know the unicorn is a legendary animal, but my unicorn and I do not care about that. We are quite real to each other, and isn't that what counts? He comes from the woods, usually at dusk, walks delicately down the hill, cropping the violets as he moves. When he dips his head to drink at the pond, his silver horn catches the last light. Through the years, he has acquired many friends, who ask, "Has the unicorn come yet?" But nobody has ever seen him except me. And, of course, I only see him at this time of year. He goes back to his own country, and where it is I do not know. But he gives me assurance that there is still magic in the world when he comes in lilac time.

A fragment of a Rupert Brooke poem, found in his notebook by a friend, is much to my liking as I ponder on the balance between ordinary reality and the extra-real in this world.

All things are written in the mind.
There the sure hills have station;
   and the wind
Blows   in that
   placeless air.
And there the white and golden
   birds go flying;
And the stars wheel and shine;
   and woods are fair.

It is true all things are written in the mind. And so I feel very easy in my mind about my unicorn. I have him, and that takes care of that!

The lilac is my unicorn's special love, and it is mine too. I suppose if I ever came back to this world as any kind of plant, it would be a lilac. Either a Lincoln, or a white lilac with lacy white-jade blossoms against the deep-green leaves. I am sure heaven is bounded by a white picket fence that never needs repainting, and with lilacs always in bloom hanging deep clusters over it.

When the lilacs are in bloom and the apple blossoms and the white narcissus, New England is an experience in rapture. I also love the lilacs because they are a faithful flower: they grow around old blackened chimneys where houses once stood; they mark out abandoned gardens. When I cut the clusters and bring them in the house, their sweetness is pure and singing as young love. White lilacs belong in old blue sugar bowls, purple in milk-glass vases.

Pale gold tulips, white narcissus, smoky black tulips (the new variety) and white lilacs from the bush by the well house make a bouquet to remember.

The texture of spring flowers is especially lovely; the feel of a tulip petal is like lustrous old porcelain.

By mid-May, the violets cover the ground and invade the lawn so that it is hard not to step on them. In the meadow, the tiny wild dark purple and the white make a rich carpet. The Confederate violets have taken over the border and advanced to the terrace, where their pearl blooms with blue centers are lovely against grey stone.

Apple blossoms mist the air with white and soft pink. We drive along the winding country roads to see the old orchards when they are in full glory. The apple is one of the most beautiful of trees because the shape of the tree itself is so gracious. The silvery grey trunk usually has a slight angle, and the branches bend in a design of beauty. If I could paint, I would first of all paint an old, very old apple tree in an old abandoned orchard with blossoms not fully out, just pinky and in bud. With a spring sky softened overhead and young grass below.

Even though we cannot spray our old apple trees, we can fully enjoy their blooming, and the gentle silvery-green leaves coming out, and the nice shade, designed for a hammock swung underneath, and then in autumn, we can gather windfalls for spicy applesauce.

The old abandoned orchards are home for the birds too. Every knothole has a busy little family cheeping in it. In winter, nuthatches and woodpeckers whip up and down knock-knocking and darting bills for nice juicy morsels of all the little things that attack old apple trees.

The birds are full of bustle these days. Most of the eggs have hatched and some of the more precocious youngsters are teetering on the edge of the nest, trying to learn to fly. They cheep worriedly, wondering whether this is what they are really supposed to be doing, and their parents call encouragement. It all starts before sunrise, when the mist is still wreathing the lilacs, and late in the evening the night birds are still talking. Stillmeadow is not exactly still in May.

When I occasionally go to the city to visit my daughter and her family, I am stunned by the noise. When I lived in New York, I grew accustomed to the endless roar of a world of noise. But now that I have been in the country so long, I find the voice of the city appalling. I can hardly hear what people say for I am always conscious of brakes squealing, trucks grinding gears, sirens screaming. Trucks grinding gears all over again.

There is nothing wrong with my ears. It is a psychic affair. At home I can hear not only all the bird talk, but also the squirrel leaping on the bird feeder, the distant bark of a fox in the upper orchard, the sound of an ax in my neighbor's woods. I hear a drip in the cellar when the tank begins to leak, and the sweet melancholy of a mourning dove in the swamp. And from the first floor, I easily hear mice skipping in the attic. But country sounds are individual against a backdrop of quiet. City noise is an ocean assailing me. In a group of chattering people, I sit glassy-eyed after an hour or so trying to count the number of times that same bus has roared past outside.

And then I notice that when weekend guests come to Stillmeadow, they are often tired in the morning because the birds got them up at dawn. And if the cockers and Irish see strange things at night and bark lustily, nobody visiting gets a good night's rest at all! In the days when our neighbor kept horses on his completely unmechanized farm, the thudding of hooves in the barn at night unstrung guests who could sleep through a five-alarm fire in the city.

It all goes to show, Jill remarks. And always adds that her feet hurt walking on those awful pavements. This is not strange, for we have not even one sidewalk in the village. We walk on grass or country roads or on garden earth. And even in a drought, these give to the footsteps.

In the country too, when a car goes by, we know by the sound whether it is Willie's car going up the hill, or the postman. And now and then we stop whatever we are doing and say, "That's a strange car. Must be on the wrong road."

The dogs know too. They are mouse-quiet when George drives over to tend the furnace in winter, check the kennel heaters, burn the inevitable rubbish. But just let someone drive by looking for Hull's Hill Road, and they give tongue. They instantly recognize the sound of our own car as soon as we get to the top of the hill when we have been away, getting our hair done in the next town.

But the only approximation to city racket is when four horseback riders clop past. Then, I admit, our cockers and one Irish could almost do justice to Times Square. This is why everyone in the area who has a timid horse trains it by riding back and forth in front of Stillmeadow. They figure if a horse can stand that, he will stand anything.

Except when something happens, cockers are quiet dogs. When they bark, it means something.

Sometimes when we have guests and the dogs begin to bark, Jill goes to the door and says firmly, "Linda, stop that this minute. Tiki be *quiet*. Jonquil, hush that."

"You didn't call to Teddy," says Steve.

"He wasn't barking," Jill answers.

"But how do you know who's barking?"

"They just use their own voices," says Jill.

Teddy (Especially Me) is usually quiet, but when he feels it is his duty to bark, he barks with whoever is nearest him, keening like Jonquil or doing a staccato performance with Tiki. But still, he sounds like himself.

This spring has brought an addition to the family, for my grandchild Muffin now has a baby sister named Anne. The newcomer is a calm, sunny little soul, who already seems to love being held and especially being sung to.

Alice is surviving very well. She reminds me of a spring flower, perhaps a crocus. She touches things so gently that nothing is broken. Her crying is like a shower — the sun is out so soon. And when she thinks something is funny she spills over with a chime of merriment.

Next to music, I find scent is most evocative. An odor can re-create a whole memory. For instance, the smell of dried lavender takes me back to my childhood. My mother had a friend whose whole house always smelled of lavender. She was a retired French professor and lived just down the block from us. She always treated me as if I were grown up, pigtails and all, and she often asked me to lunch when Mama was busy.

She gave me China tea in a fragile flowered cup, and black walnut croquettes and a green salad with her special dressing. She wore soft silk dresses with lace around the neck, and she was always cool and unflustered. I minded my manners and politely refused a fifth croquette, although it was hard. She talked to me about poetry. Those were enchanted times and I hope she knew how much they meant to me. And they come back, completely realized, when I smell dried lavender. I think she must have tucked tiny silk bags of it in her dress.

Unsavory odors can also evoke past

times. The smell of a scorched rag takes me back to the night the barn burned down, for Jill had put a couple of dog blankets on the workbench that day. There was also a mattress in the haymow (which was my studio), and for days we smelled burned mattress and blankets from the ruins.

But now, on a sunny day, I can smell the pines we set out on the site of the barn, and most comforting it is!

In our particular part of New England, pine trees are not too common. Maples and elms, wild cherry, hickory and a few butternut and black walnut trees strike the dominant notes. The chestnuts went in the great chestnut blight, and only a few white birch trees have resisted the wild winter storms we have. There is some oak, but I suspect it has always been rare, for a section near us has always been called White Oak, as if it were very special.

Our postman, George Bennett, whom we call Mr. Conservation, is determined to bring back chestnuts. He keeps a small sack of Chinese chestnuts in his car as he goes his rounds, and entices everyone possible to plant Chinese chestnuts. The tree resists the chestnut blight, grows sturdily and relatively fast and bears big glossy nuts. Korean nut pine is another planting project of Mr. Conservation, and most of us have planted Korean nut pines.

Ever since I have known him, I have found George Bennett a rare and wonderful man. He doesn't know what a stumbling block is, and I doubt whether the word *obstacle* is in his vocabulary. Years ago, he noticed, as he went hunting with his sons, that the face of the land was changing. Good soil was being eroded into rivers and streams. Cut-over land developed great gullies and the good soil washed away. Bird cover was scarcer every season and wildlife diminished. Sewage poured into the Pomperaug and the smaller streams. Forest land was being razed for housing developments for factory workers in the nearest cities. And as the trees came down, so did the water table. Wells began to go dry, brooks diminished to a trickle.

It would have seemed to most men a hopeless proposition. This particular man had never had an opportunity for training as a naturalist, horticulturist or forester. He was already working for a living when he would have liked more education. Now he worked hard as a rural postman, a quiet, pleasant man who minded his own business, and never even got involved in local politics.

But he began to read everything he could lay hands on about conservation. Government bulletins, fish and game reports, reforestation articles, books by such naturalists as Edwin Way Teale. He read late at night on weekdays, and then on Saturday afternoon and Sunday he walked the land and studied it.

"We have to do something about conservation," he said mildly.

And so began a one-man crusade which resulted, in time, in a program that is now being copied in many states, and in fact, he even has letters from Australia asking for advice on conservation there. Meanwhile he has farm folk, weekenders, retired people, young business executives who work in the nearby city, all planting, setting up feeding stations for the birds, fighting water pollution. He set up a training program for Boy Scouts because he said if they learned about the value of natural resources, they would grow up to conserve instead of destroy. And constantly he experiments with plants and trees, which he calls "just trying things out."

His wife, Ethel, who is a superb cook, is used to having people coming in at any time for meals or even for the weekend so they can as she says, "tramp around all day." I often think that Thoreau, on one of his trips to town from that hut on Walden Pond, would have felt completely at home sitting at George Bennett's table, trying some of Ethel's hot apple pie and talking about trees and birds and the weather.

Most of the garden planting comes now, and such an excitement. I sing a small tune to myself as I watch Jill moving down the stretched string marking the row.

Plant this when maples are in bud,
And feel the magic in your blood,

Plant that when maples are in leaf,
And that's the *end* of winter grief!

Of course, I cannot actually compose a true tune, but I can sing along to suit myself.

Jill follows the rows carefully, lifting the friable earth — what a fine word that is, friable. It sounds the way the garden feels, and it is even, curiously enough, a dark cinnamon-colored word.

Almost all words do have color, and nothing is more pleasant than to utter a pink word and see someone's eyes light up and know it is a pink word for him or her too. You can also get into rather warm arguments over a definitely dark-green word that someone insists is beige. Also, it is not a good idea to go around explaining about the color of the words in strange company. Some people give you such a sad critical look, and their heads shake slightly.

As the hard little pellets go into the earth, Jill moves down the rows, intent, earnest. Suddenly in the clear spring light, she has the look of a pioneer woman, tall and vital and dedicated. She has, I notice, gardener's hands, with firm squarish palms and long strong fingers, sensitive enough to cope with those maddening carrot seeds that I cannot even get out of the packet without disaster. Like a true gardener, she also is, in spring, red as a beet in the back of her neck and arms, but winter-pale as to face, because she is always bending down.

Planting is an act of faith. The small envelopes of minute hard particles have no slightest suggestion of the tender sweet corn, the snow peas, the dark and juicy beefsteak tomatoes that are somehow in them. They lie in this earth, secret and still, and then suddenly one morning a green mist seems to come over the garden. Fragile and delicate tiny etched lines mark those string rows where Jill moved back and forth so patiently.

Presently we go out and pull the fresh parsley and the rosy crisp radishes — and the miracle has begun again! From now until the black frost, the garden will be a constant excitement. The pink crisp rhubarb, the asparagus, the first carrots, the lettuce and silvery savory scallions usher in the season. How delicious is a sandwich of freshly baked bread and young scallions well salted and peppered! (We always remember with pleasure the day Jill's daughter, age ten, said she was just simply tired of being the family scallion!) As I snip the tips of the first scallions, I am always feeling that one of the most hopeful things about mankind is that we go right on planting when the season comes, despite bombs, wars, world crises. There is a basic faith in mankind that planting is a secure thing.

And how infinitely much the earth gives us for so little! Here in New England where our easiest crop is stones, and we never see the rich steaming black loam of the Midwest, we still have only to plow and rake and maybe add a little lime or fertilizer, drop the seeds in, and be reasonably decent about weeds, and we have bountiful crops!

I note the atlas says we have a humid continental climate in this part of the country. This means, in my language, that it rains too much here and it is damp.

But how the growing things love it! Jill has to hoe out rhubarb now and then — it takes over like a giant tropical creature in a rain forest. And the shy little shrubs she put in the border a few years ago have to be cut back or we could not get in the gate at all.

This is true of the pine trees we set out after the hurricane took down our thirteen beautiful old apple trees and played jackstraws with them. We set out six small modest little pines, and now we can only get to the clothes dryer out back by hacking a path between the two most vigorous ones.

The iris — ah, the iris! Jill moved and separated, moved and and separated, gave away, moved and separated, and one desperate day flung her hands in the air and said, "I cannot take it." She dumped a basketful in the swamp, since when we have iris all over the edge of the swamp, and doing nicely.

The poet's narcissus that we naturalized under the remaining old apple trees has really naturalized in a big way. It chokes itself. Every year or so, Jill goes out and spends a day trying to manage a million bulbs that are just rampant in the tall grass.

However, strange things happen. We used to have a whole border of primroses, with their velvety leaves and pale gold and rosy faces. All of a sudden they vanished. I said they packed up one night and just went off adventuring with their roots tucked under their arms. Jill said, nonsense, the soil was wrong.

"Same soil," I said.

"Doesn't make sense," said she.

I like to think our rhubarb is a heritage from the early folk who lived here. For the shining bright-green leaves open like platters down by the pond, at the edge of the garden, all along the border, back of the compost heap, and at the edge of the asparagus bed. Rhubarb stalks grow tender and rosy and big all over our place.

And as I cut up the tender pieces for a pie, I think the first woman who kept house here must have done the same thing just about now. Maybe she had a pie cupboard and set her pies on the shelves, crisp and juicy from the great Dutch oven in the fireplace.

We have some wild asparagus too. I love eating gifts from nature. Dandelion greens are as satisfying as finding a treasure in the old jewel box. Wild blackberries, and grapes, sweet wild strawberries, and the morel mushrooms — these are rare and lovely presents.

But we had no luck with fiddlehead ferns. Perhaps we picked them too late; they tasted a little like old rubbers to me. A friend who specializes in wild edible plants says you pick them just as they poke up. Ours were older than that, I think, looking back on it.

Pokeweed shoots are supposed to be elegant too, but we have never gathered them. The berries are poison, the stems and roots are poison, and I felt we had better not get involved with them at all.

Milkweed pods, sliced and fried are supposed to be delicious. The Indians used to eat them, and used them for thickening too, somewhat as we use arrowroot.

There must be hundreds of unsung heroes and heroines who first tasted strange things growing — and think of the man who first ate a lobster. This staggers the imagination.

I salute him every time I take my nutcracker in hand and move the melted-butter pipkin closer.

My father was a kind of emotional gardener. One summer he went into beans and we had beans by the million. Then he gave beans up and concentrated his furious energy on tomatoes and grapes. We drowned in tomatoes and we had grapes by the tubful. Then he pruned them all wrong and that settled that. He was a gardener who wanted results, and fast. He actually kept digging things up to see how they were doing. Mama advised against this. "Rufus, give them time," she would say.

"They ought to be up by now," he would retort.

After the bean summer, she was glad, however, that he wasn't more successful in a steady sort of way. She got awfully tired of canning beans day and night.

Father liked things in good amounts anyway, at all times. Sent to the store for a can of peas and a loaf of bread, he would come staggering in the door with a full case of asparagus, a case of corn, go back and unload a case of tomatoes. He might have forgotten the peas, but he had lots of other things. He liked the feeling that we were well supplied in case anything happened. "You never can tell," he would say.

I often wish he could have lived to see a modern freezer; he would have had the largest made and absolutely jammed. Then he could have arranged for half a pig, half a beef and half a lamb and really felt satisfied.

Nowadays at lunchtime the sun is almost summer-warm and we can carry our trays to the Quiet Garden, where the Lincoln lilacs overhang the picket fence, and the flowering crab gives a rosy glow. The lilies of the valley are spreading out of bounds, we note, and the lemon thyme planted between the flagstones half covers them. When we step on it, a sweet odor fills the air. The iris is beginning to bloom as the late tulips go by.

Some years ago we put in white pansies as a border in the Quiet Garden. They have reseeded themselves ever since but they skip from one spot to another so they are now all over the place. Also, as time goes on, they are reverting to their natural color so some of them are moonstone blue and some flecked with darker blue. The blooms themselves grow smaller each year, but on the whole I like them better than the giant size. I prefer flowers that are modest.

The small garden is the one place off-limits to the dogs, because of the bulbs and lilies. So as we carry our trays out, they line up by the picket gate and watch. Jill says someday Holly will appear with a placard (lettered by Little Sister, the neat one) saying UNFAIR TO COCKERS AND IRISH.

The Quiet Garden is not actually a true garden at all. When we moved to Stillmeadow, a half-demolished corncrib stood there, furnished with corncobs and field mice. The crib itself was too far gone to be remodeled into anything, even a puppy house, so we chopped it up and used the wood for the fireplace all one winter. Then we put a low picket fence around the spot and laid flagstones in the center, leaving a border for flowers around the edges. One side we reserved for any herbs — tarragon, chives, lavender, sage, borage (the blue flowers are lovely in a May bowl). Applemint and savory were planted. We had sense enough to plant the dill in the vegetable garden, where it can be restrained, although with difficulty.

We put in the spring bulbs and a few roses and some nicotiana. Nicotiana has leaves like a tobacco plant (it is a variety of tobacco). It grows so vigorously that Jill has to keep grubbing it out, and the plant itself is leggy and ungainly. But on hot summer nights it fills the air with an almost tropical fragrance. The flowers vary in color from a bluish white to a garnet red, but the rank growth of the leaves obscures their beauty. Never mind, the scent is worth everything.

After lunch Jill, who is never one for resting, goes off to check the rhubarb. But I decide that the dishes and the mail and the household chores can wait. I turn my chair so that I cannot see the imploring noses thrust between the pickets and I allow myself a few minutes to sit in the sun and dream. My dreams range from imagining my unicorn cropping the violets on the bank beyond the pond to wondering what would I do if I had, suddenly, a million dollars. Or I dream that I am on a freighter going round the world, seeing all the strange lands I shall never see. I am on deck, sipping hot broth, and the captain (no less) leans over me and asks tenderly if I will dance with him that night! I can smell the starch in his uniform.

However, I always have a running commentary in my dreaming. It goes like this: "Better defrost the refrigerator tomorrow. *Must* clean utensil drawer in kitchen — ants any minute. Jonquil needs a bath. Mat in shower should be washed and sunned."

Then as I dance in the moonlight over a tropic sea, I begin to worry about the telephone bill. Did I pay it twice? I often do. And where is my driver's license?

Regretfully, I leave the freighter and go inside to see if my driver's license is in the kitchen basket where everything else is.

Jill comes in with rhubarb and more asparagus, and at this point it seems inevitable that we freeze some of each. We set up the kettle with boiling water for blanching the asparagus. Get out the sugar for the rhubarb.

"I'd like to go round the world someday," I venture as I snip the tough ends from the asparagus stalks.

"I don't see how we'd have time for it," says Jill firmly.

Much later, as I take my shower and get ready for bed, I realize that I am definitely never going to get on that freighter, but that the asparagus and rhubarb in the freezer will be lovely next winter. You can't, I tell Holly, have everything. After all, we could hardly cruise the seven seas with five cockers and an Irish and a couple of cats. And besides, the children could not come out for weekends. We would miss that first tooth of Jill's granddaughter's being swallowed. We would miss the grandson's first definite steps and the clear but unintelligible lecture he gives about the wood in the fireplace.

We all, I suppose, desire at one time or another to escape. We not only wish to escape the drudgery and routine of our lives but the frustrations and worries. We yearn, in short, to be free. Just to pack up and go. To get away from it all, as the saying goes.

But there is no place so far away that one can escape one's own self. The country of the heart is always the same.

As I pick up my tray and start toward the Quiet Garden gate, there is instant rejoicing among the spectators outside. They never reproach me for having stayed inside, eating marvelous things while they starved slowly on the other side of the fence. They are too pleased to be with me again.

Little Sister bounces against my knee, almost knocking my tray down. Her bright, eager little face looks so much like her mother's. But now Sister is not the only one who is missing. When I came home from my last trip to the city, Honey was not there at the gate to meet me. Her tired heart had simply stopped beating, and although she was well over fourteen, I wondered whether perhaps she had missed me too much. It would have been utterly selfish to wish her back but I couldn't help wishing she might have been there to meet me. The fourteen years seemed suddenly a very short time. I had helped her be born and held the tiny soft ball of satin in my palm. Even just three minutes old, she began to wiggle and paddle the air with minute paws.

She was not a beautiful puppy but I felt we belonged together. Later, after we had called her a wind-hound for some time, she suddenly blossomed into a facsimile of her champion sire. She was wheat-gold with low-set long ears and dark amber eyes. She had a blocky muzzle, with a dark nose. And she followed me like a golden shadow. We had a good life together, but as I say it seemed very short.

I often know she walks beside me now.

It is Jill's theory that in every life there is one dog. Other dogs may come and go, but there is one grande affaire. I feel this is probably right and yet it worries me, for it might mean that I am a fickle person.

For I seem able to love deeply just the dog I am looking at.

I think that there is a truth about love which one learns by having a companion such as Honey. My devotion to her was special but it will never prevent me from cherishing any others we ever have. There is always room in my heart. And this, I believe, is the way it should be.

After freezing asparagus, hoeing the garden, doing the chores, getting blankets out to sun and back in again, we take a breather again at suppertime. When the sun goes down over the green hills, there is an afterglow the color of a fire opal. The valley below is already blue with evening. The stars are always a mystery. I never really see them come out; one moment the sky is empty and the next there are the stars.

As the swallows swoop by, Holly chases them, leaping high in the air. Often they stop to perch on the electric wires and talk back to her. She will never be able to fly, but it is not for want of trying! Teddy follows her as fast as his cocker legs can go. When the birds have gone, Holly finds her faithful bone and tosses it in the air awhile. Then she drags Teddy along by one golden ear until he protests at summit level. The rest of the cockers busy themselves around the yard. I notice that dogs never go to sleep gradually. They can be in full chase and suddenly they flop down and are off to sleep in a wink. When we go in the house, they get up and follow us in, and then collapse again. Now and then a paw twitches, a tail stirs, but the dream is deep.

Moonrise silvers the sky as we put the house to bed. And May, like Byron's love, "walks in beauty, like the night of cloudless climes and starry skies."

Six

This is the singing month. Rambler roses
everywhere — over white picket fences,
over grey stone walls, climbing old well
houses, blooming on lattices in old-
fashioned gardens. The whole green
countryside is laced with shell-pink, ivory-
white and rose-red. The sky sings too,
such a deep tranquil blue. I think I can
hear the horns of elfland faintly blowing

as I go out to the Quiet Garden to shell peas.

The gentle charm of old white houses is enhanced by the riot of roses, as well as by the tall pale amethyst iris and the shorter pale gold. Most of the old houses have borders of iris around the yard or flanking the walk to the front door. I like to bring iris in the house and set it in the milk-glass swan compote, where the light from the window falls on it. The petals are translucent and the color a pure and lovely note.

Faith Baldwin does not wish any flowers arranged in orthodox flower arrangements. She likes flowers as is, just put in water and left to their own devices. She is very firm about this, and for a tiny exquisite small person she is firmer than almost anybody. If she comes for tea, I am careful *not* to make arrangements. My own feeling is that flowers come into their own in the house if they are properly arranged as to mass and color and design, and related to the container, and that it is an art much like painting with living color to be able to make fine bouquets.

I think the beautiful mass arrangements in Williamsburg, Virginia, add greatly to the atmosphere of that enchanting place. They are traditional, and they are made with flowers grown in the same way as they were when Williamsburg was young.

I saw the Wythe house by candlelight once when I was in Williamsburg, and I remember the polished beautiful furniture and muted tones of the rugs but most of all the way the candlelight shone on the massed roses in silver bowls.

It is strange that the human eye finds beauty in certain forms. Why does a circle seem satisfying and a triangle or pyramid shape inspiring? The crescent may be fine because of a connection with the moon, and the moon has played a great part in our life always. In that case, the circle might be the sun. In flower arrangements I find the triangle a happy design, for the apex gives a sense of height and uplift, and the lower points help relate the bouquet to the container and give stability to it all. The main thing is to cut the flower stems in varying lengths, and to give each blossom room enough in the bouquet to look comfortable. Some bouquets one sees are stifling.

On the whole, I like bouquets in containers that are not formal vases. David says that with a whole closetful of vases, I am always making bouquets in old bread tins or pie plates. I do have a hand-hammered silvery grey aluminum casserole which is beautiful with purple lilacs, white lilacs and tulips in it! Old flowing-blue sugar bowls are lovely for pale pink roses and delphinium, and milk-glass saltcellars look charming on a coffee table filled with Tom Thumb rosebuds and forget-me-nots.

The autumn flowers, such as zinnias and marigolds, take on added glory in old copper bowls or wooden mortars, and winter bouquets are admirably suited to antique pewter tea- or coffeepots or mellow waxed wooden bread-mixing bowls (what they call trows in Williamsburg). But very ordinary containers are nice, too — a mustard jar or a fat little vitamin bottle. Or a glass from what we used to call the dime store.

One of the loveliest table arrangements I ever saw was shown at the Southern

Connecticut African Violet Show. A member had taken a piece of curved and weathered grey driftwood, tucked delicate mosses and lichen in the hollowed-out parts, and where the root formed a niche, planted a tiny Romany African violet. The fluted pale lilac of the blossoms in the setting of grey and woodsy green was lovely. And actually you might say a piece of old wood and a little wild moss and a potted plant weren't much to work with.

Boiled down, and I do mean boiled down, the rules for a bouquet are simple. Delicate flowers take a delicate container. Heavy rough-textured ones need strong solid containers. Then you gather your flowers — or if you have no garden, you pick weeds or grasses, or you buy a quarter's worth of daisies at a flower cart. Then you set up your container full of water and look balefully at it while you take off the lower leaves of your flowers. (They get gangrene underwater and smell.)

Then you put in one flower which is two and a half times the height of the container. If you are using a basin or bowl, you will have to have a needle holder or a wad of chickenwire or some sand or else you will have to glue it to the bottom, for it won't stand still a minute.

Then you cut a flower stem two thirds the length of the first and put it in slanting to the right. (It will slant right to the counter if you don't catch it.) And another, one third the length of the first, goes to the left. This is easier as it is a shorter distance. Then you fill in the interstices (a good sound word) with blooms of various lengths. No two should be just the same and your scissors will fix that. Meanwhile you put the heavier blooms and darker colors toward the bottom and make a focal point of one special one at the lip of the container, but not leaning on it. (Never let anything lean.) The lighter tones go to the top. Finally you have to be sure each flower has a breathing space and does not cross stems with any other. And there you are, with a simple bouquet. If it falls over, you have made a mistake. Very well. If the Siamese cat eats off half of it, that is not your fault.

In June the house is cool and quiet. The dogs play their games in the new-cut grass. When the day is hot, the old house never gives in to it. Roses in a milk-glass bowl look cool too. We change to soft-green candles for the candlesticks on the trestle table. But this is as far as we go for summer. I don't like to tear the house to pieces just because it is hot in summer. Rolling up the good rugs, putting on pale slipcovers, and putting away my cherished antique bottles and the milk glass to save cleaning and dusting is not for me. We get more dust in winter anyway from the furnace.

Putting the house away for the summer used to be traditional. And during the years I lived in the South, I often hardly recognized a house when the dustcovers went on, the bric-a-brac vanished. I might do this myself if we lived in a very hot climate, but in New England it is not really necessary. I do concede spraying and packing away the knitted hoods, mittens, woolen scarves and the afghans. That is as far as I go. We do not have a revolution in blankets. If I want a blanket when a cold wind comes up in the night, I want my own regular blanket. I don't want a gossamer thing that I cannot even feel.

But then, as far as my room is concerned, I do not like change. I may add something new from time to time, but I almost never get rid of anything. Jill manages to keep her room uncluttered and the children's rooms are relatively ordered now that they are away so much of the time. But my room would give a decorator a nightmare. It is a small room, and it is not only my bedroom but my workroom. It is also the television room, since there isn't an inch for the set anywhere else. In addition, it has the Franklin stove, an antique maple daybed (comfortable for the dogs) and a Pennsylvania Dutch chest (I have to have some storage space somewhere). Between the office-size desk and the maple four-poster is a low bureau which just squeezes in. It holds the radio, clock, a pile of books, magazines and the crossword puzzle I am working on.

My desk does not resemble any I have seen in those lovely colored pictures in the magazines. How elegant they are with a single bouquet, a neat telephone and one desk pen. How uncluttered indeed must be the life of the owners of those desks. Just an expanse to preside over! If there is a typewriter, it lurks underneath somewhere and springs out when needed.

On my desk I have thirteen objects, not counting the pile of unanswered mail and the two piles of manuscripts. It looks like a rummage sale. But it can't be helped. The wide windowsill back of it takes an overflow of dictionary, World Atlas, *Treasury of Great Poems* and my best white African violet.

I have only ten books on the desk itself, chiefly poetry. The pictures take up some room, although I also have the wall at the left covered with family pictures. My gentle Honey is in a silver frame next to the Severn portrait of Keats. A dreamy picture of Connie is at the right. She looks as if she might write a sonnet any minute, but actually the picture was taken of her when she was perched on the top of a stepladder. The ladder does *not* show. At the left is a portrait of Faith Baldwin taken at the time we first met. She gave it to me the first time I went to visit her, and this was quite an occasion in many ways. As I turned into the driveway in front of her house, I ran into a fairly good-sized shrub and mowed it right down. (It was an imported something or other — valuable.) I then went to the front door. There was a storm door on it, and the bell inside. I hauled on the door and broke it open with a splitting of boards and the sound of the knob being torn out. (The door was nailed shut for the winter.) I ended my visit by getting myself locked in the powder room where I wept miserably as the members of the family wrestled with the jammed lock.

This was the beginning of our friendship, and I may say I think Faith was remarkably brave to risk it! In this particular portrait, she has a grave gentle expression but with the half-smile so characteristic of her.

On the whole, I expect my desk will always be just the way it is, even to my two favorite milk-glass mugs full of pens that won't write.

Before we know it, school is over. The big yellow buses no longer come down Jeremy Swamp Road, and children feel the wonderful excitement of freedom. My teenaged friend Tommy, who is Willie's son and lives around the corner, finds everything easy except, spelling and grammar, and this past winter I think I bored him with daily spelling lessons. It got so he would bound in the house chanting "a-c-q-u-a-i-n-t" or "r-e-c-o-m-m-e-n-d." It had an odd effect on me; I began spelling to myself all the words in my vocabulary! I think we should take a long look at teaching in elementary-school grades. In this age of science, education has progressed marvelously, but after all, words are basic tools and we do live with sentences all our lives. As far as I can gather, we haven't made much progress in enlarging the horizon of the very young with regard to English.

There have been many changes in education. Jill's grandchildren and mine had to be tested for nursery school. David's youngest, Amy, who will be starting this fall, enjoyed the tests: she liked playing all those nice games. But Muffin, now safely *in,* was frightened by the whole thing. I know that city schools are crowded, but even so, I wish parents didn't have to begin worrying about education until college. In my day we just went to school when we were the right age.

For children, life is one big experiment, and they attack it with zest. I wish we could keep that sense of wonder all our lives. I think we take too much for granted, and no doubt this helps us to get our work done, whatever it may be. But I believe an hour looking at a Silver Moon rambler is a well-spent and exciting hour.

Speaking of silver roses reminds me that one of the cockers, Silver, has learned how to jump the picket fence. Usually only an Irish can do this. She has also found out that by going around the outside of the yard, she ends delightfully in the midst of George's chickens. The first we knew of it was when a guest came down to breakfast and said idly, "Who is the little black-and-white one that stays with the hens?'' We flew out, expecting an end to the flock. And Silver was lying down by the chickens, just watching them with interest.

The strange thing about it is that when she is inside the fence, she rushes at them with everyone else, whenever they come near. All the dogs make a game of flushing the hens at regular intervals, and the hens give a few conventional squawks and go on eating. Silver must have figured out in her funny little head that the chickens are part of the place.

"Well," said Jill, "I'm glad it wasn't Melody who got out." Melody is not noted for rigid self-control. In fact, she has a gleam in her eye when she sees Esmé lolling on the hearth. It really would be wonderful to play catch-as-catch-can with a cat, she thinks. Then, when I say something about it, her eyes are as innocent as a spring day.

"You misjudge me entirely," she says.

Briefly, in June, our own children drift back to touch home base again for a time. I remember how it used to be when they were in college. The girls would come with fanfare, laden with dirty laundry enough for the armed forces, with run-over shoes and broken glasses and cavities in their teeth. With boxes of books tied up with old rope, and with phonograph records in suitcases. The preliminary approach was made by tons of airmail and ordinary mail and postcards. As they got closer the phone began to ring. None of their friends, it appeared, had any idea when they would arrive, how long they would stay, or where they were going when they were mended and repaired and ready for combat again in the mysterious outside worlds parents wot not of.

The culinary department had been stocked for some days with everything that could be baked, boiled, roasted or whipped up in advance. It appeared that no food of any kind had passed the lips of the younger members of our family for weeks. In a semi-fainting condition, they fell into the kitchen and admitted they were at the point of collapse.

I wonder whether it was simpler when the children were still at home, and June brought the last events of the school year right on our own doorstep. Pageants and plays, Sunday-school projects. The children making the last ashtrays, and giving concerts on primitive instruments. There is something very odd to me in a pageant. The sight of a small boy in brown cambric, wearing his mama's fur around his head, does not actually suggest Daniel Boone to me. And when he hacks with a cardboard hatchet at a paper mountain, I distinctly do not experience the thrill of the Dark and Bloody Ground. The vision of Connie as part of a bread line, chanting, "I haven't got a job; I haven't got a nickel," had a shade more reality, as I knew she probably hadn't got a nickel.

Then there was the time when David had to give a speech in final assembly. I asked him about it, and he said, rather diffidently, "Well, it begins, 'I am an Athenian citizen.' "

Jill said, "Do you want a sheet or something for a costume?"

"Oh, no," he said, "we're going to wear our regular clothes. I just want my good pants."

The morning of the speech he got up at dawn, and voluntarily washed his face and hands. With his cowlick sopped down and his fringe brushed back, he was ready to mount the rostrum and declaim, "I am an Athenian citizen."

I wasn't able to be there that day, but afterward I asked him how it went. He gave me a solemn look and twisted his feet around the chair legs. "Oh, I gummed the whole program," he said.

I didn't press him. I suppose he forgot just what he was doing as an Athenian citizen, but he preferred to let the tale be untold.

Then there was always the school yearbook. I remember the day I found Connie absorbed in Bartlett's *Quotations,* looking for suitable verses to be printed under the senior pictures.

"I found one that just fits Mary," she said doubtfully. "You know Mary is so dumb. 'Be good, sweet maid and let who can be clever.' Do you think that would get by?"

"No, I don't," I said.

"Then we found a lovely one about a quiet mind is richer than gold," she went on, "but we couldn't think of anybody at Bradley with a quiet mind. It's really very difficult."

"We always used 'Queen rose of the rosebud garden of girls,' " I said reminiscently, "and 'Her voice was ever soft, gentle, and low, an excellent thing in woman.' We used that for someone we just couldn't fit to anything else."

Connie sighed. "I've got to be in a play, too, and I'm tired of being abstract Truth and Wisdom. I wish just for once I could be a regular character."

Pageants, plays, parties. Oh, yes, parties. And Barbara's first evening dress for the Junior Prom. That time it looked as though Jill would have a nervous breakdown as an aftereffect. Unless you know how fourteen-year-olds are, you would think that a city the modest size of New York might have an evening dress or two for a high-school dance. But it turned out to be more impossible to find a dress that Barbara would wear than to pile Pelion on Ossa. The question of the evening coat was worse. One solitary evening coat was at last found and delivered, and turned out to be a size too small.

"You'll have to wear your sport coat," said Jill.

"I won't," said Barbara desperately. "I can't!"

"Then you'll have to take my white wrap."

"No, I can't wear that, either." Barbara was determined. "I just won't wear anything."

"You will too," said Jill. "It's too cold to racket around in a sleeveless wisp of silk." They eventually compromised on my heavy lilac shawl.

By the time Barbara was groomed, gowned and off to the dance, Jill and I both felt that we had earned a stay in a sanatarium. Nowadays I suppose Barbara would need a certain brand of jeans or one special type of denim jacket. But although the styles may change, I suspect that the crisis is always the same.

Then there were our early struggles with their music lessons. Barbara had been taking piano lessons for about two years, rather idly, but at least taking them, when Jill decided it was time for David to "take" something too. Tooting penny whistles and bursting paper bags under our noses had gone on long enough, she felt. So she told him she was getting him a trombone for his birthday.

"I don't want any old trombone," said David firmly. "I won't look at it."

Jill described the joys of a trombone. David burst into tears and retired. For about a week life consisted of hysterics, violent scenes, bouts of tears over the trombone. But David always rejected anything new, so Jill persisted. On his birthday he unwrapped all his presents and was very happy. Then he said, suspiciously, "Is this all? Every single thing?"

"Well, no," said Jill. "The trombone will be out tomorrow."

She dragged him off for his first lesson. The next time I saw him, David came bounding at me with this large shining thing.

"Listen here," he said. "Listen here!" He shot his arm out and a loud blast nearly blew my head off. "It's my new trombone," he said proudly. "The man says I can prob'ly be a great artist — a great one — like Tommy Dorsey! I got a natural lip!"

And a few weeks later Jill had to turn in his beginner's trombone for a bigger and better instrument at a much higher price.

Shortly afterward Jill met some prominent musician at a dinner and was discoursing on David and his trombone, as a mother will do.

"But why did you pick a trombone?" he asked. "A trombone is always played by guess and by golly. It's all in how far you slide your arm out. And did you hear the Philharmonic Sunday? In the trombone solo the fellow never hit the right pitch one time! What did you pick a trombone for?"

Jill blushed faintly. "Well, I always wanted to play a trombone myself," she said.

No need to explain why I got Connie a guitar.

Now the grass grows high in the

meadows and fields. And every lawn is deep velvet. It is the time of the lawn mower, and the smell of newly cut grass fills the air. Since we have what you might call a natural lawn, we also have the scent of newly cut dandelions and bluets and a dash of wild onion. The gardens are green with lettuce and chard and pea vines; squash is about to bloom; tomato plants are set out; corn is thriving.

Early in June the asparagus goes by and begins to grow tall feathery tops that will bear scarlet berries in fall. But the new peas, cooked with a mint leaf, need no apology. It is the time of strawberries too, big, dark red and juicy. Every roadside stand glows with strawberries.

Jill gave up raising them after three or four years because she said you had to practically lie down to take care of a strawberry bed, and it was a constant battle with the birds. It was easier to buy them from the hermit down the road.

Our hermit is not a religious hermit, just a live-alone hermit. He is neither young nor old — I doubt if anyone can tell his age. He looks just as he did twenty years ago, except for being a trifle more weathered. He is thin, dark and voluble. He wears khaki work pants and a sweat shirt. I have never seen him in a coat or with a hat. He lives in a shack that looks like a chicken house. A stovepipe sticks through the tar-paper roof, so he must have a stove of some sort. There is a pile of rubbish and junk around the outside so there is barely room to get to the door.

But nobody goes on his land anyway. The etiquette is to stop the car and blow the horn and wait until he slides out from the shack or materializes from the strawberry bed. His berries are the biggest and sweetest, and they are no ordinary berries. They are pedigreed. He advised Jill which varieties to plant when she started our own bed, and even parted with a flat of plants.

"You won't take care of them," he said morosely.

Sometimes he sells honey, now and then raspberries. He has a few fruit trees, and a vegetable patch, and may put squash out on a rickety table by the road if he feels in the mood.

He has no chickens — unless he keeps them in the house! Or under one of those strange rubbish piles. So I suspect he is a vegetarian. He walks to the village occasionally but I think he buys flour and salt and that is about all. He has very nearly gone back to basic survival, and one wonders why. But there is one remarkable thing about our village, which is the attitude "Live and let live." Perhaps it belongs with the Yankee independence of spirit. He is there, he is a hermit and it is his own business.

In any case, whether you buy them or grow them or pick them wild in a sunny meadow, strawberries are for June. A big blue bowl heaped with freshly picked richly ripe strawberries and a subsidiary bowl of powdered sugar is as handsome a centerpiece as one could ask for. So is a strawberry shortcake, made the proper way. Not a spongecake dotted with small berries and topped with a fluff of whipped cream — not a cake at all — but a rich old-fashioned baking-powder biscuit enriched with sugar and baked until the top is golden. Baked in a pie tin, then split and buttered — yes, buttered, and never mind the calories. And then the berries — which have been partly crushed and set to warm a little on the back of the stove to bring out the full flavor. The berries are ladled well over both layers of the shortcake.

With this, a comfortable-sized pitcher of thick Jersey cream, not whipped, just at hand to pour over as is, so little smooth brooks of cream make their way to the ruby sea of juice below. Ah, that is fine fare for a June night supper.

It is best to give yourself up to it and not add anything else to the meal except a pot of boiling-hot black coffee.

Perhaps I should add by way of a postscript that there is only one true shortcake, and this is how to make it:

Sift together 2 cups of flour, 4 teaspoons of baking powder, ½ teaspoon of salt, 2 teaspoons of sugar. I work in ⅓ cup of butter and gradually add ¾ cup of milk. I toss the mixture on a floured board, patting it rather than rolling it. I bake it in a deep pie pan in a hot oven (425°) for about 25 to 30 minutes, then split it and butter both halves.

I pour the berries on the bottom layer of the shortcake, pour more on top and serve immediately. This will probably serve four, unless they are dedicated! I like it in shallow soup plates so the juice is easy to spoon up.

This is a good time of year for a picnic, especially if you do it the easy way. I pack a basket with some fruit, a loaf of fresh bread, a small jar of sweet butter, a wedge of Wisconsin cheese, a sharp knife for cutting and a thermos of coffee. Then we stop work around noon and drive half a mile or so to the trout brook or the little waterfall and eat in the warm sun. We seldom talk much. Jill is never a talker; sometimes I ask her a question and never do get an answer. I talk in spurts, sometimes spilling over like water over a dam, sometimes with just a trickle. But it is good to sit silent, drinking the hot coffee and looking at the stream flowing by. Silence can be a communication too. There is peace in the stream, in the green of the woods, in the cloudless June sky.

And in the fact that we do not have to do anything about anything at the moment.

When we drive home, the garden needs attention, the cockers all need baths, dust has gathered on the trestle table, and the well house definitely must be repainted. But we have had a piece of time without pressing responsibilities and we are ready again to go to work.

We busy ourselves too much, I think. Now and then we well of our spirit needs time to fill up so that we can draw from it again. And when someone says to me that he or she cannot bear to be alone, I always feel sad, for it means the level in the well is so low that no bucket can reach it.

In June I find it easy to drop everything and sit in the garden and watch the butterflies and admire the opening roses. Suddenly I feel the wideness of the universe and gain a new sense of well-being. My thoughts are not profound. I think about how much the lemon thyme has spread over the flagstones. I think, without anxiety, that we ought to do something about the rose canes next fall.

I think the wasps should not gather right under the arm of my chair. But chiefly I am absorbed in just being.

Then, restored, I am ready to shell peas again!

By mid-June it is hot enough for summer clothes. But I have problems with my summer wear. I shop by mail at my favorite shop. I have a catalogue with lovely colored illustrations of two-piece and three-piece outfits and what are called casuals. I fill out my order blank faithfully, wanting that lilac wash-and-wear to go with my good violet sweater. But on the order blank there is a space for second choice. And inevitably the second choice is what I get. So my dress is sage green and I haven't a thing to go with it. When I appear at the market, Eleanor Hoxie says, "Well, I never knew you wore green!" I suppose it is a good thing, in a way, for I never willingly wear anything but lilac, seashell-pink and blue. I also order the same style of dress year in and year out. By appearing in second choice, at least I get a variation!

The most extreme fashions seldom reach us here in the valley. But of course we know all about them, for we see them not only on television but also on visitors. We have many travelers going through our village, and after the isolation of winter, it is hard to get used to a stream of cars and a marketful of strangers, all stylishly garbed. It reminds me of a man who asked how to tell the natives from summer people. "The natives are the ones with clothes on," said the Yankee.

Assembling the right wardrobe is not my only problem, however. Maintaining any sort of proper hairdo is another. Most of the time I settle for a sort of feathery whisk, but for state occasions, I need emergency measures. For instance, there was the time when a photographer came out from the city to take some pictures of me for a magazine. He was to take an early-morning train on Sunday. Occasional trains do come in to Seymour, which is about nine miles away, and has *our* bank and the beauty parlor and a few stores — in fact, it has a Main Street. Marilyn, our hairdresser, found out about my coming ordeal when I asked her to put a net on my hair so it would *keep* longer. Whereupon Marilyn secretly arranged with Jill to bring me early to meet the train.

"But we'll have to sit and wait," I protested.

"No, we won't. Marilyn is coming down to open the shop and fix your hair." Jill was firm.

It meant that Marilyn had to get up early too, on her free day, and drive from Fox Drive in Oxford to Seymour, open the shop and comb my hair properly.

"Because," she said firmly, "I knew you'd be a mess, Mrs. Taber, a perfect mess."

She couldn't have been more right. In my life-time a good many well-wishers, both hairdressers and friends, have tried to teach me *how* to manage my hair. And every single one, alas, gives up in the end. It is not that I don't try. And Marilyn says my hair is so manageable and easy to do and stays so well.

"Now just brush it," she says.

So I do. My recalcitrant hair then

stands up straight in the air as if I had just seen a tiger in the kitchen.

Usually when I go back to the next appointment, Marilyn closes her eyes when she sees me.

Then she tries to comfort me so sweetly. "But I couldn't write a book," she says as she whips my mop into shape.

Today our dear friends Alice Blinn and Margaret Cuthbert are coming for supper. I sit and think, while Jill bastes the roast, that I wish I could write a whole book about them, not for their brilliant minds at all but for their rich warmth of personality. Many people are brilliant; few are also unselfish and giving, deeply loyal and belonging to the grand tradition of honesty and faith and kindliness we were brought up to believe in.

When one falls to thinking of life and its various vicissitudes, one realizes that friends are the bulwark of the whole edifice. With Alice and Margaret, all they need to know is that someone needs them, someone is ill or in trouble. They gear their lives to it without a thought of any sacrifice involved personally.

This is a fine and comforting thought. Selfishly we also know that if ever we were in trouble, we would say, "Call Alice and Margaret."

Steve and Olive Stephenson are like that too. In fact, I feel we are blessed with friends who would give willingly. And in what I term a kind of cut-and-come-again civilization that cannot be overestimated.

I like things that wear well, from friends to cooking pots and pans. No matter how many new shining utensils I get, I always reach for the old wooden spoon that has been through so much stirring with me. And I often pass over the elegant white-and-blue casserole for an old cracked brown one. It takes living with things to love them. And somehow the aura of happy meals when the children were little clings to those old things.

"One should never get attached to things," said a visitor the other day. "I think it should always be that you could go out the front door, turn the key and never come back at all, and never miss a thing." This is a good stern philosophy,

I thought, but not for me. I love to give things away; it is not that. Anything anybody needs I am glad to part with. But things like Mama's monkey pitcher and the deep green goblets from the captain's attic in Maine — these have a value for me, I admit, far beyond any value they should have.

The monkey pitcher happens to be valuable, experts say, but the reason I love it is not so much the soft smoke-blue color and the odd little figures capering on it — monkeys they are, I know — or the graceful flowing lines. But it was one of the first objects I noticed as I was growing up, and I can look at it any time and see Mama's face as she dusted it.

I have just been reading about the latest research into the cycles of bodily rhythm and I reflect that I myself have always been a night person. This is as much a part of me as my flyaway hair.

Nevertheless, I cannot help feeling it is somehow not moral to waste the golden morning hours. It just does not seem right. And I believe most people afflicted with "night person" rhythm feel the same way. I have two dear friends who rise at six and by ten they have accomplished the day's work. Sometimes they drop in around ten thirty and find me weakly drinking coffee and not dressed.

"Oh, aren't you up *yet?*" they say. "I thought you'd be up by *now.*"

"I worked until midnight last night," I remark doubtfully.

I can just see them thinking this is peculiar. Why didn't I go to bed early and get up early?

But I remember the days when I had to rise with those misguided birds to get Connie off to school. And when we used to leave at six thirty for a dog show. I managed it, but I had a headache and felt thoroughly dispirited. By afternoon I was operating satisfactorily and by the time the sun set, I was ready for anything.

Now that I've learned about day people and night people, I begin to think the rhythm is inherited. My mother hated to get up early and was always pretty quiet until mid-morning. Father got up around five thirty and managed to be patient until

272

six, but then he got lonely. In summer he arranged things by mowing the lawn under the bedroom window. In winter he ran the car out in the driveway (under the bedroom window) and gunned the motor, slammed the car doors, banged the hood up and down.

When Mama gave in and got up and came downstairs, he would say, "Oh, there you are. About time you got up. It's seven o'clock. Where's Gladys?"

Mama didn't dare say I had been out late at a football dance, because he would instantly say, "I don't want her ramming around at all hours. She ought to stay home and get to bed."

Mama got me up, if he was in the mood to make an issue of it. If not, she distracted him by making waffles for breakfast. With her iron waffle maker, three people could not eat waffles all at once anyway, so this was a successful maneuver.

"No use wasting the day," he would grumble as he poured half a cup of maple syrup on his waffles. "Not healthy to lie around."

He went full tilt all day — in fact he

was known on campus as the professor who never walked but always ran. Then around nine o'clock at night his terrific vitality suddenly ebbed.

"We better get to bed," he would say, "or we'll never get up in the morning."

And when he went to bed, so did we.

I used to shut my door and douse all but one small light and read and write poetry (I called it poetry). Mama used to tiptoe to the sewing room and shut that door, and Father never heard her pedaling away, for once he fell asleep the trump of doom would not bother him.

I was always able to rise at six to go to the lake or play tennis, but this was a triumph of love over self. I would also have walked through fire with equal determination if my dearly beloved had been on the other side. But when I got to college, I tried to take courses that did not have eight o'clocks. One reason I almost lost the battle of Advanced Algebra was that I had to take an eight o'clock for that. But I loved the night seminars — how I loved them!

I was exciting to walk out of the

dormitory and savor the night and to leave early enough to be able to go by way of the lake and see the moon coming up. And the corridors in the building were empty, for there were very few seminars at that hour. The classroom had a magic it never had in daytime, glowing with light and smelling of chalk. I sat near the window so I could see the stars. And I always got an A on an evening exam. The world seemed full of promise, unless I happened to remember that eight o'clock would come the next morning.

Years later, when I was teaching at Columbia, I took the afternoon or night classes and found them a delight. One way or another I have managed to avoid too much of this early-morning business and I am so sorry for people who have to get to work early every day — until I reflect that some of them must be day people and would purely hate to begin work at four in the afternoon.

Lately the coffee party has come to my valley. My neighbor Wilma recently gave one, and when she told me about it I asked just what time it would be.

"Ten o'clock," she said.

"Don't ask me, Wilma," I begged.

So she didn't. She said everyone had a wonderful time, and I am sure they did. They had hot muffins and fresh-baked sugar cookies and a gallon of coffee.

And this reminded me that I might have managed the coffee but that would be all. And my contribution to the gaiety would have been to sit and stare into space.

For I am out of step on this hearty breakfast too. I know one should have a third of the day's calories at breakfast, to work up energy for the work of the day. Lunch can then be negligible and dinner a few ounces of lean meat, half a cup of two green vegetables, a green salad and fresh fruit. But the time I am really hungry is around eleven at night. Then I begin to dream up recipes and think happily of lobster thermidor or fried chicken. I am very fond of eggs, except in the morning. I like crisp bacon, but not until lunchtime.

So I think appetite has a rhythm too and everyone does not have the same pattern. If I have to eat breakfast, I would prefer something like baked beans or macaroni and cheese, and who would recommend that?

Father's breakfast was a special one. He had shredded wheat or oatmeal with cream and crumbled bacon and syrup or honey on it. Then he tossed off a couple of eggs or a few slices of French toast, with syrup. And four cups of coffee. He said it kept his strength up!

Father never heard of a calorie. I thought of this when I heard the charming English actor Robert Morley say in an interview, "I don't believe in calories. I never saw one and I never tasted one, so I simply don't believe they exist."

Father was raised in a pre-calorie era and the eight children in the family ate fried fish or chicken, fried potatoes and apple pie for breakfast. Father died at seventy-seven of a heart attack due to climbing a mountain a bit too rapidly. Some of the others were carried off at early ages such as seventy or even sixty-nine. And life expectancy wasn't nearly as long then as it is today. Grandfather died in his mid-seventies from trying to lift a corner of the barn to put some timbers under it.

So either the heritage couldn't be licked or the diet was fairly satisfactory, right up to the three teaspoons of sugar to every cup and a pot of coffee always on the stove. All of them, especially Father, felt they liked light meals, such as roast beef, mashed potatoes and plenty of good rich gravy, steamed, buttered cabbage or a side dish of baked beans topped off with apple pie (their favorite).

Now that eating has gone out of fashion — I mean real eating — I sometimes think of the suppers at Grandmother's. I forgot to say there was always hot bread too and clover honey or strawberry jam for spreading. As I tick off a thousand calories a day, I wonder. . . .

But of course that family never sat still, except at mealtimes and in church. Whatever they did, they moved at full speed. And even the girls spent plenty of time outdoors climbing mountains or fishing. All that exercise must have made the difference.

June light is gold as afternoon lengthens. It is queer that light is never the same in any two seasons. June sun is like a Chinese lantern — warm and richly glowing but not yet too intense. It is life-giving, and it is dreamy. The hot dry spell is ahead. The lawn grass is almost too green to believable. The garden grows overnight. Some of the early lettuce begins to bolt. The rosy chard and spinach have lustrous leaves.

The Japanese beetles have not yet come, so we do not have to spray incessantly. Everything is quite perfect. Nights are cool enough for a small fire on the hearth. Days are full of poetry, from the first silvery webs on the grass to the fireflies carrying their lanterns in the dark.

The leaves of the spring bulbs begin to turn brown and lie down. But it is a world of blossoming with the roses and the late, late lilacs. It is good shampooing weather for the dogs, for they can roll in clean grass and dry in the sun. The Irish lies flat, paws upheld, and lets the sun bake her.

Inside the house now in daytime, the

light is green and shadowy, for the maple shade overhangs the roof. It is a little like living underwater, and the milk glass is opalescent as shells. The wide oak floors have a soft glow, and the ruffled curtains are snowy. The house smells of lavender, for we have tucked it in with the linens and in the drawers. Jill planted lavender in the border of the Quiet Garden and it is a rewarding herb, lovely when in bloom, so fragrant when dried.

Neighbors drop in, easing aching backs as they sit down. The talk is of gardens, naturally, and whether we shall get the tomato blight again this year. Everyone has a theory and a remedy. The sweet rocket is spreading, someone says, and so it is. It has taken over half of the side yard. Someone else says he will plant potatoes this year, trying for a succession crop. His first planting is up and those will be pearl nuggets, but he wants enough to "put down" because potatoes have been so poor the past few years.

In the pale green light of dusk, the neighbors go home to finish the chores, let the cat out, let the dog out, let the cat in, let the dog in. And after supper, to reach for a bottle of liniment for those garden-weary muscles.

Jill gets out the garden encyclopedia and announces that our new little mimosa tree should eventually be eight feet tall!

Seven

July brings still blue days, with heat simmering over the fields, crackling in the long corn rows. The Farmer's Almanac says quietly, "Hot, sultry, bit of a drought, but let's not pout or shout."

This should settle the pronunciation of that word *drought* anyway. I have always rhymed it with *south*.

The hottest time of the year in

New England it is; the heat is actually dramatic in its intensity. At suppertime we like to sit down by the pond, where the cooling air rises from the water. With Alice and Margaret, our neighbors from down the line, and Steve and Olive from the old red house by the watercress brook, we wait for the hamburgers to broil and the buns to toast while we talk, idly and with long pauses.

The real art of conversation implies an ability to sit quietly now and then, I think, without any sense of strain. Even brilliant talk with no intervals gets wearing. Also it implies listening as well as talking.

I have known people who deliver fascinating monologues, but conversation takes at least two.

Yankees are traditionally closemouthed and this is a good quality.

It is not true, however, that Yankees are dour. Not Connecticut Yankees at any rate. A passing farmer will stop and chat at any time, provided that you ask him a worthwhile question, such as how the corn is getting along.

And when friends get together,

conversation is never a problem. The only difficulty is that it is hard to sort out what is being talked about. I catch bits like, "What they ought to do with the international situation is — dip it in egg and milk, then flour lightly — and the doctor said he should be operated on immediately and so they — ordered a new truck for the fire department last Tuesday."

Our small talk, however, might seem rather scant to an outsider. When I go to the market, I always take time to chat with Eleanor Hoxie, who is at the checkout.

"It's a beautiful day!" I say.

"Beautiful," she says. She is beautiful herself, in a soft-blue skirt and sweater. She has shining eyes and a lovely smile and is, as always, fresh as a meadow violet.

"The swamp," I say. "I wish you would come and look at it."

Now to a Southerner with flowing, easy speech, this wouldn't sound like much. But to New Englanders, it sounds just right. We are sharing our feelings about the beauty of nature, though we don't use many words to do it. I go over to the meat counter where Louie, one of the three brothers who own the store, is sharpening a murderous-looking knife.

"How are you?" I ask.

"Can't complain," he says. "Lovely day."

The second brother, Joe, who could have been a singer if he hadn't wanted to stay at home with Peggy and the children, is checking the price lists.

"Hi, Gladys!" he calls. He knows the name of every person in town, or so it seems, and he always makes a point of greeting you by name. When Joe is in the store, you feel as if you were being welcomed into somebody's home.

"How have you been, Joe?" I say. That's all, but I head for the car in a glow of happiness.

Sometimes, of course, I get caught up in a real conversation when I should be buying the milk and deciding on the meat for supper. Yesterday I spent some time discussing the state of education with George, the oldest brother, who acts as general manager. I admit I am always distracted talking to George, for he is one of the most beautiful men I have ever known. I do not say handsome, for to me that implies a kind of slickness, and good-looking is not enough. There is no true reason that I can see for confining the word beautiful to things feminine, anyway. George is slim and dark and with eyes as blue as the October sky. He is tired-looking, quiet and has a radiant smile.

His older son graduated from Colby College, and the younger son is in school here.

"Do you think television is responsible," he began, "for the fact that young people don't seem to read?"

"Partly," I said. "Not all."

"Well," he sighed, "I had a time trying to teach my boy last night the difference between 'illusion' and 'delusion.' How would you tell him?"

"Well," I said, "I think some illusions are delusions, if that helps."

We both agreed that when we were growing up, we read voluntarily, not just for assignments. And that few students nowadays seem to have a passion for classic literature.

"I read Shakespeare when I was a boy," said George.

"Partly it is the overemphasis on science," I said. "People seem to think it's more important now to advance in science than to acquire the richness of a cultural background."

George finally got called away by a salesman, and I was so busy thinking about education that I forgot to consult my list and went home without milk, fruit, butter and bread. I walked right past them planning a television hour in prime time (sounds like roast beef) which would encourage reading. It would not be a course with credits; it would be intended simply to create excitement about reading and reading the best. I do not like the word *classics,* for it sounds dull and formal. I would call it something like There's Magic in Books.

When our own children were growing up, they read whatever they found around in the bookshelves. But we never had a comic or a Mickey Spillane type of book in the house. I suppose we established an unconscious censorship but we never thought about it.

David's favorite reading was, for some time, the dictionary. He would hunch his thin leggy frame up on his bed and pore over such items as "Na-ga-na, n. A disease of horses and other animals produced by the action of *Trypanosoma brucei* and carried by a variety of tsetse fly."

No doubt this foretold his later decision to become a doctor. On the other hand, we often felt he was destined to ply between some tropical islands on an old freighter, since he read everything about boats he could find.

Connie read the romantics, from Joseph Conrad to *Wuthering Heights,* and the poets, from Keats to A. E. Housman.

Barbara had one fixed goal. She wanted to read anything that had some poor underprivileged character or someone who needed help. She did not, however, want any but happy endings, or she would burst into tears and rush from the room.

Of course they all read the regular children's classics; the *Oz* books were worn to a shadow. Hans Christian Andersen, *The Wind in the Willows, Peter Pan* and *Treasure Island* were favorites.

I am sorry to see fairy tales in such poor repute, for there is something in fairy tale and legend that is vital. No amount of factual books can replace the delight of the Snow Queen in the palace of ice, or the charm of Sleeping Beauty wakened by the Prince's kiss.

I am also sorry that reading aloud has gone out, at least in so many families. To be sure, the family now gathers around the television set, but that is not quite the same as gathering around an open fire and listening to the roar of the wild seas as Moby Dick bears down on Captain Ahab, or hearing the childish ghost voice of Kathy crying, "Let me in, let me in."

Jill and I put off buying a television set for a long time, feeling that with books and records and a puppy or two for company, we did not really need TV. But finally we decided on a month's trial. We saw Jacques Cousteau exploring a coral reef, listened to the Boston Symphony, watched an unforgettable football game and attended a Senate committee meeting. And we decided that television was worth having after all.

By and large, the dogs and cats ignored the strange new box when it was installed in my bedroom. But Teddy loved it. He was especially fascinated by Lassie, and he would sit alertly, tail wagging, eyes never leaving the screen. He was following that collie every step of the way. Esmé liked to watch birds whenever they appeared, and the funny bouncing dot of a tennis ball during the championship matches.

From the very beginning I looked for music and news. I tried to avoid the animal programs because I didn't want to see the rattlesnake bearing down on the baby field mouse or the hunters in their helicopter zeroing in on the mother wolf. But Jill watched them all. All, that is, except for one very popular comedy series which starred a large, mournful-looking basset hound. Jill tried one episode, then turned it off in disgust. "I don't see why that dog is so famous," she said indignantly. "She can't even act!"

Like most people I know, I deplore the amount of violence shown on television, especially at times when children may be watching. And I am glad that our own grandchildren are restricted to nature programs and the gentler children's shows. I am glad, too, that whenever I ask for suggestions about birthday gifts or Christmas presents, the grandchildren's answer is always the same: "Books, please!"

I will always remember the winter evening years ago when our Virginia friends Harriet and Ida Fitzgerald came for a visit. Late one evening we got to quoting poetry. We matched bits. When we missed lines, we helped each other out. It was a lovely evening. Ida began with an old-time favorite — "Here's a sigh to those who love me, and a smile to those who hate" — so we did Byron for half an hour. "The isles of Greece, the isles of Greece! Where burning Sappho loved and sung." On through the love lyrics, "Maid of Athens, ere we part" and "She walks in beauty, like the night"; bits of *Childe Harold* and *Don Juan*.

We were practically drunk with George Gordon, Lord Byron, before we moved on into the intellectual ether of Keats with "I stood tiptoe upon a little hill" and the magnificent tones of Shelley's "Ode to the West Wind." Some of the lyrics we stopped over: "Rarely, rarely comest thou, Spirit of Delight!" and the lovely "Music, when soft voices die."

Rupert Brooke, Sassoon, Millay — we had to get down the books now and then, owing to our habit of forgetting the last line of the octave in a sonnet. But we ranged high, wide and handsome until the night was a sliver of moon in a thin sky. Then I realized, coming awake in the "dead vast and middle of the night," that Connie, then aged twelve, was still up, hands linked around her knees.

"Mercy on us," I said.

"My goodness," said Connie, "who knew *you* knew all those poems?"

Administering this coup de grace, she moved off to bed, while I, nothing but a parent, let the dogs out, let the cats out, let the dogs in, let the cats in, and crept to my middle-aged sleep, while outside the snowy night was still full of stars and dreams.

Recently someone sent me a copy of Keats which belonged originally to a John Mitford, Esquire, in 1845. This is a precious book, an 1841 edition, and came enclosed in a special box to preserve it. Clergyman John Mitford was the son of a John Mitford who was in the navy and mentioned in Nelson's dispatches (as an ''insane rogue''). My Mitford had a bookplate with a plump cherub enveloped in the waving forked tails of a sea creature or maybe of several creatures. Could he have been a son of Triton? The sea is quite agitated around it, in any case. In the flyleaf, Mitford notes in a spidery hand that for Keats's death see Shelley, etc.

The ivoried pages are marked now and then by a respectful pencil. I think I should have liked this John Mitford, Esquire.

Now the little cinnamon-colored volume

lies on my desk, and although the singer is gone, the song still sounds in my New England ears.

When Faith Baldwin went round the world, I made only one request, "Go to see how Hampstead Heath is, where Keats lived." She went, with an English-woman who had never been there. The plum tree where the nightingale sang — "thou wast not born for death, immortal bird" — is gone, but another plum is planted. The wallpaper is new, but that is because when they did some repair work, they found a small piece of the original and copied it. It has a green feathery design, says Faith.

"No hungry generations tread thee down," wrote Keats. So many hungry generations tread so many things down, I thought. But it is good to know that the little house in Hampstead has withstood the bombing and has a new plum tree and that the wallpaper has been restored.

For who of us does not need a shrine? Even people who have never heard of Keats have in some way profited by his outpouring of lyric ecstasy. For I think all beauty adds to our heritage, whether it be the flawless purity of the Greek in the Parthenon or the rich and lavish splendor of Dylan Thomas. So my Johnny Keats saying, "Beauty is truth, truth beauty," gives a lift to us today in an uneasy age.

In the letters I find a great deal worth remembering. I wonder, sometimes, whether he realized as he dashed them off to this one and that, that one day long after he was laid in the Italian soil in Rome, readers would reread his letters.

"My prime object's a refuge as well as a passion," is memorable. For this is so true of most of us. Work we love, work we struggle hard at, is at once an easement of the spirit and an excitement. This is true of our George, who farms only the rocky Connecticut soil, but finds in the filled silo that his prime object is a refuge as well as a passion.

Having been raised with poetry, I am astounded at the lack of it in young people nowadays. Although we began in school reciting, "The snow had begun in the gloaming — and bus-ily all the night —" and went on to "Lars Porsena of Clusium by the nine Gods he swore," still we did learn that words went in form and pattern sometimes. But recently a young man asked me, "Just what is a sonnet anyway?"

"A sonnet is a moment's monument," said I, quoting Rossetti rapidly. "Memorial to the soul's eternity." And then I wondered, is that Rossetti? Then I saw the blank stare on my listener's face, so I sat down and folded my hands and said meekly, "A sonnet is a poem of fourteen lines, and it has to be fourteen lines, and it has a definite rhyme scheme, either English or Italian — Now the Elizabethan —" But he wasn't listening anymore. Quatrains and sestets meant nothing to him; he was pulling a burr out of the Irish ear nearest him, and I thought, well that is practical and constructive anyway and Dante is still Dante and Shakespeare is still Shakespeare and always someone — as long as we are on this odd little planet — someone will read, "When in disgrace with fortune and men's eyes, I all alone bewail my outcast state." Or, "Life has no friend; her converts late or soon, Slide back to feed the dragon with the moon."

This is the dry month in New England, so when it rains we are grateful. It is the only time in the year we are grateful for rain, this being our chief product come summer, come winter. But in July the patter is sweet on the old roof and on the lawn. You can see things turn greener after a rain. Bean pods plump up. Chard stands more erect. Lettuce looks brisker.

The pond shines darkly clear; the scum disappears. We swim without sweeping motions of our arms to clear the way. And such a lovely pale light comes after the rain is over, like a love song in sweetness.

Jill is what I call a sometime swimmer. If she is busy training Holly to do the Long Sit or Tiki to take the jumps, she says, "You go on. I'm busy."

Then I give up waiting and swim. Maybe she will get around to it, maybe not, but hot weather means nothing to her; she was raised in the hottest corn-growing Illinois territory and she rather likes to steam. I do not. I like to be cool.

I like to sink slowly to my chin and feel the cool gentle water all around me, and if the small fish whisk past, I do not mind. Connie says they nibble her toes, but I wear large heavy tennis shoes anyway, as I do not like mud on my feet, and the bottom of our pond is plain Connecticut mud. I wear my glasses too so I can see where I am. I suppose the sight of a woman in tennis shoes and an old skirted suit and glasses wheeling dreamily along the pond is fairly amusing, if anybody came by to look. All I can say is I do *not* wear a garden hat, as one of my friends does, to protect her complexion. She wears a scarf first, then the large straw hat, and as she swims, it does look like a misplaced garden party but it has a very nice effect nonetheless. Especially when the hat has flowers on it. The sight of a flat circle of pinks floating around is very interesting.

Water is not man's natural element, but it is strange to think how the deep green seas have always lured us. From the early divers who plunged down after pearl and gold and silver in ancient galleons to today, when frogmen slide down to adventure in the glimmering depths, man has always felt a strange kinship with the sea. Does it perhaps go back into time when all life was seaborne?

In any case, when I first saw the ocean, I felt a quickening such as I never had felt before, a sense that all mysteries were immediately mine — rather the way I suppose a mystic feels at certain times. The rhythms of tide on shining sand are basic rhythms; they speak of God and eternity.

Our own sweet-water pond has a small echo of this too. The brook tumbles in down the ferny hill, the sky and the clouds are in it and on clear nights the moon and stars shimmer there. Although it covers only about a third of an acre, it is nine feet deep and it has a life of its own with skimming waterbugs, darting fish, polished emerald frogs and the blue heron and his family.

Recently, though, when my daughter came for the weekend, she took one look at the pond and said, "Oh Mama." I suspect parents need to be nudged frequently about various things. Connie said there was so much algae in the pond that it was dreadful. We should take a broom and *sweep* it, she said. I never believe in taking a negative attitude with the younger generation. So I said yes, we should sweep it. Well, as I've said, the pond is nine feet deep in the center, and swimming with a broom in one hand turns out to be quite a proposition! It is practically impossible to swim and sweep simultaneously. In the end, the algae took its own course.

The truth is that you may have a Hollywood sort of pool with a painted bottom, tile sides, water pumped in and out, or you can have just a plain farm pond, plus frogs, turtles, waterbugs and algae in season. Also a water snake now and then gliding along the edge. A natural pond is edged with wild iris, forget-me-nots, and the water is often muddy. Minnows swish by, frogs jump in and out, birds skim over looking for insects. In autumn, leaves spread over the surface, and my last swim is usually quite leafy. The brook purls in cool and ferny from the upper reaches. I like it. If we dumped something in to kill the algae, we would have just another swimming pool.

Jill spends the dry hot days in the garden hoeing and spraying and picking potato bugs and Japanese beetles. She carries pails of water from the pond to encourage the succession planting of lettuce. When the squash leaves fold up, she carries more pails. She comes in with her hair a damp cap on her head, her sweat shirt justifying its name.

"Those colored pictures in the catalogues," she remarks, "never mention how much work is involved!"

Once she figured out that the radishes we grew represented about five dollars apiece. But when we have stuffed baby pattypan squash for supper, she allows it is well worth the labor. Or zucchini in a casserole with tomatoes and onion and Parmesan cheese. People who do not care for squash are usually those who rely on store vegetables. A crook-necked squash should be picked when it is not much thicker than two thumbs. The skin is pale and waxy, not knobby and mustard yellow. It should be easy to slice with a table knife.

The slices, dusted with seasoned flour, can be sauteed in butter with a suggestion of diced onion in it. This is squash as it should be. By the time a squash must be peeled, I am losing interest in it.

Cucumbers, on the other hand, are delicious when they are ripe. They turn to the color of a new-minted penny and are large and plump. Then we split them lengthwise, scrape out the seeds and stuff them with anything from poultry dressing to creamed chicken. And bake in seasoned milk, not quite covering them.

Baked stuffed cucumbers and a tossed green salad make a gardener's supper. For dessert a bowl of ever-bearing raspberries with sweet cream, and plenty of coffee. Afterward Jill decides she will plant another row of cucumbers next year.

One treat that the grandchildren always ask for is melon. We love all kinds. Pale green balls of honeydew, served with a wedge of lime to lift the sweetness, or cubes of golden cantaloupe in a chilled white bowl, or simply a thick old-fashioned wedge of watermelon, dripping with juice and cool as sherbet. They all have the bright taste of summer.

This is a month of violent thunderstorms. They break the heat and bring mint-cool air and sparkling-wet leaves. All the same, I distrust them as much in July, when they are such frequent visitors, as I did in May, when they first began to arrive.

Fears seem to be instinctive, although some experts say there is a reason, buried deep within us, for any fear. Why then does Teddy panic at the first rumble of thunder and hide under my bed, while Holly leaps to the windowsill to watch the storm with interest? Both were raised exactly the same way.

My personal fear is of spiders. I know perfectly well that the average house spider is a shy and retiring soul, interested only in catching mosquitoes, not in crawling on me, and that we really should be glad to have spiders around. Still, they do make me nervous, especially the large black ones with lots of long legs. Recently, while David and his family were visiting, we were peacefully eating supper when a huge spider appeared on the wall by the trestle table. David rose to deal with it, casting an anxious glance at me.

"Why did you go and kill that spider?" asked Jimmy.

"Because we didn't have a jar handy to put him in," said his mother calmly.

How I admired her! She did not say that one peculiar adult couldn't stand big spiders. She made it sound circumstantial, and Jimmy was satisfied. I decided the next one would be ignored at any cost. However, I reminded myself he didn't exactly need that spider. He already has more pets than he can keep track of.

A good place for the Fourth of July picnic is right in your own backyard. On that weekend the roads are jammed with cars, the picnic spots and beaches are crowded, and I do not like to spread the lunch by a quiet brook and then have a bevy of small boys begin to set off the firecrackers right under the grill where I am turning the hamburgers.

Even the lonely and secret places are hard to get to without threading the highway traffic. It is strange how Americans have to go somewhere in order to get back. And I remember when I was a little girl it was the same. Fourth of July always found us with the old car stuffed with hampers, people and Timmie, the Irish setter, while Father went speeding to the farthest possible distance for the Fourth of July picnic. Then we always had to eat in a hurry so we could get back to town in time for the fireworks. Mama produced fried chicken and sweet corn and a bowl of homemade potato salad packed in ice, and of course there was a huge thermos of lemonade and plenty of watermelon. But leisurely picnicking was out of question. We had to gobble everything down in a rush.

Now on the Fourth I set out almost the same menu in the little screened house beside the pond. Only sometimes we grill hamburgers instead of having chicken. There is plenty of time to eat slowly and chat quietly and watch the sun go down behind the big butternut and the mist begin to gather on the surface of the water. If the children are here, they may go over to Lake Quassapaug to see the town fireworks. Jill and I generally stay at home. After all, we do have the fireflies and the stars.

The past and present are closely intertwined here in New England, and nowhere more so than right in our own valley. We do not need to wait for a patriotic holiday to be reminded of history.

Sometimes when Jill and I drive out on a clear evening, we go down to Ridgefield and stop to look at the tablet marking the Battle of Ridgefield, when British and Revolutionists fought and fell together. It is a most moving memorial, it seems to me, the patriots companioned by the men they died fighting, who in their own death became the patriots' guests. It is strange to think that this green peaceful valley was once, just about two hundred years ago, in the battle-torn heart of the war.

The inscription reads:

In Defense of American Independence
AT THE BATTLE OF RIDGEFIELD
APRIL 27, 1777
DIED
EIGHT PATRIOTS
WHO WERE LAID IN THIS GROUND
COMPANIONED BY
SIXTEEN BRITISH SOLDIERS
LIVING, THEIR ENEMIES, DYING,
THEIR GUESTS.
IN HONOR OF SERVICE AND SACRIFICE
THIS MEMORIAL IS PLACED
FOR THE STRENGTHENING OF HEARTS.

This battle, I remember, was won because Benedict Arnold came spurring his big white horse down the winding road and flung himself into the wavering line. He was in New Haven when word came to him, and he swung as lightly to the saddle as any young Lochinvar and saved the day.

There is no doubt that Arnold was a reckless and brave man and if he had been managed with tact, the history of a traitor might never have been written.

Nathan Hale's birthplace is not far from

here and I often think of this young patriot schoolmaster who combined ardor and loyalty with a rather astounding lack of shrewdness, being so easily caught. It probably shows that the academic dreamer should not essay practical plotting.

I note from my reading that Connecticut was one state which turned in supplies for the army without fail during the Revolution, delivered its quota of soldiers and always responded to any appeal. Sometimes, I gather, men would disappear and go home for the plowing and the haying but generally they came back in due time. One wonders how Washington ever won this war with such a casual roster. Half the time nobody got paid either, and the food was limited to what happened to be around. Clothing was negligible; ammunition was always short.

I suspect if ever one man did win a war, it was Washington, for few leaders have ever had so little for so long. And one wonders at his great heart when, after it was over and he expected to go to his beloved Mount Vernon and raise his fancy fruits and vegetables and hunt with the foxhounds, which I think

Lafayette imported for him (anyhow, they came from abroad), he had to begin all over again to pull a sorry, tired, impoverished band together and make a nation grow. *good*

It used to be popular to debunk all heroes. But nobody could ever debunk Washington for me. It seems to me that he pinpointed the whole struggle for independence, and I am heartily pleased every time I cross the Sandy Hook bridge to think that General Washington forded the river here.

During the Revolution, the Glebe House in our neighboring town of Woodbury was the home of the first Episcopal bishop in America. Since he represented the English church, he was of course eyed with suspicion by some of the local patriots. Finally, he was forbidden to minister to his flock. However, since nobody could be arrested on Sunday, he preached his sermons in the parlor on Sunday and then slipped through a secret door next to the fireplace and escaped somewhere via a secret tunnel. It occurs to me that the local citizens were admirable. Because he had to be within reasonable distance of the manse to get there every Sunday for the services. So why was he never discovered during the week? True, many of the early houses had secret rooms, but as he was slipped from one to another somebody must have seen him.

I would like to go back in time for a few hours and walk around my village as it was during the Revolution. I'd like to know where Captain John Minor, the town clerk, had his office. And I'd like to see a post rider pulling up his horse and calling out the news of Bunker Hill.

It was 1784 when the French troops with General Lafayette came down the valley. They camped between Middle Quarter and White Oak and the soldiers whose tents were near the Sherman house are reported to have eaten twelve bushels of apples and drunk seven or eight barrels of new cider. This must have made them merry at the ball given for the officers, for the sound of music and laughter drifting out was better than the sound of cannon.

I never tire of the story of the doughty

husband who locked his wife in a secret closet back of the chimney when the French came down, so no French officer would cast a roving eye at her beauty. I think she must have been divided between rage at missing the ball and pride that her own husband thought she was too beautiful to hazard in public!

I'd like to go back and be there when the news of the defeat of the British finally reached this remote spot. With the thankfulness and the triumph, there must have been women weeping and wondering how to go on alone. And there must have been anxiety about the future and more hard times to come.

And I think the valley looked strange to the men straggling back, bone-weary and hungry, and sick of war. Peaceful with the sweet-running brooks and the fertile fields and green hills. But with so much work to be done, they must have paused and prayed to God for strength.

The past came to life for me in a different way last week when I attended a meeting about enlarging our church.

In 1732 the Congregational Church went up, and around 1800 the Methodist Church was erected half a block down the road. Eventually, a few years before we settled in at Stillmeadow, the two tiny congregations finally joined and a Federated Church was formed. A few extra Episcopalians came into the fold, and possibly an odd Presbyterian or two and some unorthodox Jews.

Half the time the services were held in the Methodist Church, half in the Congregational. Communion in the Congregational Church involved individual communion cups passed around, while in the Methodist it meant kneeling at the altar. When it was very cold, the service was moved to the church with the better furnace. During Easter the bigger church was used.

And then suddenly, in our day, it was discovered that some change had to be made. The church was *growing* as the town grew. The new young minister sparked the Sunday-school program; more members came to church. For over a hundred years the beautiful little buildings had stood firmly, and with repainting had kept on. Now, it seemed, there was an urgent need for Sunday-school space, for heating, for rest-room facilities for the increasing Sunday-school group. The choir needed a corner for robing. And the kitchen needed a good sink and a few shelves and a new stove — in short, just lugging water and working on a deal table were not sufficient for the faithful Women's Guild.

After a year and a half of committee meetings, the building committee drew up recommendations. It was proposed that we move the smaller Methodist building in back of the larger church and at right angles, join them with a small connecting link and get everything under one roof, and by raising the foundations for the Methodist Church, add a whole story for Sunday-school groups, a parson's study and so on.

And here the interesting study of a historic community was illustrated. There were those who wished no change at all, under any circumstances. As the churches had been built, so they should stay. The small back lot where the horse-and-buggy congregation had parked was good enough for the founders of the church, and as for the current members, let them park on the highway or wherever. There was also the problem of the Methodists wanting to move their church back someday if the Federation ever was done away with. Then there was the problem of raising the money for the whole project.

When the church membership gathered to vote on the question, I was impressed with the way the young businessmen who had done the planning undertook to iron out all the objections. I myself felt the church was a growing proposition and might better serve the community with adequate physical equipment.

But the high point of the evening for me was when the oldest deacon raised his voice and said, "I would like to ask, Mr. Moderator, whether the heirs of the Browns were paid off when we bought the parsonage in 1842."

The head of the Congregational Ecclesiastical Society rose to answer and said soberly, "We have five deeds of the twenty-three heirs of the Brown family, but I haven't at hand the rest. I would have to look them up. However," he said slowly, "this is not possibly pertinent to the matter at hand."

It is one of the most delightful things to me to live with the past going along currently. I remembered, as they spoke, the friend of ours who told all about the fire in their house and when I asked, in shocked tones, what night that was, she said, "It was in 1850, and we lost almost all the furniture."

And another friend who told me that her best china had been dumped in the Pomperaug. I asked about that, and it turned out her great-grandfather had remarried, and one of the children had carted all the best china out and tossed it, in resentment. This was possibly not more than eighty years ago, but gives one a nice sense of continuity about life in our valley.

I think this sort of thing may be peculiar to New England — at least in America — for many of the families here have roots which have never been disturbed.

The names of a good many are the names of the original group that came over from Stratford and made a thrifty deal with the Pomperaug Indians for land in return for a couple of kettles and a few beads. I may do them an injustice — perhaps they also gave a gun or two and a few hunting knives.

Be that as it may, the Indians were friendly hereabouts, and none of our doors have tomahawk gashes in them such as you see in the houses in Old Deerfield farther up, in Massachusetts.

The arrows which we have turned up from time to time are delicate bird arrows, well shaped and usually of white quartz. Most of them are so small I cannot see how any marksman could shoot them and strike the prey. They must have been phenomenal hunters.

The camp must have been where our pond now is, for the brook would be rushing and big then, flashing with trout and fringed with watercress. Pleasant too for boys and girls to play in. One feels the Indians were a grave race, but I know the small ones played some. And I love to think they lived on our land, and the little Indian dogs hunted just where our merry cockers hunt.

On a midsummer evening, many things in the valley look just as they always have. The villages hereabouts have no streetlights, fortunately, so the gleam of lamps shines from the windows of the old houses. The white church spires catch the last flare of the ebbing sun. The villages still keep the look of New England, but the countryside is changing. The old stone fences diminish as people quietly drive out to take the best stones for terraces, paths, fireplaces or barbecues. A good many stone foundations have the best of old stone fences in them. Farmers sometimes string a few strands of rusty wire along the top of denuded walls to keep the cattle in.

Meadows are still rich, and occasional herds of black Angus raise their furry heads to look at us as we go by. The calves look like overgrown teddy bears. A few sheep and some Holsteins and Guernseys are pastured in the good grass. But all too often a good farm has been sold and bulldozers are at work. Candy-box houses spring up and Pleasant Valley development is on the way. It was a pleasant valley once. The houses have yards just big enough for a clothesline. Soon they may be even smaller, since most people use dryers nowadays. The picture windows have a good view of the house across the street.

I do not blame the people who want inexpensive homes outside the industrial centers. I do heartily blame the real estate men who would sell twelve-foot lots if someone devised a house that could be built in ten. There is naturally more money to be made if you have more lots. It is easier to level a stand of pines, flatten an old orchard, than to tuck the houses here and there with a piece of the green world for everyone.

But when I see a two-hundred-year-old white oak go down, I hope the development men have an uneasy sleep that night. True, they may gain space for a garage, but that oak could cast grateful shade on children for many years to come.

Now that the farms are being sold off, I miss the haying time. When we first came to Stillmeadow, hay wagons came down the winding roads at dusk, smelling of summer. By lantern light, farmers would still be forking the last loads into silos. A farmer moves effortlessly; as he bends and lifts the golden weight he is just plain beautiful. I know there is a poetry in the mechanized farming of the Middle West and Far West, but I haven't been intimate with vast harvesting. All I know well is the one-man farm, where the land runs up and down hill and is rocky and resistant. Acreage is always small, and a single barn houses the few cattle. But the New England farmer has few equals for industry, integrity and independence, and I am sad to see the end of his era. In fact, we are stubbornly preserving our one arable acreage above the swamp, and one of the neighbors grows hay on it. He limes the land, plows it, seeds it to good grass and cuts the hay, and this gives me the greatest satisfaction.

One sure sign of July is a field foaming

with daisies. They are cheerful, sturdy flowers. They seem able to put up with anything, from a parching dry spell to a lashing downpour. They seem even to ignore the fumes of passing cars, for they flourish along the highway. Indoors, arranged casually in an old ironstone mug or a small beanpot, they stay fresh for days. And later, when the midsummer flowers — black-eyed Susans and butter-and-eggs and Queen Anne's lace — begin to appear, the daisies will mix sociably with them all.

A July night has a special quality, the hot air is ebbing over the meadow and a faint cool breath steals in, delicious and exciting. Mist brims the meadow now, and a silvery look is about the world.

The moonlight is whiter than pearl over the pond these July nights. The small businesses of the day and the worries are magicked away by the soft glow. You can step from the door of the little white house into a white foam of moonlight on the crest of the wave of night.

Esmé steps delicately, on her cinnamon

velvet feet, along the terrace where the dew has not fallen. Her eyes are lit with moonlight; they are sapphire flame. On the fence black Tigger sits, his body melting in night, but his eyes shining too, pure topaz or sea-green as the light reflects in them. The dogs move quietly, shadows among shadows.

In George's barn, a cow gives forth a soft mooing, and a strange dog bays in the distance. How still it is, here in the little fold of the valley on a hot summer night! I feel the world revolving around me; I hear in an inner ear the troubled voice of the times. But the stars come so bright and clear upon the sky, and the moon rises so slow and steady that I cannot feel the turbulence of life, only the steadfastness of the seasons.

Suddenly I feel I am everywhere, and this is a strange feeling. I am in the rose garden of my Bombay, India, friend, whom I have never seen. I am in an igloo on the deep green-black icecap with the son of my friend in Washington, living on K rations just to see if this is possible. And I am in the desert with the mountains rising so purple and violet above the golden sand.

I am in the eighteenth-century bakery in Williamsburg talking to Parker Crutchfield as he bakes the gentleman's bread and the household bread in the great ovens. Candles flare, the night is hot and the life of yesterday moves against the life of today.

But I am actually right on the worn doorstep of the old white farmhouse, and I call the dogs in and close the door. I may have been a thousand miles away in five minutes, but I am, after all, at home.

And the moon is right over my apple tree, and this is July in New England. The mind makes many journeys, but the heart stays home.

Eight

The turning wheel of the seasons rolls slowly now, in August. People walk without hurry. Cows seek the shade of oak or sugar maples in the pastures and chew their cud dreamily. The wild country cats tiptoe along the stone walls at dusk, instead of racing with tails flat out. The dogs bark in a halfhearted fashion when they tree something. Even our neighbor's haying lacks the feverish haste of early summer, for his barn is almost full. Pumpkins and squash are ripe; corn silk darkens in the corn patches.

There is a hiatus between the hard work of midsummer and the brisk days of woodcutting, filling woodsheds, chopping kindling, to come. Weeding in the garden is about over. From now on, the vegetables can hold their own, weeds or no. High time too, says Jill, after all the tending they have had all summer. Nature and man both seem to me to move on a light rein for a short time, a restoring time.

I wonder whether the fact that so many vacations come in August is because of the heat itself or because it is a natural time for man and Nature to relax. I have read that energy is highest in October, and it may be so. If this is true, then August is the time for dreaming, for taking a thoughtful look at life and for letting some chores go by the board.

However, if we have a litter of eight cocker puppies, there is not much time for relaxing. Last week we had to be away over the weekend, and my daughter,

Connie, came to baby-sit, while Curtis and the little girls stayed in the city. According to the report she left for us on the kitchen counter before dashing back to New York, it was not exactly a restful holiday.

Dear Mama:

Arrived safely. And spent first two hours cleaning puppy pen, and occupants. Ate an egg. Went to bed. Got up. Fed puppies. Went to bed. Let Sister out. Went to bed. Let Sister in. Went to bed. Got up. Fed puppies. Went to bed. Let Teddy out. Went to bed. Let Teddy in. Went to bed. Got up, played chase-the-mouse with the cats. (Esmé was darling, tossing it.) Went to bed. Got up at one A.M., screamed at dogs, all yelling. Barked until three A.M. (lonesome for you). Read for a while.
Friday. Up at six to feed puppies. Let out dogs, put in dogs. Cleaned puppy pen. Chased strange terrier through hole in fence. Closed hole. Removed Jonquil's collar, which

stuck in her teeth. Caught Holly, who escaped by opening gate. Lured her. Let dogs out and in. Fed puppies. One fell in Pablum. Gave him warm bath. Went to bed. Worried he might be cold. He was. Rubbed with warm towel an hour. Went back to bed. Up to let Jonquil in. Brought large very dead thing with her. Now understood why she didn't come in earlier. Caught her. Removed THING. Turned green.

Saturday. Mice in bedroom wall so not much sleep. Cleaned puppy pen and puppies, fed them. Holly had eaten through fence. Chased to excited cheering of cockers. Got her back. Propped shovel against hole, wheelbarrow against shovel. Dropped both on toe, am limping. Callers dropped in. Defrosted chocolate cake, made coffee. Nice time they had. Noticed a headache, remembered no time for lunch and only coffee for breakfast, as Melody was eating little Sister's breakfast at the time.

Leaving for train in fifteen minutes

— no, Holly is out again. If you get back in time, phone Steve.

And thank you for the MOST exciting weekend I've ever had, and why don't you come to the nice peaceful city for a REST?

Connie

Our Quiet Garden definitely sags in August. Jill says she can never keep things blooming in all seasons. Time gets the best of her, she says mournfully. Before we ever get all the spring bulbs tended to, the roses are all over everything and the Japanese beetles are there, and then my white pansies give up in the heat and the ivy border springs out over the flagstones and then the weeds come in where the lemon thyme is struggling. Succession bloom, she feels, would be a joy, but she needs four more hands and a couple of extra backs.

When we eat supper in the garden, I look at the pale white clematis climbing the fence and admire it as we cook the hamburgers and dish up the cucumber mousse. But Jill leaps to her feet and whips up a clump of weeds from the edge of the border. She takes a bite of her toasted bun, darts over again to the far side and wrenches a tuft of something else up from the lavender bed.

"Just relax," I say, "such a lovely evening—"

Jill sets her plate down and gets on her hands and knees and begins to weed the thyme. "Just a minute," she mutters. "This is in terrible shape —"

The true gardener's eye, I think, is always focusing on the needs of the garden, the state of the soil, the moisture problem, the pests, the pruning, the thinning — if you really add it all up, you wonder how any soul is staunch enough to attempt to grow a single rose!

In the vegetable garden, the blessing of the hot still days is manifold. The rosy ripening globes of the tomatoes, the amber silk on the sweet-corn ears, the gleaming emerald peppers and the royal purple of the eggplant — the color and richness and textures in a vegetable garden are a recurrent miracle. When I walk down the bean rows, I think of Yeats and his "Lake

Isle of Innisfree."

> I will arise and go now, and go
>   to Innisfree,
> And a small cabin build there,
>   of clay and wattles made;
> Nine bean rows will I have there,
>   a hive for the honey bee,
> And live alone in the bee-loud glade.

Somehow there is a magic in the number nine. However, if he were to live alone in the bee-loud glade, I wonder what he would do with nine bean rows? Maybe they were very short rows? Or maybe the faery folk would gather in the bright of the moon to pick and eat beans? Otherwise, I think Mr. Yeats would have had little time for his golden singing, at least in summer. He would just pick beans!

The shape of a bean is a lovely thing to see. When very young, it curves like a small scimitar; later it lengthens to a lance. And the color is beautiful — the golden wax has a glimmering tone and the green is a rich blue-green like an agate.

To really savor beans, you must eat

them when they're young — young, tender and butter-sweet. Therefore it follows you must grow your own and pick them your very own self. Nobody, but nobody, ever picks beans young enough. Those large robust things like chopped-up bits of garden hose which are labeled frozen string beans are barely edible. The limp piles in markets have lost their goodness long since and were too elderly when gathered in the first place.

But picked when delicate and young, cooked quickly and not long from suppertime, dressed with warm butter and a sprinkle of rosemary and served in warm bowls — this is fare for the gods. Sometimes I add a spoonful of sweet cream at the last moment, if not too involved in dieting.

And now the first ears of corn begin to ripen. I feel, as Thoreau said, "And pray what more can a reasonable man desire, in peaceful times, in ordinary noons, than a sufficient number of ears of green sweet corn boiled, with the addition of salt?"

There is only one way to eat corn. Like

beans, it should be last-minute fresh. You put the kettle on, a big kettle, with salted water halfway to the top. Then you dash to the garden and pick the corn as fast as you can. By the time you strip it, the water is boiling and in go the ears, for three or four minutes. Then serve on a warm platter, with plenty of butter, salt and pepper. This is not a silly gardener's idea; it is a fact that corn loses its flavor rapidly after being picked.

Naturally everyone cannot have a corn patch at the back door. It is possible to eat corn which has stood around, so to speak, if you must. For this, you add some milk and a spoonful of sugar to the water in the kettle, and you cook the ears longer, testing with a fork for tenderness. The older the corn, the longer it takes to cook.

I don't mind picking corn, but whenever I pick golden wax beans or cut the rhubarb chard, I wish someone had devised a way to grow vegetables on shelves. Leaning over in the hot sun is not my idea of comfort, and I never have been able to adopt the graceful, easy crouch that is pictured in garden photographs.

Jill, however, is never really happy standing upright. The crouch position seems to be her favorite. She goes along on her knees with her nose practically in the earth. When I see her out among the lettuce, I feel sad to think that she had to spend so many years in the city, being what is called "gainfully employed." If there was ever a born dirt farmer, it is Jill.

When the dew falls, it is hard to believe it will be hot and dry again tomorrow.

We must carry water from the pond for the wilting garden. Even the optimistic chard is discouraged. The lettuce looks like a dried sponge. And I expect the corn to pop any minute.

I wrote a note to the Turners saying: "We'd love to have you for the weekend. Please take your baths before you come."

For last week the well ran dry. Fourteen showers a day finally wore it down, and when I tried to water the herb bed, one faint gurgle was the requiem. The well, they told us, hadn't run dry in a hundred years. But perhaps the pioneers didn't take fourteen showers a day. I suspect what washing they did was done in the brook.

As for us, there's nothing to do but wait until the rains replenish the water table. Meanwhile, we will have to bring pails of drinking water from George's spring and also do a lot of swimming.

The rain came sluicing down at last, long silver sheets of it. Jill went right out to check the garden and came in wet but beaming. Then, since she had to stay indoors, she settled down to go over the fishing tackle. I have a new and splendid bait-casting rod from my friend Ida in Virginia, sent with a firm note: "This is for you to learn to cast with." My previous attempts at casting have been startling. First I caught two bushes and the seat of Jill's breeches. Then I got my own neck. Finally I was embroiled in a birch tree. I wonder if it would work better if I turned my back to the water and cast off behind me. I always seem to get something tangible in the rear.

Then another thing. I like to catch fish,

even very small fish. And standing on the bank of Eight Mile Brook, dropping a simple worm as bait, I can be sure of getting at least a mud turtle or a salamander. But when you cast expertly, I understand you get either a real game fish or nothing. For me a sunfish in the hand is worth ten trout in the water. So I expect that Jill and David, who is here for the weekend, can go on playing games with their rods while I bring home the bullheads. Eight Mile Brook is my dish. I know it's chiefly occupied by turtles and water spiders, but it is so beautiful. It gives me a sense of release just to stand at the bend and look up the stream.

After all, catching something is purely a by-product of our fishing. It is the act of fishing that wipes away all grief, lightens all worry, dissolves fear and anxiety. Why this is, I don't know. But when you fish, you simply forget all the world. No thought of dinner or supper or unpaid bills mars the surface of the water. The only thing of import is a small cork, generally lying tranquil on the bosom of the stream.

We have very nice waders, although it is a fact that I can hardly walk in mine. We can all, by now, cast very nicely when we bait-cast for pickerel or bass. But to date we have never caught a trout. The art of flicking a fly and actually getting a fish on it is a complicated one. Trout just aren't ingenuous. Sometimes I wonder if they ever get hungry, with a real natural appetite.

For trout, you have to fish the Pomperaug. It is running strongly now after the big rain. The smell of summer is in the air, and the sound of birds, which I can't identify because my hook is caught on a willow.

The veteran trout fishermen come up softly on the bank, letting no shadow fall on the water. I can't help it; I have to laugh when I see them. They look like Christmas Day before the presents are opened. They are hung at every conceivable spot with creels and tackle boxes and rods, and their hats are stuck full of flies. Landing nets hang limp from their belts, and their faces are radiant.

Jill was upstream with her back turned

when one expert made a perfect cast, and his fly caught Jill in the middle of her shirt. "You'll never get a bigger trout than that," said his companion happily as Jill came back and the poor man unhooked her.

This was a pleasant introduction, so we fell into talk. Most real fishermen are friendly and kind to novices. These two gave us some extra live bait they weren't using and suggested we try in certain deep holes the trout love.

And we all talked about The Trout. I suppose every stream has one, an almost legendary character. This trout has lived in a special hole near the rude bridge that arches the flood, and he has been there since time immemorial. Nobody can catch him. Everything known to man has been offered to him: dry flies, wet flies, natural nymph creepers, beetles, grasshoppers.

"Probably some boy will get him with a worm," said one of the men.

We all crept up on the bridge and lay on our stomachs and looked down. There in the shadowy depths he lay, perfectly visible, a king in his own right. I would, of course, give practically anything to be the one to catch him; and yet, at the same time, I keep hoping he never will be caught. My emotions are always getting underfoot in this irrational way.

"I come over every week during the season and spend a day on him," said the second man wistfully.

"He's not going to bite today," the other assured him, "come on down to the riffles."

Jill said, "A boy got a big pickerel in that side water yesterday."

"Funny about pickerel," said the first man. "I saw a swampy pool right in the middle of a cornfield the other day as I was going across to trout water. There was an old hick countrywoman in blue jeans and with a felt hat, standing there and just whanging down on the water with a bamboo pole. So I asked her what for, and she said she was catching herself a pickerel. I said, 'You can't get pickerel here, lady,' and she said she could. Whang, she went. She'd lift that old pole with both hands and come down like a brickbat with it." He laughed. "Next thing I knew she came up with a pickerel big as your arm. She put him under her arm and started away. She said, 'Every day I get a pickerel here. Every day I catch one and the Lord sends another one.' I figured she must make 'em so mad whanging at 'em, that they bite out of pure rage. But what they're doing in the cornfield I wouldn't know.''

''Pickerel's a peculiar fish,'' asserted the other as they left us. ''True enough, one always comes back to take the place of a caught one.'' They waved at us and waded downstream with a final ''Let us know if you catch the Old One!''

Shadows were falling on the water. We had a few fair strikes and no fish. I knelt to take a last look at the Old One, secure and royal in his twilight pool. The water was clear amber now, darkened with the evening light. Overhead the sky was tinged with pale, pale apricot, and the banks were still and dark.

David packed up the tackle. Wading in the swift icy water is hard work, and the footing none to easy to maintain. Water dripped from Jill's waders as she climbed out.

We took the suspiciously light creels and started home. True, we had no trout. But we had some hours spent in the summer woodlands. We had friendly talk with some fellowmen. We had the sight of the Old One moving a fin.

"Didn't we have a wonderful time," said David happily.

"Perfect," said Jill.

"And now about supper," said David. "You said we'd have fish tonight."

"So we shall," I said placidly. "Crab soufflé."

Reading an article recently about hobbies, I wondered whether I am not just all hobbies! This was a disconcerting thought. And would I put cooking first? Collecting milk glass? Folk songs? Flower arranging? Just what is a hobby anyway? Well, I rushed to the dictionary and found out it is a small Old World falcon.

One can always depend on the dictionary for a surprise. It was formerly flown at such game as larks.

Reading further, I found it is also a

small or medium-sized horse. Hobbyhorse must come from that.

Finally I came down to a favorite occupation, topic, etc., pursued for amusement.

Well, my favorite occupation actually is writing — writing almost anything. If I have no ideas for stories or books, I write letters like mad, or poems which I can toss afterward. Or just little notes to myself with observations such as "The chickadee's neckpiece is three-cornered. It is a cravat of jet silk." Or "The single birch in the swamp is like a pencil of moonlight."

But could one say I pursue it for amusement? Not at all. For writing is not an amusement; it is work. It takes just about all you have got, all the time. No, not a hobby.

It is very often painful when the lovely images in the mind will not compose themselves into even reasonable facsimiles, in words. It can be so painful that I long to throw the typewriter out of the window and scrub floors all day. With a floor, I feel, you can see progress, you get somewhere.

Books and music cannot be hobbies. They are half my life and cannot be categorized as pursued for amusement.

Then how about dogs? Neither Little Sister nor Holly would thank me for suggesting that having dogs is a hobby. Over the years, reviewers and interviewers on radio and such have rather typed me as a woman with dogs and cooking and gardens as hobbies. But I never read such comments to the dogs. Raising puppies may be my favorite occupation but is a serious one — nothing slight about it.

Just possibly birds could be a hobby. But the relationship between me and the birds is a deep and profound thing. I do not feed and cherish them just so they amuse me, not at all. I heartily respect and admire them and appreciate their beauty, but they are much too wonderful and mysterious to be anybody's mere hobby.

A hobby, one feels, should be a light thing, a sometime affair. And viewed in that light, I decide I have only had one hobby in my life, for even cooking is far from a hobby, it is a lifetime work.

My hobby, and this is obvious when analyzed, used to be doing jigsaw puzzles. There was a time when I always had one set up on a small table, and every time I had a few minutes I would go and try to fit in an odd piece of blue which should be sky and wasn't.

As for Jill, photography is not her hobby but her vocation. Gardening is her job. Obedience training is a serious field in which she pursues her way, in snow, in rain, in hot sun.

Building furniture and redoing antiques might qualify for her — but it isn't always amusement, however; it's often to get us some furniture.

So that leaves her with detective stories and me with my onetime jigsaws. I think we should really establish hobbies for ourselves, on thinking this problem over. Like making ceramics or painting on glass.

I am always amazed at the way we New Englanders are proud of our weather. When we get a January blizzard, it is the worst blizzard in history, and now in August, we feel sure that it is much hotter here than anywhere else in the world.

All our thermometers play a game — no two ever get the same answer. "Right by the barn door it was a hundred," says one neighbor at the store. "Ninety-eight is all I made it," says another, very conservative. "Over a hundred when I went up the hill," says George.

Weather in New England is always dramatic, and always personal. I myself am in a constant conflict. Shall I peer every half hour to see just how high the temperature is climbing, or shall I ignore the whole thing?

This is the season to be careful that dogs have plenty of fresh water and are as cool as possible. I am by nature a mild woman, but when I see a dog shut in a car with the windows closed, I tremble with rage. After all, noboday *has* to have a dog. There is no law. If one chooses to have one, some decent kindliness is obligatory. That is all there is to it.

At Stillmeadow we refill the water dishes every little while all day, and if it is a scorcher, we sponge the faces of the old ladies now and then, and encourage them to stay inside on the damp cool stones of the hearth. We do not encourage ball chasing. For we have learned that hot weather is more lethal to dogs than cold. If the very old ones pull through the heavy humid heat of August, they face the blizzards with equanimity.

Holly keeps jumping around — nothing quenches the Irish. She likes to lie on a snowbank in February and in the broiling sun in August equally well. Her shining coat seems to insulate her in a strange way. Just as it sheds water. Giving Holly a bath is quite a thing, for the suds just slide off and drip down in the tub. And when you have sixty-five pounds of dog to get over, it makes quite a problem.

With the cockers, the main problem is finding them. The minute Jill uncorks the shampoo, we suddenly have no dogs at all. We can hear them arguing under the bed. "You go first."

"No, you go first."

"I think it is not my turn."

Once they get in the tub, they enjoy it. We have never had a dog that did not like to be clean. After they are dried with soft towels they act as if they were at a party, leaping around and wagging and racing in circles around the yard. Then they settle down to find one place in the yard where there is no grass so they can roll in it and come back in with sand and gravel on their washed selves.

Jill says I am such a fiend for cleanliness, she is rather surprised I don't whip the chickadees in at least once every winter for a quick shampoo!

But of all bathing, the bathing of a Siamese takes the primary prize. I seldom speak of it, for many cat experts feel it is murder ever to wash a cat. However, our cats have always had occasional baths. They have lived to ripe and happy old ages; they have had no skin diseases, no fleas, no mites, no hairballs. When the air gets full of flying leftover fur, and a tentative paw begins to scratch an ear delicately, I say, this is it. Jill gets out an orange sack. Pussy goes in. Tigger endures stoically but Esmé screams with outrage. A good mild dunk follows, and a rubbing with a warm bath towel.

A brushing with a soft brush afterward

makes the fur look so shining and fine, and a nice clean kitten curls up by the fire, making only a gesture at washing one paw, which she opines we left over.

I know cats scrub themselves endlessly, but I don't see why they shouldn't get a little help.

In recent summers Jill's two older grandchildren have gone to camp, and of course they learn all kinds of skills. The programs amaze me because when Jill and I went to camp we just swam and canoed and sang around a smoky fire. There wasn't much organization. We got fed and someone looked out to see we weren't drowning! In school we learned out of books. We didn't have dramatics until high school. But Davy had a part in a play last winter, based on an Irish folk tale. He was a tree. He was supposed to wear a green shirt and brown pants.

"You'll have to wear your gray pants," said his mother firmly. "You don't have any brown."

"But what'll I say when they ask me why I haven't got on brown pants?"

"Just tell them you are a silver birch," suggested Barbara.

So the silver birch was added to the production and the play went on!

In winter, the fire on the hearth is the center of the life at Stillmeadow. In summer, life flows outward. Someone is in the backyard typing on the old card table; someone else is in the Quiet Garden reading. The girls are out in their summerhouse; David and Curt are playing badminton in the newly cleared stretch of ground behind the wild blackberry bushes, and Val has just finished washing his car. Jill is down the meadow with Holly "seeking back" an old glove. I, of course, am in the kitchen.

Sometimes our casual spreading around causes trouble. We still talk of the day when our friend Johannes got locked in the studio. The studio was in the old haymow, and the old double doors had a way of swinging back in a breeze and locking. Johannes went up to Be Alone and finish the novel he was writing, and alone he really was, for the doors swung back and when he tried to come out, he found he was tightly shut up.

At first he was not worried. He leaned out the window and called mildly. Nobody paid the least attention except a couple of spaniels who were after squirrels below. They barked loudly. He raised his voice. So did they. The kennel took it up and a thunderous racket ensued, with Johannes yelling. Then he worked at the door, the nice heavy old chestnut door. Nothing gave except Johannes. So he went back and called again. But he had asked for an uninterrupted time to work and he got it.

Finally it came to him that not even for lunch would the family interrupt art. Who would intrude on a love scene with crab salad? He had a new idea. Being a Viennese, he is a fine yodeler. Or perhaps not all Viennese can yodel, but he is our only friend who can. So he yodeled. He yodeled with the very best yodel.

But the cockers had never heard anybody yodel before, and when they heard that sound from up above, they made noise enough to drown a bombing attack. They went really wild. Yodeling and barking went on for as long as Johannes could breathe, and then he gave up and resigned himself to a life in the studio, starving and helpless but with his manuscript beside him. He mopped his brow and eventually located a coat hanger. This he wrenched into a kind of bar, with which he managed to pick the latch and escape.

We were serenely stringing beans for the freezer when he appeared. I thought he must have been working very hard, he looked so hot and tired.

Jill looked up. "I hope the dogs didn't bother you," she said. "For some reason, they have been making an awful racket this morning."

Now the big golden moon makes night so bright that our normally quiet dogs are apt to get barking sprees just when they should be still.

When the dogs really get in full chorus, nobody can sleep. I have to get up and go to the back kitchen and switch on the kennel light, and speak harshly to the dogs that are in the house. The kennel will become violently silent as I switch on the lights. All the dogs rush inside and sit looking at the light in surprise, and this stops the noise. But not permanently.

If it is around two o'clock, I can't get back to sleep. All the assorted worries that any woman acquires wait to pounce on me. I worry about the world situation. I go into anguish over the possibility of not being able to pay next year's income tax. I feel perfectly sure Muffin will marry some no-account man who will be an albatross around all our necks. Anne will be misled by some charmer who dances well and has the brain of a hubbard squash. Neither girl will choose the right career, either. My sinus and arthritis and a lot of unknown diseases will do me in within a week or so. There will be nobody left to make popovers for the family. The dogs will miss me. Nobody else, I say, thumping my pillow, will care. Somebody will ruin my typewriter and somebody else will turn the stove on in the well-cooker and burn the precious aluminum out.

These and other two-in-the-morning thoughts keep me occupied for some while. All those dandy little articles on not worrying run through my head, to no avail. I know I should think of pleasant things and relax, but I can't think of any pleasant things to think of. I relax so hard that both pillows fall under the bed and I have to get up and fish them out. My mind goes like an electric mixer on high.

Summer is almost over, but I prefer to think so in the midst of sunlight and the brimming garden, not in the night. Nobody should ever say good-bye to summer in the wakeful hours of the night. Better to take the blow while the zinnias make a flare of color and the cosmos are beautiful in the sun, promising that there will be another summer.

When the grandchildren come for an August visit, I notice that they never seem to have any footwear. Anne, the baby, lies on a blanket wiggling her pink toes in the sun, while Muffin skips barefoot over the grass. Connie and Curt do own sneakers and sandals, but seldom bother with them except for trips to the village. I envy this. The cool grass must feel wonderful.

But I confess that I am glad when I see a sign in the market or the post office banning bare feet. They are fine on a clean beach or a country field, but not in town. In my day, of course, everyone always had to be properly shod, even for swimming.

When our own children were small, Jill usually left to me the task of escorting them to the shoe store. One particular trip stands out in my memory with a sort of awful clarity. For although buying shoes for three youngsters may sound perfectly simple, in our case it was unbelievably complicated. For we had not one ordinary, common garden-variety pair of feet in the whole assembly. David's were flat — flat as a pancake turner.

I said to the salesman, "He has flat feet."

"And how," said the salesman, with awe.

David galloped up and down the carpeting chanting loudly, "Flatfoot Dave, I am, Flatfoot Dave." Then he mounted the shoe stool and rode over what must have been the far Western prairies, waving a measure in his hand. Heigh-ho, Silver! The Lone Ranger!

Connie had pronated anklebones, and Barbara had that and some other odd quirk that made her feet look as if they belonged to somebody of a different pattern.

Connie wailed, "Oh, Mama, I don't need wedges again!"

Barbara stared abstractedly at her Oxfords and said, "Oh, how big my feet are!"

"Do sit down, David," I begged, completely distracted by the Lone Ranger.

"Whoopee!" sang David. He sped past me, leaping high in the air and calling, "What I want is shoes I can run in! Shoes I can — run in!"

"I want white shoes with a brown piece around the middle." Connie always knew what she wanted.

"My feet look simply *enormous* in these!" Barbara protested sadly. "Don't my feet look enormous in these?"

"They're smart," I offered tactfully.

Barbara, clop-clopping up and down gloomily, looked like a young blue heron on a wet beach. David, whirling past, exploded with happy laughter: "Look at her big feet!"

The situation was pretty tense before seven pairs of shoes were sorted out in separate piles.

When I was a child feet were simply feet — they were pedal extremities. When I needed shoes, I just went into a store and bought shoes I liked. If they didn't have my size, the salesman gave me a size larger, saying I could just grow into them. All the children had foot ailments, I am sure of it; but nobody noticed it. For years I thought an orthopedist and a chiropodist had something to do with zoology, as indeed in a way they have.

I can remember walking painfully home after a few hours of tennis, played in thin, flat sneakers, and looking for stones or bits of broken brick. I would step so that the stone pressed on my arches, if possible, so that my whole weight was on the stone with my toes and heels in air. Oh, the heavenly aching pressure of those stones and bricks, or the edge of the gutter, on my arches — which I suppose were completely disintegrated, with every bone out of place. Today I would have had aluminum arches, no doubt, shaped to fit my foot by a specialist.

But it didn't actually cramp my style. I could dance for hours, never giving my metatarsals a thought until the music ended.

As August draws to a close, mornings are cool. Autumn is already in the air. The signs are small, but a country eye sees them. The grass no longer seems to grow overnight and need mowing. The peppers begin to turn rosy in the vegetable garden, and the tomatoes ripen. The lettuce begins to run out.

The silk on the corn is darker too, and some of the broccoli shows yellow florets in the heads. But the whole garden still bears luxuriantly and the squash is all over everything. Grapes turn purple on the vines at the edge of the garden and the apple trees seem to sag with the fruit.

It is a time to can, to freeze. A time to gather the herbs and tie them in bunches and hang them upside down (poor things) in the woodshed. Mint and sage make the air savory. Herb vinegars stand in neat rows on the fruit-cellar shelf. Bay, tarragon, mint, basil and dill are our favorites.

Comes the day when Jill goes out with the pitchfork and just tries one hill of potatoes. No bigger than a pullet's egg, the pinky potatoes tumble out. Scrubbed and cooked with a mint leaf they taste as good as any gourmet dinner. This is a happy moment, yet with a touch of melancholy. The season is changing; goldenrod and chicory mark the way. And some of the birds begin flying in formation instead of singly. They are doing practice flights. They wheel and circle and talk a lot, and a few just cannot seem to fall in line. How do they know that they must fly a far distance before long? Some of them will get as far south as South America, but who tells them this? How do they know they should get ready for the fall migration?

But when they begin to swing over the peaked roof, we know it is a sign. Summer is already walking the path to yesterday.

Nine

One morning I go out to pick wild asters and suddenly it is September at Stillmeadow. I think the first sign is the smell of the air, like wild grapes and windfall apples. I know fall is here, although the world is still green with summer. And I feel an urgency to gather in all the loveliness of the past blazing days and star-cool nights and keep them forever.

The Stillmeadow road is edged now with gold. From the picket fence I look up the hill to the mailbox and see the wave of goldenrod, accented with the purple of wild asters. It gives me a sense of sadness, lovely as it is, for goldenrod is the forerunner of the bright, cool autumn which will make our valley blaze with glory. Hal Borland tells me he once counted three thousand twenty-three individual flowers on a spray of goldenrod. I don't know whether I was more impressed by the number or by Hal's matchless patience, I would have been in a state of collapse by the time I got up to forty-five. And when Hal went on to say that with a magnifying glass he studied the individual florets and found there were twenty thousand in an average plume, it seemed unbelievable. What invention of man could be more intricate than a spray of this country weed?

Days grow shorter now and migrant birds begin to leave according to their own mysterious schedule. Squirrels fling themselves from tree to tree in a burst of activity. I always hope they will store enough hickory nuts and acorns, but they never do. What they do is eat the bird food from the feeders and clean up everything put out for the chickadees, nuthatches, woodpeckers and juncos.

Later this month, two major events will occur — the line storm and the black frost. The line storm can be like a hurricane, with terrible rain and heavy winds, and I have to stuff bath towels around the windows and doorsills. The frost comes after a still day, and we do not need weather reports to know it is coming. We feel it. The day after it comes, the vegetable garden looks as if it had been ironed. Flowers hang limp on blackened stalks. There will be more balmy weather, of course, and Jill says that if she could just wrap that frost up and put it down cellar, there would be more tomatoes, more corn, more everything. And I answer that I have had enough of canning, preserving, pickling and freezing, and the sight of one more jelly bag dripping in the kitchen will drive me out of my mind!

I drove to the village yesterday along the golden country road. At every farmhouse a group of children stood waiting for the school bus. Hair brushed, shoes polished, pencil cases clutched in tight clean hands, they looked so earnest, so vulnerable to the world. As I passed, I waved at them, and they waved back. It is hard to remember back to the days when schoolchildren went to school in a world that seemed very safe and steady.

Now we live in such tension that any strange object in the sky is possibly the end of the world. Anxiety is the keynote as we go on building more destructive weapons and polluting our environment. It is no longer possible to assume that if we learn our lessons and are good girls and boys, all will be well. We have learned that the innocent and young are thoroughly expendable.

But musing on this, I thought it is a very fine thing that the children do go to school in a free school. That in America we are coming more and more to see to it that all children, all races, all religions, all colors shall have the same basic educational opportunities.

What an encouraging thought this is, I said to myself as I turned to the post office. For instance, take the hot-lunch program alone. When I was in grade school, children who could not go home for lunch, or whose parents did not pack one for them, could slip out and buy a couple of lethal sinkers at the little Greek stand, drink some pop, and face their lessons with large greasy lumps in their stomachs. Charity baskets at Christmas and Thanksgiving went to all poor families, and they were elegant. Coal was delivered to the needy, and the little town was a kind town, no doubt of it.

But the idea of general balanced feeding of schoolchildren had not been heard of. At least not in my part of country.

Now and then I would sneak over and indulge in a sinker myself. But I had to ride my bicycle home a couple of miles for lunch so I could have a hot meal. Mama didn't know anything about vitamins because they hadn't been invented yet, but she was a very sound dietitian by instinct.

The sinkers were very large and very heavy, very dark and extremely greasy. If you bit in with valor, you came on a lump of red stuff, supposed to be real jelly. The dough inside had a pale chewy texture. After consuming a couple of these, I went back to my arithmetic class with a very queasy stomach.

Just when thermos bottles came in, I cannot remember. I do recall our first one was a kind of squat jug made of some kind of clay material. We just adored it. But it was not to carry to school, any more than a gallon gas tank.

I went on thinking about the advances in our way of life for the young. We now have, in our village, a school doctor. We have eye examinations and dental care; we have balanced sport programs. And our principal arranges fascinating trips and cultural programs and even excursions to Washington — it seems like a dream when you add it all up.

So after all is said, our children are inheriting many fine things along with that hydrogen menace. And with so much good, I wonder whether we should fear annihilation?

There are still all too many places in the world where children do not stand rosy and confident waiting for the school bus to take them to a free school. But we can hope to help, at least a little, with projects that provide food and books, and this is a heartening thing to consider.

Now that school has begun again, I listen for the school bus to swing along Jeremy Swamp Road. It carries my young neighbor Tommy, who pops in and out daily, just as his father Willie and Uncle George used to do when they were his age. But now he can only come after the bus drops him off, and how eagerly I await his visit. He gives me a report on what has gone on in a world I cannot enter. I almost envy his teacher, for Tommy has a quicksilver mind and great sensitivity.

I may be wrong, but I think country children have an early sense of responsibility that apartment children do not get. "I think I'll clean out the woodshed," says

Tommy, "before the cold comes." Or, "Time to get cedar chips for the kennel." Or, "I'm going to see if I can hammer the gate latch back."

He fixes a great many things for me. And his latest project was rebuilding a discarded sewing-machine motor.

"Of course you can't do anything with it," he said modestly, "but it runs!"

"Well," I said, "the most important thing is that it runs."

After all, I reflected, much in life seems to have no tangible result, just as many roads we follow seem to have no ending. But it isn't necessary always to have a useful practical result. It's the going ahead that matters.

Tommy's stories of school bring back memories of my own. When I was in high school we had a dancing club — actually a dancing - eating club. To the inspiring phonograph records of "The Skater's Waltz," and "Ivanhoe Two-step," we whirled blithely from the dining-room door to the front porch, and back again. Everytime we got to the dining-room door we popped in for a little nourishment. We even gave a formal. I must have been fourteen — I had braids flapping down my neck. In our little town braids were almost required up to a certain age. I had flat patent-leather slippers, polished vigorously with Vaseline. I had a rose-colored crepe with little pink rosebuds for a belt — it was just beautiful.

My escort borrowed his father's tuxedo. He was a tall, broad-shouldered boy, but his father was rather large, too. The pants came down over Bill's patent pumps in little ripples. The trouser belt was nipped in oddly with safety pins. He looked like the Prince of Wales and Beau Brummel to my fond eyes, but unfortunately, in the middle of every dance, he was apt to get a glazed look in his eyes, break from me with a mutter and bolt upstairs. After the sixth exit I insisted upon an explanation.

"My shirt," he said unhappily, "my shirt." The stiff front belled out like a barrel. He placed one hand on it. "It keeps coming up," he said desperately. "The pins don't — they don't —" and he bolted again.

The evening was a little jerky. I decided formal clothes were quite a responsibility. But when I really fell in love at the age of fifteen, I decided to dress up if it killed me. My poor mother, up to that time, used to wail, "You'd go out in a gunnysack, if I didn't watch you!" Suddenly I was changed. I went to the ultimate length of sewing fresh white collars on my navy serge middy suit! I have never forgotten the clothes I had that year. The pink ratiné two-piece dress with the flounce on the skirt. The ratiné stretched out of shape almost at once; I must have looked like a bag of potatoes. The corduroy suit trimmed with brown fur. The pale-blue evening dress.

And I had a rose velvet evening bag with powder and a puff in it! I carried it to my first formal banquet, and that was also my first public appearance as an after-dinner speaker. The staff of the high-school paper gave the dinner, and a solemn lot we were, seated around the long table at the Menasha Hotel. I had a lovely speech about the future of the publication, and I was going to read it.

It was in the evening bag. I had been clearing my throat all day, and sucking lemons. I seemed to have swallowed a block of pavement during the night.

But there was a new boy sitting on my left. He had just come to our school that year; he was from away. It was all over for me with the soup. The dinner passed in a kind of dream, and I didn't even rise when I was to speak until he poked me nervously and whispered, "Get up, get up!"

I got up. I never even took my speech out of the bag. The bag was in his pocket, because he was "seeing me home." I must have delivered some kind of speech, but I shall never know what it was about. There was only one thought in my mind. "He's got to like me! He's got to like me!" Fortunately, on the way home, he said he did.

The poor boy led a stormy life from then on. I was feverishly jealous. I took it very hard. Romance didn't seem so easy as in books. If he walked a block with another girl, I was wretched. Once he even took a rival to a picnic. She had large black eyes and black curly hair. None of us "spoke" for a week, and then I had it out.

You will have to choose," I said dramatically. "Choose between me and her!"

I know now some adult sense of pity must have been wakened in him as he solemnly chose.

Here I am now, among the vegetables and the cockers, and farther from that little town of yesterday than any space. But I can still feel how terrified I was, how lost and desolate. Suppose he had chosen her!

When Barbara reached the boy era, she was in a girls' school. She spent half a year trying to get David, who is three years younger, to introduce her to the boys in his school. She said, slanting her eyes at him. "Now Dave, if I should just happen to be in the schoolyard, and the boys are there, what's the name of the big tall boy with blond hair and blue eyes?"

"Oh, him?" David was bouncing his soccer ball. "That guy's Babe Ruth."

"Well," said Barbara, "if I happen to be there, suppose you just introduce me to him.

"What for?" David bounced the ball again.

"Never mind what for. You leave that to me." She spoke mysteriously. "All I want is for you to simply say, 'I want you to meet my siter, Barbara.' "

David stared at her. "You want me to get my face pushed in?" he asked. He was disgusted. "Do your own introducing."

"But I can't — You'll simply have to —"

"I'll get my face pushed in," he said with finality. "Then the whole gang'll sock me."

Now is the time to finish drying the herbs. We had apple mint and spearmint growing wild when we came to Stillmeadow, and catnip. Jill planted dill in the vegetable garden and it nearly took over the whole area. It is better to plant dill off by itself somewhere. She put in chives and garlic by the raspberry bed, and in the Quiet Garden she made a plot for sage, rosemary, tarragon, borage and savory, with lavender and parsley as a border.

There are a number of ways to dry

herbs but we like hanging them in the woodshed rather than drying them in the oven. Perhaps the best part is how good the house smells when you package them. Herb vinegars are easy and delicious. We bring the vinegar to a boil, drop the herbs in, and bottle the infusion. The tarragon and dill are my favorites. Jill likes the mint vinegar with lamb, but I prefer melted currant jelly as a sauce.

The tarragon died out and after several tries we gave it up. Possibly our winter was too cold. The sage spread and throve. So did the parsley. I like parsley in almost everything except pie. The borage has a delicate blue flower, nice to float on punch, and it is also pretty in bouquets. Jill has never tried bay, but the herb shelf is never without it. I do not think a meat loaf amounts to much without bay leaves pressed in the top.

A pinch of rosemary glorifies green beans, and is fine with sage in stuffings. Savory is good with beans and in salads, stews and ragouts.

Herbs, I feel, must be right at hand or the cook won't bother with them, at least not my kind of cook. I want to reach and tilt right by the simmering pot. So a narrow shelf runs along by the range the whole width of that wall.

This serves two purposes: it provides easy access to the seasonings and makes my meal-getting romantic. For the whole world comes into the kitchen with saffron and sesame seed, chili powder, curry, basil and bay.

For instance, bay, which is laurel, or called sweet bay. I think of the golden days of Greece when I lift the jar, and victors' brows bound with laurel wreaths. It was then, I believe, a symbol of immortality. I think of Edna St. Vincent Millay, who plucked two laurel leaves from the graves of Shelley and Keats and kept them always pressed in a book — and I wonder, was it Aeschylus?

This leads me easily to remembering bits of Millay as I cook.

> For the sake of some things
> That be now no more
> I will strew rushes
> On my chamber-floor,

I will plant bergamot
At my kitchen door.

The laurel leaves she loved were buried with Edna, and I feel it very fitting.

Many poets have loved herbs, and this is not suprising, for even the names are lyric: bergamot, rosemary, rue; savory, thyme. They strike down deep, to a kind of race memory; they suggest far-off shadowy things in the beginning of time. Old sunny gardens, ladies in sprigged lawn . . . copper kettles steaming over great fires, Kit Marlowe's gay young laughter, and the bright dark gaze of that lad come late from Stratford, Will Shakespeare. . . .

Every gardener should reread Will's garden notes, scattered richly through the plays. I like the "wench married in an afternoon as she went to the garden for parsley to stuff a rabbit." That's love — gardening and cooking — in one packet. Then I enjoy the "neat cookery" of Imogen, who "cut our roots in characters, and sauc'd our broths as Juno had been sick and she her dieter."

Will didn't neglect my favorite dogs either. Launce aptly says, "She hath more qualities than a water-spaniel, which is much in a bare Christian." Much indeed, Will! . . . And Proteus sighs, "Yet, spaniel-like, the more she spurns my love, the more it grows and fawneth on her still."

My own spaniels, I admit, wouldn't like the spurning. Will's must have been a tougher breed, those lusty Elizabethan bowwows. Anybody that tried to spurn Linda would get a surprise.

The line storm, as we call it, usually comes in the middle of September. Rain falls with a clean, driving force. It makes a tangible wall of dark silver. George looks like a deep-sea fisherman as he splashes in from the kennel, his sou'wester pouring with water.

The pond brims to be the top of the spillover, cascades into George's brook. The air is incredibly fresh as we dash out for the mail. Beautiful is the color of the countryside, dove-grey of sky, charcoal of tree trunks, silver of rain blending into a kind of twilight for the world.

When the line storm comes, we know a profound sense that autumn is going to slip away into winter before long. The line storm is as definitive as a backfire on a prairie blaze. Wind whips away all of summer; rain sluices the air. Branches fall. Windows rattle. Smoke backs down the chimney. The dogs get as close to the fire as possible. Especially Me heads for my lap, because storms frighten him.

The hearth fire seems especially snug and the teakettle whistles merrily. I actually don't think a teakettle should whistle right out loud — I always jump at the piercing note — but that is the modern way of telling me the water is exactly boiling. And tea must be made with freshly boiling water, in a freshly scalded teapot. We like ours steeped not quite four minutes, strong and comforting.

Very, very thin-sliced bread and butter is the best accompaniment for tea. For company, however, we may have a sugary tea cake fresh from the oven or cinnamon toast bubbly with butter and cinnamon — or tiny hot thumb-size biscuits spread with white-clover honey.

Conversation at teatime should be tranquil, I think. Not the time for world problems or controversial issues, but a time to rest the spirit, remember pleasant things. Everyone needs such a time, and tea goes well with it.

After the storm, the world is polished and shining. The light is so golden, we feel we have never seen the sun before. The battered zinnias shout with color; the asters, flat on the dark earth, make little pools of violet and deep rose. We are in for a spell of perfect weather now, every day luminous, every night brimmed with stars. Picnics at noon, supper by the applewood fire at night, a walk in the cool moonlight before bed.

Last night I spent the evening making tomato honey. On my desert island, I shall call for a copy of Keats, a bar of soap and a few jars of tomato honey.

Tomato honey must have been invented by Circe. Cleopatra brought a crock of it in her purple-sailed barge; Helen fed it to Paris when he came for tea that first day.

I make it the same way, and feed it to unromantic New Yorkers, who say simply, "Pass that jelly or whatever you call it."

To make tomato honey, you take 1 pound of yellow pear tomatoes, cover them with boiling water and let stand until the skins can be slipped off. Add 1 pound of sugar and let stand overnight. In the morning, pour off the syrup and boil it until it is fairly thick; then add the tomatoes, 2 thinly sliced lemons 2 ounces of preserved ginger cut in small pieces. You cook it until the tomatoes have a clear look and the syrup is like honey. Then cool; fill jelly glasses with the mixture, seal and store.

This is one of the very best of all preserves, good on toasted English muffins, good with cold roast duck, good with turkey. If pear tomatoes are scarce, a similar effect may be obtained with large yellow tomatoes.

The first time I made tomato honey, I spent half a day. Jill was out, weeding and raking, and cleaning the kennel. When she came in she said briskly: "Well, where's your canning?"

"There!" I said, pointing to three two-ounce jars.

"What!" She stared at me. "You mean to say — all this day — that's all you've got to show for it?"

I left the room.

Now I do better. I don't skin every single wee tomato and count the seeds.

As summer wanes, we cherish every mild dreamy day. I love the soft blue haze. I know summer still walks the lanes, but the frosty slipper of autumn is just behind. We now get up early — or what the books call betimes — for dog shows, as the last outdoor shows are being held within striking distance.

Having been involved for a long time with obedience training, we have developed a routine. We get the dumbbells and the box of fifteen scent-discrimination objects and the leashes and the bench chains in the car the night before. We put the entrance papers and the show directions in too, as often we have gone many a mile and found they were at home in my desk drawer.

Groggily, we get up early and Jill pops dogs in the kennel who are *not* going to the show. I pack a lunch. We locate the sunglasses, in case it is hot, as it may well be. I explain to Little Sister that she is a Utility Dog and all through and can't go now, and she sits looking sloe-eyed at me saying I betray her every time I set forth with this paraphernalia.

The current dogs, Tiki and Holly, jump around in the back seat as we take the long road.

"I really think we should give this up," says Jill. "Keep an eye out, please, for that route number."

"Yes, we should," I agree. "After all, we have twenty-four obedience degrees — that is enough."

We drive on. Eventually we get to a heavy crush of traffic on some side road. We pass station wagons loaded with collies, poodles. A dreamy old English sheepdog leans a shaggy head out of a sedan and eyes us solemnly. We begin to feel the excitement of the show.

We invariably get lost. So do other show travelers. We line up, back and fill, lean out and ask directions. Some brave soul leads. We are off.

Comes the show ground. We fumble for our entry cards. We park. It may be a mile from the ring; it may be in a poison-ivy nook. But we park, and we now go forward with at least two dogs, sometimes three, winding themselves around our legs as they get excited and forget to *heel*. We carry also the lunch, a collapsible canvas seat, all the obedience articles, two purses filled with Bufferin and salt tablets. Plus a comb and brush for the dogs. We acquire a catalogue, which I may carry in my teeth, having no other way left.

The sun is very hot, unless it is pouring rain, in which case it is very, very cold. We find the ring, we set up the folding chair and we learn that the judge has not arrived. If it is hot, we try to make a little shade for the dogs under the chair, which is too small. If it is raining, we drip. And wait.

In the end, our special darling lopes into the ring, looking askance at judge, stewards, spectators, and our hearts jump into our eyebrows. Maybe this is it, and maybe it isn't. Some small boy whistling at the ringside may call our dog to a happy reunion, quite outside of the rules.

Perhaps we do the exercises correctly, and then the day is lit up with glory. The blue ribbon and the silver ashtray mean a great deal. They mean days of heeling and sitting and staying and retrieving and work for both dog and handler, and no silver mink could ever be as precious.

During the lunch intermission everybody sits around and tells just how well Buffy does at home. What he does in the ring is a dog of a different color, but at home — well, you should see how he takes those jumps!

Finally we load ourselves and all the junk — and by now it is all junk — into the car and start the long drive home. The sun goes down; the dogs sleep on the back seat. I nibble a stale sandwich.

"Now the next time," says Jill, "I am going to give Tiki more of a workout before we get in the ring."

And so we begin again.

There have been many dogs in my life, and for that I am grateful. Someday I shall write a book just about the dogs I have lived with, for no two dogs are alike. Father felt it was disloyal to have another dog after Timmie, the Irish setter he gave me when I was in high school, died. In a curious way, which many people seem to share, he felt it would be an insult to Timmie's memory.

"We shall never have another," he said.

And he never did. When he came to visit Stillmeadow years later and the yard was full of cockers, he tightened his lips and tried not to look at them. At that time we had Snow In Summer, who was an exquisite red-and-white gentlewoman. She could easily have won her championship if we had wanted to bother with it.

We ate on the lawn that day and Snow went directly to Father and laid her muzzle on his foot. She turned her dark amber eyes up to him and wagged her tail so hard she shook her whole rear end. Father stood it for some time — he was a strong man. Finally he gave her a pat.

"I suppose she's all right for a scrub

dog," he said grudgingly.

Now and then when he wrote, he would add a line, "How's the scrub dog?" But he never really forgave me for having any dog at all after Timmie.

My position is that love should not be so limited. I did not feel I was betraying my Honey's memory when Jonquil came along. It is true there will never be another like Honey, but I do not expect Jonquil to be a copy of Honey. Two cockers could hardly differ more, except in the deep golden color of the coat. During the fourteen years I had Honey, Jill used to say my shadow was golden. If I got up from the desk in a hurry to answer the telephone, I had to be careful not to step on her. She was a dedicated cocker, quiet, with no sense of humor. She loved only me, and that was her career.

Jonquil, on the other hand, is merry, outgoing, gay, and everything seems funny to her. She is perfectly happy with anyone and everyone, a completely adjustable dog. She is always the life of the party when we entertain, whereas Honey retired under my bed until the last guest had gone.

I have never felt it necessary to measure my portion of love for each of them.

The whole countryside is bright with color now. Not the tender colors of spring, but the vital tones of coming autumn. Goldenrod follows the line of the fences with its feathery spikes of minted gold; the chicory sets deep-blue stars adrift on every line. The gardens are like a Mexican fiesta, with countless shades of zinnias.

My favorite zinnia color is the soft pale salmon, and I love to mass the blossoms in an old dark-blue sugar bowl. For the sharper oranges and reds, I use an old wooden bucket or a copper container, just right with the brilliant shades.

Zinnias are the most independent flowers! You get them all arranged so nicely in a bouquet and an hour later they are standing up stiff as ramrods and facing in the wrong direction. I have given up doing a good arrangement with them; I just pop them in and leave them to their own devices.

The second blooming of the Chinese

delphinium goes well with zinnias in an antique copper bowl. We keep the house filled with bouquets now, anticipating the frost. And when the leaves begin to turn, Jill brings in branches of rosy red leaves for the stone jug by the hearth. The swamp maples turn first, and their color is incredible. They really burn with color.

Midday is still soft with summer, so warm and dreamy that it seems it must go on forever. Comes the blue dusk, and a cool knife slices the heat of the day. But there is a feeling in the air, nevertheless. We keep a wary eye on the Farmer's Almanac, and an alert ear to weather broadcasts. For the hurricane season approaches.

I may admit that so far we have never had adequate warning of a hurricane that arrived. We have had many warnings of those that did not come. But the most severe hurricanes we have had came without being announced, except by our own country senses.

A hurricane is preceded by a strange stuffy smell in the air. Nobody has ever mentioned this, as far as I know, but it is as if the whole air were shut up in a small space. People sometimes tell me I am silly to say I smell a hurricane, but so I do. Then comes a black sky and a rain shepherded by a dark wind that seems to come from all directions at once. When you cannot tell which way the wind is blowing, it is time to batten down. Often the storm seems to be going over, and then I hear a sound, half wail, half roar, which comes also in all directions at once. At this point, we lock doors and windows, get out the candles and try to make fresh coffee before "the electric" goes off.

We no longer fill up the bathtub with water, for (a) it takes a lot of water from the well and (b) we never need that much.

We spend our energy bringing in wood, for a hurricane, at any time, is cloaked with cold. I haul out extra comforters for the beds. Jill races about with lawn chairs — it is not good idea to have them flung against the windows. We fill a water pitcher — not for us, but for the dogs. We can drink coffee heated over the fire in the fireplace but the cockers and Irish need fresh water.

My first experience with a genuine hurricane was long ago when I thought this was only a bad nor'easter. I was alone at the time, with the cats (three), a litter of small puppies in the kennel, a houseful of grown cockers. I thought it was a big storm. It was blowing so hard that water flowed in under the sills. I got sacks of onions and potatoes newly dug, and laid them along the sills. Then I got all the bath towels in the house and stuffed the windows with them. I was tired of the whole business by then, but I looked out in the yard and saw the kennel door had given way under the impact of the wind and all the puppies were blowing about the yard like windy leaves, while branches crashed from the old apple trees. The puppies were frightened and screaming. I hauled the onion sack from the back door and flew out and spent quite a time scooping up wet puppies. I was hampered by the wind and the rain and by being able to carry only three at a time. The fourth just fell through. Finally I had them all in the kitchen and got the range going with the leftover wood from a packing crate. I next burned up an old chair. Then I got the fireplace going with the last logs in the woodshed and made a pot of tea. I lit the oil lamp and fried an egg in the embers at the edge of the hearth. I got out *Wuthering Heights* and read five chapters. I always read that in a crisis — it rests me.

Quite a storm, I reflected, checking on the puppies, who had stopped shivering. Then suddenly the current went on and the phone began to ring.

"Are you all right? Is the house damaged? Are the dogs safe?"

"We are all *fine*," I shouted (the connection was fuzzy). "But I had to use undiluted evaporated milk for the formula — they love it."

I had been too busy, fortunately, to notice that the thirteen lovely old apple trees in the back yard had gone down. I just thought the storm was noisy as I rubbed various puppies with towels. And I hoped the water pouring in wouldn't spoil the potatoes and onions!

Subsequently, during other hurricanes, I found that I was always too busy to worry. But I did learn a few things in that first hurricane, which was local but devastating. Now when the sky takes on a greenish tinge and the air gets that funny smell, we mobilize. Fill pails, fill teakettles. Wash lamp chimneys, trim wicks. Lug in enough wood for a siege. Get out all the candles in the house. Make coffee. Stack bath towels for handy mopping when something gives way.

Then we sit it out. We always hope the cables on the two-hundred-year-old sugar maples will hold, but when branches crash, we are thankful the roof has survived.

I always think of the unfortunate people who lose their homes in such a hurricane. And of those who get flooded out. Stillmeadow, built below the hill and away from the stream, is sound. But how many lose all they have when Nature lets her fury loose! I feel such an identity with all homepeople who lose everything in flood, fire or hurricane that as I lug in one more sack of onions to brace against my own door, I utter a special prayer for those less fortunate.

Hurricanes can strike us all, one way or another. Even those who are outside the natural hurricane belt may be subject to hurricanes of the spirit, the heart. And there is only one way to meet any kind of hurricane: batten down, ride it out, face it with courage.

As Hugh Walpole said, so wisely, "It isn't life that matters, it's the courage you bring to it."

"I suppose you never travel far," said a recent visitor. This was a much-traveled person who had made an extra trip to see Stillmeadow.

I thought it over. No, I do not travel far, in a way. I would like to go to far-off islands in the South Seas. I have always wanted to visit Hawaii. My husband and I did visit Europe, including Italy, before war had laid a mark on it. I was the most avid sightseer that could be imagined. I kept on looking at things and walking to see things until my eyes swelled shut and my feet flattened out. But in my memory now I remember most of all going to Keats's house in Hampstead

Heath, and in Rome visiting his last dwelling place and going to the cemetery where he was buried under the stone with the pitiful words, "Here Lies One Whose Name Was Writ in Water."

On that trip I ate a lot of indigestible fabulous foods in elegant places. I looked at masterpieces. I prayed my own prayers in all the cathedrals. I saw opera in Paris, when the swan broke down in *Lohengrin*. I saw, and did not climb, the Swiss mountains. I heard *Parsifal* in Munich. I did not miss anything, so far as I knew.

But now what remains is the memory of a bare and rather uninteresting house on Hampstead Heath and a grave in Rome. And I had traveled with Keats for a long time in his books.

"No, I do not travel far," I said to the visitor.

But I travel as far as my mind will reach, I thought. Any day, any time.

Physical traveling can get you around, but only travel in the mind can be satisfying, for I saw many people on my one trip across the ocean who spent their time deploring the absence of bathrooms and hot running water such as they had in Iowa. The galleries were just a lot of paintings and were chilly. And room service was sketchy. They had a hard time getting ice for their drinks.

Now, except for short weekend trips by car, I confine my travel to our annual visit to Cape Cod to look at the ocean. It takes over five hours to get there, and after the first hour we begin to worry about home. Did we turn off things and turn on things? Did we leave enough notes for everyone who might come? Did we tell the cocker-sitter to add a teaspoonful of this or that as per the Rx from the veterinarian?

We often stop midway to phone back and be sure everything is all right. But the more miles we go, the more we worry.

"I forgot to tell the laundryman not to stop," I say in Providence.

"Did you leave a note about watering the house-plants?" asks Jill as she heads toward Taunton.

No matter how homebound we are, we all need a small vacation. We go away, as our neighbor says, "to rest our heads," and this is about what we do. We head for Cape Cod, and as we drive over the Sagamore bridge the salty, piny air leaves us breathless. I stop worrying over whether the meter reader will leave the gate open and let the dogs out. I look at the canal, wide and deep, and see a freighter in the distance. Across the bridge we drive between scrub pines and sandy banks. The narrow land lies between the ocean and the bay, and if it is windy, sand blows against our cheeks as we drive. Gulls begin to wheel over, crying and crying.

When we get to our special place, we do not bother to unpack. We go out and look at the ocean, with the waves rolling in and breaking on the bright sand. The crests are silvery and foaming, but the underpart of the waves is a black-green. There is nothing so timeless as the breaking of waves on a long beach. I can look at the horizon and know that Spain is the nearest shore. I see a ship moving steadily against the edge of sky.

Suddenly I stop worrying about that coffe-maker at home. If we left it on, let it burn out. It is not vital. What is vital is to watch the breakers, and count to see whether the seventh wave is truly larger — or is it possibly the ninth one?

The beach itself is a lesson in time. I pick up a tiny shell which has been polished and shaped by the waves but still keeps its original shape. As time goes on, it will become part of the sand. Here and there, a shiny pink pebble is left when the tide ebbs, and this too is on a course. It will roll and sweep forward with the tide and retreat with the tide. And always it will be shaped, smoothed, rounded and lessened until it too is a grain of sand.

As I pick up a cool pebble and hold it in my palm, it seems to me that the tide of life shapes me in much the same way. An edge is polished off in a great storm of grief. A jagged point is smoothed away by disappointments, disillusionments which have been face. Gradually life polishes the stone. The surface of a small pebble is satiny. It feels cool to the palm.

So it is with people, I think. If the core of the stone is sound, the wearing away by the tide results in a smooth oval. If the core is soft, there is no pebble left after a few nor'easters. I have known people buffeted by life mercilessly who still give me a sense of serenity. The integral core was sound. And I have known people who disintegrated at the first blow as a bit of clay exposed on the great beach dissolves in the first turn of the tide.

But perhaps the great lesson of the sea is that small things do not matter. The horizon is limitless and my own becomes limitless too if I look a long time at the edge of sky and sea.

There is color on the Cape in autumn, but not the flaming passionate colors you find inland. There is some low oak with brown-red leaves, there are thickets that turn rosy brown, and there is the lovely grey-blue of the bayberries. And of course the cranberry bogs, which spread like a jeweled carpet. And finally, there is the ocean, which is every color there is, according to weather and light. Is it more beautiful as the sky turns apricot and the sea is washed with pink as the sun sinks — or when the great blue-green seas reaching out toward Spain deepen to indigo at twilight? Is it more beautiful when the tide is out and the clam flats are polished pewter, with pools of pink pearl here and there — or when the white crests roll in at full tide, flinging salt spray on the great beach? And at night, when the moon floats on the deep sea of sky and casts a shining path over black deep water — perhaps this is loveliest. I am glad I do not have to choose. I can have them all.

The summer visitors leave around Labor Day, usually going back to jobs and school. Cottages are boarded up, boats lifted from the water, beaches are wide and quiet, and it is rather like the curtain going down on Act III. Then villages lie in tranquil sunlight and people walk slowly to the post offices, no longer dodging cars. The opinion of the Cape Cod residents is, "I am sorry they have to go, poor things, but I'm glad they're gone."

Now the year-rounders have time to see their friends again and September is a time for catching up. Life returns to normal after Labor Day, and then casual suppers, afternoon parties and coffee-and-desserts begin. It is as if they had all been on a long journey and had at last reached home port. I visit Charlotte and Ruth in their exquisite house with the whole sea spread before it and sweet gardens frilled around it like ladies' Victorian laces. I take a Sunday afternoon ride with Bobby Gibson and see roads I never saw before. (Sunday afternoon rides were the high point in my childhood, and I wish they would come back). I watch football with Millie and Ed after a superb dinner. I sit by the fire with Helen Beals and talk books. I discuss world affairs with Barbara and Slim and local politics with the Barkers. Or worry over an impossible crossword with Margaret Stanger while we eat her famous baked beans. There are just a few of the happy meetings that belong to September.

And I wish it could go on forever. I do not even mind paying a dollar and a half for fourteen small, undernourished pieces of firewood, although at Stillmeadow our woodpile reaches to the windowsills outside two rooms and the wood is prime.

One Sunday on the Cape stands out in my memory. My cousin Rob and his wife,

Bebe, were coming for breakfast. On Jill's advice, and remembering from childhood Rob's sturdy appetite, I decided to go along with the experts who advise a hearty one. I set the time at twelve, figuring I could be wake up then. I splurged on Rock Cornish game hens on the theory that they are lighter than chicken. I made a pilaf because something had to go with the birds, and since I had a can of beets I fixed Harvard beets to give a color contrast.

Rob had gone out at six, however, and found a clam bed, so our guests arrived with a huge pail of clams. We began with a platter of cherrystones.

These are my favorites in the clam family, and their official name is quahog. They are known as cherrystones in the city and as "the little ones" on the Cape. To dig your own, you need a clam rake, a wire basket and determination—that's all. Somehow the clamming itself is sheer joy, for the water is still and lovely, and the only sound is the lonely cry of gulls riding the air currents. Sometimes, as you stop to rest, you see a freighter far out, bound for a distant land.

The clams are cool to the touch and almost iridescent. I have never learned how to open them, but Rob says it is because I make them nervous. He evidently calms them, for we have a platterful in no time. Rob likes a sauce of hot horseradish, lemon and catsup, but there's a lot to be said for plain lemon juice and pepper. The Cape clams are delicate pink and honey-sweet, and all you need for a meal is fresh Portuguese bread with garlic butter. And plenty of hot coffee.

However, on this occasion we also had, as I have said, several other dishes! When we finished the cherrystones, we then consumed half a gallon of steamers with a pint of broth to each. Then came my part of the meal. And as he finished his Cornish hen, Rob suddenly said, "You forgot the salad!"

It is now referred to as "that breakfast with no salad."

September is a good month for the Irish and the cockers. Raccoons are about, eating the best of the corn, woodchucks come right in the backyard at times, and the squirrels are there for chasing. The dogs like to stay out late hunting things they almost never catch. What they *do* catch is nettles and sticktights and burs, but that is part of the game.

The other day Holly took a notion to bring in some fallen branches, one by one. Trying to fetch just half a branch through a regular-size door kept her busy for quite a while, but she figured out that by going sideways she could get through. She laid the branches on my bed, scattering twigs, of course, all over the floor. Then she lay down on the bed next to them and slept with her paws folded tenderly over the branches.

We had, once, one golden cocker named, incorrectly, Silver Moon (she was white when born). Moon killed snakes. We must have had a couple of hundred dogs when we were raising them, but only Moon would come to the house proudly bearing a snake.

They were hard to carry, and Moon would have to stop now and then to adjust her grip. I always knew what was up, because Jill, the quietest person I ever knew, would utter a sound like a fire siren as Moon approached with the present.

It is interesting to speculate on mankind's common fear of snakes. I've been told it is because primitive man feared the snakes that dropped on him from trees. But why do my dogs have the same aversion? All summer Holly and the cockers pursued a snake that lives in the terrace. (Holly has a particular snake bark, and there is fear in it. The cockers whine with excitement.) The snake always got away. Yet I am sure Holly could have caught that snake in a minute if she'd had her heart in it.

Jill dug potatoes this morning. I am a poor digger, for I always manage to chop the best potatoes in two with the pitchfork. The first potatoes are a delight. But as Jill caried the basket in, she said the air was so still, we could get the black frost that night. It always comes toward the end of September, after an utterly windless day.

As we rush to bring in everything that

will be spoiled, I reflect that a parsnip is a pleasant vegetable. It likes to sit in the ground until after the freeze.

The back kitchen overflows with tomatoes, peppers, grapes, the last roses, zinnias and delphinium. Carrots, celery, chard, cabbage can take care of themselves, as can the acorn squash. We bring in the pattypan squash, however. Ripe cucumbers must come in to be baked or made into pickles. There is a great flurry until at last we know nothing more can be fetched in. Then at dusk on the day of the black frost, I open the door and breathe that sudden, sharp air. "What's out tonight is lost," I say, quoting Miss Millay.

"If we had one more tomato, we'd have to move out," says Jill. And it is true that we can hardly thread our way across the back kitchen floor.

"I don't mind saying," Jill comments, "that I have had enough beans for a while. Let them freeze. Who cares?"

There is — there has to be — a moment the next morning after the killing frost, when the heart is saddened. The zinnia stalks are blackened and oozy, the garden itself has flattened out as leaves wilted. A few clusters of unripe grapes hang amid drooping sorry leaves. This is good-bye to summer, flower and fruit and vegetable.

But there is inevitably a spell of warm weather next. When we walk down the country road, I think, "And straight was a path of gold for him," because the goldenrod does make a path of sheer gold. I learned from Edwin Way Teale's *Autumn Across America* that the English call it "farewell summer." This is what it is. Joe-pye weed frosts the meadows with rosy violet. Swamp maples flicker into flame. The birds are leaving. Farewell summer it truly is.

Ten

Every season has its own glory in New England, for every month has its separate identity, different personality. October is the dramatic month — everyone knows about autumn in New England. More and more tourists come during October, and eager travelers stop all along the roads taking dozens of pictures.

The air is as cool as an old coin

teaspoon, and a faint tang of blue woodsmoke spices the wind. The color of the great sugar maples is so dazzling, it seems I must have dreamed it. The maples give forth light, like closer suns. The oaks glow with a garnet fire, and all the thickets blaze with scarlets and pale gold and cinnamon. It is like the music of a trumpet.

After the black frost, a few flowers bloom again, spikes of goldenrod gleam by a split-rail fence, a spray of hardy clematis shines white in the garden, and now and then one finds a rose, smelling of summer and warmth.

Poking around in the vegetable garden, Jill always unearths some tomatoes which have been sheltered by ragged growths of weeds. She says it is a lesson not to weed too much in late summer. Broccoli is still there, and of course the cabbage and acorn squash and carrots go on happily. The chard tends to toughen, bracing for more cold weather, but is still edible. Some lettuce can be had, but most of it is gone.

Now is the time to go out to the woods

for butternuts and hickory nuts and hazelnuts. The upper pastures are grey-green and tranquil, the deciduous trees flame against a sky as soft as the breast of a dove. The old grey-stone ledges are warm; the light is golden on the fallen burrs. The butternuts are dark and sticky; the hickory nuts have a green plastic case and underneath are as smooth as ivory. The hazelnuts are fringed with cinnamon on the outer case and have an exquisite tricornered shape.

George's cows stand in pleasant aimlessness in the driftway as we go by. A big buck rabbit goes lippety-lippety into the thicket. A wandering country cat pauses to eye us soberly, then sleeks away on her own serious business.

We carry old gunnysacks and we fill them — it is impossible to stop when the treasure is there for the gathering. Midway we sit on a big rock that is frosted over with lichen and eat our ham and cheese sandwiches and drink the hot coffee from the thermos. Even as we eat, nuts plop down, surely bigger and better than any we have yet gathered! The squirrels have been at work too; many of the nuts are only shells by now.

Staggering under the weight of the sacks, we finally come home, feeling we have done a very worthwhile thing. Never mind that we never do get all the nuts shelled. We crack some with a flatiron on the hearthstone, but we never really get to them all. I surmise it is more fun to adventure in the autumn woods than to dig out the tiny meats afterward with a pick.

This is the season of the Hunter's Moon, and when it is full it casts a pure brilliance over the countryside. One can almost read by it. The light gives a glow to the trees. When the leaves begin to fall, the moon gilds them. If I walk in the yard I can see the lights from the neighbors' houses. I cannot see them at all from mid-May until autumn, for the foliage is so thick all the way up the hill.

I am particularly fond of the smell of fallen leaves, a rather musty odor. The smell of blue woodsmoke is lovely and the essence of leaf scent is in it. It is rare now, for most folk use the leaves for mulch or in compost pits or to bank around house foundations before piling pine branches up. I have a small burning of the garden weeds and always stand around sniffing it with pleasure until there is only ash left.

What does the season mean to me? I think about it as I circle back to the house. The one word that expresses it would be splendor. October is the jewel set in the hand of time.

The Indians who named the Hunter's Moon are gone, but as I go out with the cockers and Holly for a last walk about the yard at moonrise, I sometimes think I can see tall, dark figures walking leaf-light at the edge of the garden. Occasionally Teddy will sit back on his golden self and bark loudly, so I expect an Indian dog or two is there also. It reminds me that I do not own this piece of land, not even this house. I am, in a way, lent it for a time. The house belongs to a sturdy man who built it in 1690. The land wasn't his, really; it was the Indians' home place before he came. We are all, I think, sojourners.

This year I have been making strenuous efforts to learn Spanish. I have read so many articles about keeping up with the children's interests, and Connie and languages are practically synonymous. And when I realized that she was about to receive her master's degree in Linguistics, whereas I still could speak only English, I felt I should take steps!

Since it was reputed to be easy to learn, I began to study Spanish. I may say the struggle has been epic. After some months, I now have reached the stage of being able to hold a conversation in the language, provided that it is confined to the subject matter of my textbook. Most everyday subjects are far from my ken, but I can say that the General Gomez is going to the war, but the king will not go until tomorrow. The queen, quite properly, stays at home; but alas, the son will also make the attack presently.

I can also speak with feeling about my uncle and aunt, who lead a strange life. They are either going to the country, or moving to a new house, or being very,

very ill. My aunt does not drink wine.

There is a great deal of trouble in my book. The family has a hard time. they get up *a las cinco,* which is five in the morning, and they eat stale bread and drink black coffee. Juan had to walk the streets five days trying to find work when he went to Mexico. Luis cannot take a trip because he has no job and no pesos.

And there is a nasty little brother, who will not study, will not work, spends his time in cafés, is always asking for money and is really no good at all.

Even the automobile, which ran well yesterday, will not run at all today.

Poor Luis hardly closes his eyes all night and cannot eat and has *dolor de cabeza* (headache) because his uncle died in Cuba a month ago. (Oh, those uncles!) His uncle was an outstanding character — the whole world loved him — but even so, I admit I was rather glad to see the last of him.

My poor aunt constantly *tiene los ojos llenos de lagrimas* — has her eyes full of tears — and you can't blame her when you think of what her life is.

And, as if there were not already trouble enough, the books which were ordered did not arrive, although some nice views of Mexico City were sent instead.

In the supplementary reading, there is an amazing story, which has a real moral. A certain Don Pedro came home late for dinner and the soup was cold, *fria*. In a regrettable moment of anger, he threw the soup out the window. Whereupon the servant, quite properly deciding to teach him a lesson, threw the rest of the dinner *por la ventana* also, together with the chairs, table, dishes, forks, knives, spoons and everything else that wasn't nailed to the floor. "It's a beautiful day," he said. "I see the señor wishes to eat outdoors!" Thoroughly chastened, Don Pedro went on eating cold soup the rest of his life and never said a word. This is one way of solving the servant problem. Don Pedro's man must have been an uncle of Ted Key's indomitable Hazel.

My adventures in Spanish have led me to think about education very seriously. Adult education, I believe, is the answer to a good many of the problems we have today. We tend to grow in our own circumscribed worlds, and enlarging our horizon is a magic thing. We can go to classes or just consult our local librarian for a good reading list on some special subject. Whether it be history, or philosophy, or how to plant petunias, no matter. Of course, if you decide to take up something like pottery, you might do well to start with a teacher. But crewel work you can do on your own. I couldn't, that is, but I know people who have.

We do not migrate as the birds do, but I notice there is a change in the rhythm of our life when the season ebbs. Nights are cool, days dreamy with blue haze. There is a quickening in the blood, a restlessness. Suddenly we are full of projects, which may be our own manner of migrating. Now the firewood must be stacked, handy by the back door, the woodshed filled with kindling. That cellar window, broken last spring, must really be mended. The cellar itself is piled high with the debris of summer, as well as broken flowerpots, extra mason jars, a mousetrap that does not work, and a few antiques that need to be done over.

Weeds and old raspberry canes must be burned now. Cornstalks should be destroyed with fire to kill any leftover pests. We wait for a good damp day and get the permit from the fire warden, and then I have a nervous spell, being mortally afraid of fire. This is not due to any peculiarity in my personality. It means that I remember when my father's house burned to ashes in New Mexico, and how it was when the barn went up in flames. And that I clearly recall the day when a brushfire nearly swept away our whole home place. Fire isn't a symbol of anything in my unconscious or subconscious; it is just something I have had experience with. So when Jill gets the permit and begins to burn the garden debris, I shudder.

For many years, George always came over to help with the burning, but finally he had to take on an extra job driving trucks for the town road commission. When there is a real need, however, a neighbor always seems to appear, and this time was no exception. Joe Vanek, who lives up on Hull's Hill, offered to help us out. Like George, he is an experienced countryman, and when he came by the first time, Holly took one look at him and rose up to lick his chin. His wife, Erma, came too: a small, quick person, bright as a bird. I was just struggling to fold my big bedspread to take it to the village laundry. "Why not let me have that," Erma said. "That's too pretty to send out. I'll just do it tomorrow when I do my own washing. No trouble. And if ever you have anything else —"

Yesterday Erma and I did some fall house-cleaning while Joe and Jill cleared out the woodshed. It was such a bright warm day that I decided to hang some of the laundry in the backyard. Soon blankets were blowing on the line as the October sun and wind gave lovely freshness to them, preparing for the stuffy winter rooms.

All our blankets have stories about them. There are the two fragile homespun ones which Grandma Raybold had. They are a pale honey color, and invading moths have nibbled the edges in some pre-mothspray day. They remind me of my little precisely garbed quiet grandmother with her gentle voice and wise eyes. As I hang them on the line, I am minded of my Uncle Walter, her son and Mama's brother. He was the one man I ever knew of whom it could be said he "saw life steadily, and saw it whole."

He was a quiet man, self-educated, and in the paper business. Nothing glamorous or spectacular at all. And yet every life he touched had a glow from his touching it. When he died, even the Pullman porters who had been on the run he frequented on business trips made a personal grief of his going.

What I remember most is that when my mother died and a number of personal difficulties outside were crushing me, Uncle Walter took me for a walk after supper. The streetlamps cast a pale lemon glow on his erect figure, his careful hat, his impeccable shoes. All he said was so simple and so short. We walked, and the light fell on him, and the shadows moved.

The new-cut grass on the lawns smelled sweet. A little dog nosed along the curb and vanished.

"The Raybolds have always been heavy burden-bearers," he said quietly and as if that were quite to be expected and accounted for.

At that moment I felt myself one of a dim line stretching back and back and back, of people who went about their business and just bore their burdens. He never said another word to me about mine; he just let me assume I was to bear mine in the family tradition.

That simple statement has sustained me down the years.

One autumn chore that I enjoy is checking the pantry supplies. In case we get snowed in, it is comforting to have plenty of staples on hand.

Jill has been cleaning and sorting the onions, and storing them in the fruit cellar. She saves out the largest and plumpest for stuffing and baking, and some the right size for glazing for Thanksgiving. Onions are basic to good eating, I think. There really is no substitute for an onion when you need a onion.

It has a long history. The Egyptians spent the equivalent of two million dollars on onions during the years they were building the Great Pyramid. There were countless workers, of course, and the pyramid took twenty years to complete, but this is still quite a budget for onions. I have not found out how they ate them. I would suspect they ate them raw with some kind of black bread.

I do know that the Romans felt onions gave strength (my own opinion too) and they ate them as a breakfast dish with honey. This seems very odd, but then I remember that I make glazed onions with catsup and honey, baking them and basting until they are rich with the sauce. By the sixteenth century, onion juice was dropped in the ear as a remedy for deafness, and in the eyes to clear the vision.

The Spanish exported onions to the new world, but there were native varieties already there. I suspect onion soup must have originated in France, for its fine bouquet seems so French. And many a peasant soup of the Middle Ages may have been raised to elegance by a judicious adding of onions.

Holding a round, firm onion in my hand, I think how wonderfully it is made. The delicate papery skin is faintly pink or ivory, and the concentric circles inside are a marvel. Nature casually produces this gift to mankind and we take it quite for granted. Of course, everybody has onions.

When the shelves are all in order and the garden is put to bed properly, the bird feeders and suet cages come out. Jill brings home the first twenty-five pounds of wild-bird food and chunks of creamy suet. The birds are waiting. Five minutes after the feeders are set up, they flock in. And how they do eat! For seven months now, we will wait on the birds. And we will worry. I know that wild birds ought to be able to set their own table. If they are silly enough to stick around in blizzards, why is it my responsibility? Nevertheless, I shall be skating across the icy lawn all winter with pans of food.

As the winter birds are settling in, the others are leaving. The wild geese went over early one morning this week. Why this is so moving, I do not know. All of us feel it; in the village store someone says, "I heard the geese go over," and there is a moment of silence. We seldom make much of the swallows or other migratory birds when they leave, although we are very likely to note the redwings when they come back in March. But the geese — ah, that is to feet a quickening of the heart.

High and lovely, they wedge through the sky, their faint cries drifting down to earth, and for a brief time we seem to fly too. How do they chart their course? How many miles do they travel? How many of them fail to make it? How do they know when they've reached their destination? And how high do they fly? Perhaps higher than other birds. . . .

A group of us were talking about the relationship between people and pets the other night, and I thought Helen Beals settled the question.

When her son, Young Joe (who is still called Young Joe, although he has four children), had to board his rabbit, he was disconsolate. But the family was going on a trip and the rabbit had to be boarded. They got back late at night and no sooner had they unlocked the door than Young Joe suggested they go and fetch his rabbit.

"It's too late," said Helen.

"I want my rabbit," he said. "I want my rabbit now."

"But everybody will be in bed."

"I'd like my rabbit," said Joe.

Finally they gave in and drove to the boarding place. The man said, "I don't have any lights in the hutch, and I don't know where your rabbit is."

"I want my rabbit," said Joe patiently. "Let me go and get him."

"But I don't know which pen he is in," objected the man, "and I have a lot of rabbits out there. You better come back tomorrow."

"I'll find him," said Joe.

In the end, they went out to the rabbit quarters with a dim flashlight. Young Joe started down the line of cages. He went slowly, thoughtfully. He picked up a rabbit, put him back, picked up a second rabbit, put him back. Then he picked up a third, felt him carefully, rubbed the rabbit's ears.

"This is my rabbit," he said definitely.

All the rabbits looked exactly alike, Helen said, especially in the dark. But young Joe carried this one rabbit to the car in his arms and they drove home.

Now this was Joe's own rabbit and they were sure of it when they put him in his special little house, for the house had a main room, a bedroom, and a corner bathroom. The rabbit hopped at once to his bathroom, then whisked into his bedroom and flopped onto his bed. Somehow the boy and his rabbit had a communication that was no mystery to them but surprised everyone else.

Of course, the dogs communicate with me, but they bark. Holly also squeaks and chants in a contralto singsong.

"Jonquil wants some lettuce," Jill calls. "Shall I give her what's left?"

Or, "Linda says the laundryman has

just turned the corner."

Or, "Holly says there is a lovely man at the gate and she does not know him, but let him in!" (We sometimes feel a bit jealous at her adoration of men.)

It is a great help at night to know just what is going on outside. Loud, emphatic welcome sounds mean Erma is coming over, happy-happy sounds signal the arrival of Steve and Olive. Lower, rapid barks mean a stranger is in the yard, and the attack-barks are a sure sign a possum has wandered in from the woods. There is, fortunately, a very special whoop which gets me out of bed in a hurry. For this is the announcement that a skunk is on the grounds and I get the dogs inside in nothing flat. So far, the only one to get involved is Holly, who is so curious that she had to go and see what this thing was! She saw.

Queer things can happen with dogs. My friends the Tovrovs, on Cape Cod, have a fine pedigreed black Labrador named Smoky. Not long ago they missed him when it was time for supper. Their house is on a back road, some distance from the town, and the yard is unfenced. So far as I know, nobody fences in anything on Cape Cod. It is not a farming country, so fencing for cattle is not needed. Land boundaries are usually marked by small cement posts over which the bayberries and the wild roses grow.

On this night the Tovrovs went out and called Smoky, and he did not appear. Orin went to the beach, and Smoky was not there either. He was not visiting his favorite neighbor. Thoroughly alarmed by then, the Tovrovs were rushing to the car when the phone rang.

"I've got your Labrador here at the police station," said Chet Landers. "He just happened by."

So Orin drove down to the station, opened the car door, and a happy Labrador jumped in. When they got home, he followed Orin into the house, greeted Midge, ate supper and curled up on the sofa.

About an hour later Midge went to let the cats in, and following them was a black Labrador, who looked with disfavor at the empty feeding dish. The phone was ringing, so she answered it in a hurry.

"Listen," said the voice of Chet Landers, "I'm calling about that Labrador."

"We've got two," said Midge, "as of now."

"Both perfectly at home," added Orin, who was sorting them out. The first one was *not* Smoky, but they not only looked as alike as two black peas but, as Orin said, they acted alike. And how did the stranger know where the food dish was kept and which was his spot on the sofa?

I turned out that after Orin had gone happily home, a frantic owner called Chet to report his prize Labrador missing — they had looked everywhere —

"Think I know where he is," said Chet.

So the police department chalked up another successful rescue, and the Tovrovs are still wondering why the lost dog acted as if he had always lived with them. He didn't even investigate the corners — just went straight to the kitchen. It is a little strange, the more you think of it.

A New England town meeting is a lively affair. This last one was called specially to discuss zoning. We got to the school on time (which is always a mistake) and found people milling about in the corridors, tempers already rising. The gymnasium, where we meet, was not arranged with rows of chairs and the moderator's table. It was arranged with the basketball team practicing for a game. It was, in fact, full of whopping boys.

It took half an hour to find some other place for the meeting, and eventually someone opened up a classroom and everyone jammed in. It was unfortunate that it was a classroom for very young children or midgets. Some of the men just stood around the wall. I wedged myself in a child-size desk chair wondering who would haul me out. It took another half hour to get the zoning maps up on the walls. I had time to memorize the verse on the blackboard. The teacher told me later that it came from a new version of the familiar church hymn, "Old Hundred," which I used to sing as "Praise God from Whom all blessings flow."

From all who dwell below the skies
Let faith and hope and love arise.
Let beauty, truth, and good be sung
From every land, from every tongue.

I thought it was a fine message, provided these children would know what beauty is, or truth; they are difficult concepts for many adults. Faith too is something hard to understand, difficult to define. However, I thought, squeezing my knees under the desk, the children probably would know the meaning of "all who dwell below the skies."

By then, some of the maps had fallen down and the zoning commission kept putting them back up again. They were beautiful, impressive maps but impossible to read. I did discover that what must be Stillmeadow's area was dark grey, although some part of the maps were pink, which is more cheerful. The meeting had been called to order when a scout reported the gymnasium was now free, so down came the maps, out we went and we began all over.

Now zoning is a hard subject. Everyone wants it, but not for himself. It's all very well to zone a future business district, but a hardheaded Yankee may figure he might want to put up a filling station or a hot-dog stand on his land, which is in the so-called residential section. This is further complicated in our rural area because until lately the residential section consisted of farms. The business area consists of a few buildings, country store, post office (in the store), garage, doctors' office. When we acquired a drugstore we wondered whether we might be getting too citified.

The moderator opened the meeting (when the maps were up) and at last the town meeting was under way. Four or five men jumped up at once and began to argue. They jumped up and some jumped both up and down, so the floor vibrated. They all talked at once, as usual, and nobody waited to be recognized by the moderator and given the floor.

The objectors declared they had owned their land and paid taxes (taxes are a red flag) and they were not going to be told what to do with it.

"If I want to sell off half an acre," said one, "it's my half acre. Who's to tell me I have to sell in three-acre pieces?"

"If I want to put up a barn, I'm not to be told where I can build and where I can't."

"We've got along all right here since we drove the British out and we'll get along all right as we are without a lot of fancy new rules."

The moderator banged away but it was hard to quiet things down so the head of the commission could answer questions and explain the maps.

"This is one of the very few rural areas left in Connecticut." He spoke firmly. "Circumstance has protected you up to now — namely a lack of transportation facilities. This won't last."

He moved to one of the maps and used his pointer.

"Hartford, New Haven, Waterbury and Bridgeport," he said, "are reaching out already as the new highways go in. You are now eleven minutes from Newtown instead of twenty-five. You will soon be eighteen minutes from Waterbury. Your valley is more accessible every year."

It was a grim picture. Business was bound to come; light industries were already shopping for land. The quiet country farms were already going and developments would take over. He finished by saying that just how the village developed would depend on us. With proper control, it would grow with beauty and grace.

When he finished, the argument began again. The meeting never really ended, and nobody decided anything. Around midnight people began to drift away. This is typical of a town meeting. After the session, some time elapses in which the argument goes on at the grocery store, at the Grange, after church. Eventually another meeting is called at which everyone is even madder than at the first. I once heard a farmer say furiously to another, "I'll punch you in the head when we get out of here."

"Try it and see," said the other.

But I knew the next day these two would be amiably discussing crops, because that is the way it is in our valley. What sounds like plain murder is just independent Yankees exercising democracy.

The next town meeting will undoubtedly vote to set up a zoning commission to study the problem further. Eventually, of course, we will have to have some sort of plan to guide future development. Somehow we must protect the wooded hills, the greening meadows, the clean sweet-running brooks and the historic white houses — these are a precious heritage.

Sometimes in October we manage to return to Cape Cod for a few days to walk the great shining beaches, drive along the dune roads and watch the moon over the old unquiet ocean.

The gulls go over and drift on the bosom of the air and cry their piercing lovely cry. The little boats are asleep in the harbors, waiting for the tides of spring to come again. And the air smells so strongly of pine and salt that it is a wave of beauty in itself.

Colors are all intense on the Cape — possibly the sea is the cause, or the lack of high woodlands. The old weather-worn houses are silver; roses still bloom; the dark red ones against a split-rail fence have a jewel quality.

We rent a small cottage whenever we go for more than a weekend, but someday we will build a house of our own.

Alice and Margaret were with us this time, and Glenn and Burton flew in from Ohio. Burton is an old friend from my husband's college days who now teaches at a conservatory in Ohio. Glenn is his best student, a tenor who is just beginning his professional career. They often fly East together for concerts. I always admire people who fly so casually. For Burton often phones from Akron at night and says, "How would you like to have me for lunch tomorrow? Or I'll make it by four in the afternoon anyway."

As for Glenn, he would rather fly than do anything except sing or fish. He flew one of those early planes put together with bailing wire and loved it.

His wife, Peggy, usually stays at home, for there is a house full of small children, but Glenn promises that someday soon,

Grandma will mind the flock so that Peg can come along.

On this particular trip, everyone arrived in midafternoon. Alice and Jill went clamming. I could see their bent busy figures as they raked around in the icy water. There is nothing more fascinating than bringing up those big greyish-purple quahogs, plump and cold and clean. Glenn had not been allowed to bring his tons of fishing tackle, since he was supposed to sing his current concert for us, but he found an old bamboo pole in the cottage garage and began fixing it up at once.

Margaret and Burton talked music while keeping an eye on the ardent clammers. I skimmed through the *Cape Codder,* which I dearly love, and was pleased to read the news of this curiously separate little country. I was sorry to hear that Mr. So-and-So's career was cut short at age eighty-two when he ran into a telephone pole on a rainy night.

The Cape Codders, I believe, think nobody dies on the Cape except by some accident. They are all strong because of the fish they eat. And certainly all the scallops and lobster and clams and oysters must do something! But it may also be the relaxing quality in the air, so tensions are less. I notice people tend to move more slowly, to take things as they come. And not to bother about doing anything today which could just as well be undertaken next week. Or some other week, for that matter.

They are not lazy, though, not at all. The fishermen work long hours in the wildest of weather; the tradespeople struggle with the roaring tide of summer folks. Nevertheless there never seems to be any pressure about anything.

The clammers came in, with a pailful of clams. The chowder was under way in no time, salt pork diced and browned, onions sliced, potatoes cut up while the clams were ground medium-fine in the grinder. Then the simmering, then the hot cream. Plenty of true chowder crackers split and buttered and warmed. Plenty of coffee.

Later on Glenn sang his concert, standing by the fireplace, looking as poised in his old blue jeans and plaid shirt as if he were appearing with full orchestra in the most elegant concert hall.

I like to hear his new songs very much, but I also want all the songs I ever heard him sing, and as Burton points out, that covers a lot of time. He just can't sing everything he has ever sung all at once!

After he finished, Margaret leaned forward and said sharply, "Young man, is your voice insured?"

Glenn grinned. "No," he said, "but my outboard motor is!"

Which I felt was a very good summing up of his fisherman who happens to sing like an angel.

After the singing was over, Burton fixed a hot toddy and we were very merry talking the good talk of people at ease. The tide was coming in, laying a line of dark silver on the sand, a high fall tide, very slow and strong and beautiful. The gulls were crying, and the light over the horizon was mother-of-pearl.

Today I laid in a good supply of orange-and-black jelly beans and candy corn, together with small boxes of raisins and little bags of peanuts. Before we know it, All Hallows' Eve will be here.

When our children were small, Halloween at our house was strictly a family affair. It was a time for funny masks — nothing very scary — and homemade costumes. The door-to-door trekking was brief, and a parent always hovered in the background as the small ghosts and pint-sized clowns made their rounds. Connie and Barbara used to argue. "It's my turn to be the witch this year." "No, it's mine. You did it last year." David quietly stuck to being a tramp. I think the dirty-face part appealed to him. We had plenty of cider, of course, and a bowl of apples to bob for and a big plate of freshly made doughnuts. And in the front window, a cheerful pumpkin face with a rather lopsided grin.

Now I am glad to see that the grandchildren are growing up in the same tradition. My own branch of the family is here this Halloween. The jack-o'-lantern is finished and Connie is drying pumpkin seeds for the bird feeder. Curt sprawls flat on the floor with a borrowed sewing machine. He learned to sew in his bachelor days and now he is stitching some strips of sheeting for Alice, who plans to be the Ghost of Stillmeadow. Small Anne is propped nearby, watching with fascination. The dogs have been shut out temporarily and they whuff curiously at the crack, but the cats have retired sensibly upstairs, where it is quiet. They will all reappear later in the evening, when the children have finally been tucked in and the grown-ups have settled down in front of the fire to watch the last embers and wait for the Halloween candles to burn out softly.

As October ends, the air begins to smell of windfalls that have been frosted. The leaves drift down, and most of the branches are bare. We see more sky. Night shuts down early. I miss the long summer twilights, when day seems to linger indefinitely. But the mornings have a sparkle, and I love to see the shadow of the house silver with frost when sun has melted the rest of the crystals on the lawn.

Next week, I think, we might take the screens off.

Eleven

Now in November, the leaves spread a cloth of gold and red on the ground. The open fields take on a cinnamon tone and the wild blackberry canes in the swamp are frosted purple. The colors fade slowly to sober hues. The rain falls with determination in long leaden lines, and when it stops, water drips from the eaves. The voice of the wind changes, for winds are seasonal too. Summer winds blow soft, musical with leaves, except for thunderstorms. Hurricane winds scream. In blizzard time the sleet-sharp gale has a crackling noise. But now the wind has a mournful sound, marking the rhythm of autumn's end. The first beat of winter is not yet here, and country folk tend to spend extra time doing chores or puttering, just to be out of doors.

When Indian summer comes, nothing indoors seems important. I must carry my breakfast tray to the terrace and eat in the wine-bright sun. There is always a haze on the hills, making them dreamlike. Perhaps it is such an enchanted time because it is a promise that another summer will come, after winter goes. Actually there is no set date for Indian summer; it comes when it is ready. Sometimes it seems to come after a cold spell in October, but it may even come around Thanksgiving. The later it comes the better, I think — like an extra dividend.

Usually it ends with a swift drop in temperature and grey skies. Frost whitens the lawn and too soon snow lace drops on the bushes. We proceed with November.

Every month has its special kind of rain. In November, the rain is so steady, so determined and so fearfully grey. It can rain so hard in our valley that it looks as if a wall of water were advancing; you cannot see a hand's length ahead. The sky is pewter. The roads run with water and the brooks make a thunder down the hill. George's barnyard gets flooded and he wades hip-deep with his boots flooded, his oilskins dripping.

This is hard weather for cockers and Irish, particularly for Irish. Holly keeps sloshing in and out, racing around the yard, racing in the house. She reminds me of a child: "What can I do now, Mama?" And I wish I could get her interested in a crayon book or cutting out paper dolls.

Little Sister is very philosophical; she just goes to sleep. I suspect this is an ancient wisdom we would all do well to copy. Work on a fine day, Sister would advise, and when it is a terrible day, rest. Her small black-and-white cocker figure looks almost like a Staffordshire figurine as she lies so still.

But the third day, usually, the wood gives out. This makes everything just dandy. We sally forth for logs that look as though they were brought up from the bottom of the sea, and burn equally well. Even the cannel coal for the front fireplace is getting low. There is water on the windowsills. The icebox looks as if a fire sale has been going on in it. In short, there is nothing good in anything.

I finally decide to go out for some shingles to revive the fire, and I get out last year's ski pants. I can't get them around my middle this year! No amount of breathing in or pushing or struggling will get me inside those pants. The awful implications in this literally drive me distracted. It is the zero hour.

Then the next morning, when I wake up and look out, I see it is raining even harder. It isn't possible, but it's true. As I watch the long lines of water fling themselves at the soaked world, all at once I feel a reluctant kind of admiration creeping over me. Nature is nothing if not thorough, I think. An all-or-nothing girl.

It is dramatic the way this rain builds up and builds up. The weather is so foul, it is beginning to be exciting.

I climb into my old corduroys, wrap up my head and go right on out. I suppose I feel vaguely the way Alpine guides feel as they pick out a nice slippery glacier and mount it. The rain soaks right through everything, and the yard is a running swamp. Go on, see if I care! I slosh down the road for the mail.

And it is very beautiful just because the rain is so intense. The world is nothing but water. George Bennett, our postman, drives up and reaches to get the mail out with a long arm. His eyes smile, his wise Yankee face is framed in rain. Water swishes down the hood of his car.

"How long will this keep up?" I ask. "You think it might clear up tomorrow?"

"Well," he says, "might, and might not."

I feel perfectly content as I wade home. I also feel perfectly sure he knows just what the weather will be. But he won't commit himself. I respect the fact.

There is, of course, a good deal of pure

tripe written about us Yankees. As a reclaimed Yankee, I can count myself in on it. It was only an accident that I was born in Colorado and lived all over the country half my life — South, West, Middlewest and New York, which is a very special locale. It gives me a good deal of pleasure to recognize many of my traits as pure unadulterated Yankee. Close-mouthed. Mind your own business and never rush in and try to push people around your way. Never talk big about tomorrow's eggs.

Washed back into the house, I am laughing to myself about a nice exhibition of it last week when, at a neighborhood party, one man asked another if he got his haircuts in Woodbury. There was a full five-minute silence. Finally, having revolved the whole question pro and con, the second man delivered his answer.

"Well," he said slowly, "no."

After the foretaste of winter, we usually have a brief reminder of summer.

It is so warm today that all the doors and windows are open. I wish somebody would settle for me when Indian summer is supposed to be. So far we have counted five Indian summers this season — a tribal procession decked in scarlet leaves. There was that hot spell in October when we decided we could have one last swim before packing away the bathing suits. It was a mistake; there was no summer in the trout stream, Indian or otherwise. Then there came a vigorous bout with winter, followed by three more deceitful Indian summers. And now in November, comes this blissful drowsy weekend. Probably it is the papoose of them all, trailing after the tribe.

For some reason this weather reminds me of another morning, just like this one, years ago when the children were small. I sat on the old stone steps that morning, paring potatoes. Star, the black cocker spaniel, sat beside me. Whenever I lifted my eyes to watch the smoky blue haze over the Connecticut hills, Star stuck her muzzle in the pan and flew away with another potato. She was a quick little thing; of all the cockers, she moved fastest and thought of more things to do.

The three children had taken the rest of the kennel up the meadow. I heard their voices, diminished in the soft November air. The sun was warm as melted honey, but Connie was wearing her winter coat anyway. Her passionate love for that coat had nearly driven me frantic. She wore it well into May, until I hid it. Immediately upon its appearance that fall, she gave a cry of joy and got into it. She wore it up the meadow, her face red with heat but her eyes serene. She guessed she could wear it in November.

Barbara, then eleven, went along garbed in sleeveless cotton, short socks and tennis shoes. She wore this costume all winter, whenever she could get away with it. David, at nine, felt that the well-dressed gentleman always appeared in either a fireman's suit or the Lone Ranger get-up.

As they came back, they were talking about school.

"Are you scared of your new grade?" asked Connie.

"No. I'm not scared, but my stomach is," said Barbara.

There must have been more important

days that November but this is the one I remember.

Teatime comes early at Stillmeadow now. I hang the kettle over the embers, bring out the toasting fork and open the sweet-clover honey.

My mother and I used to have tea every afternoon when I was growing up. At first I had cambric tea, but later I grew up to a real cup. She used her mother's old silver teapot, and I use it now, and when I sit down by the apple-wood fire and pour the tea from that little fat teapot, my mother seems very close to me.

Mama liked strong black tea. Last year Jill and I got one of those tea taster's packages and tried to decide which was really the best. And I confess I loved every one of them. Earl Grey is very special, but so is Darjeeling. I like smoky teas and jasmine-scented teas and every other kind.

The teapot must be boiling hot when the tea goes in. And the tea should steep four or five minutes. Thin slices of lemon pricked with cloves are all right; so is colored sugar. But for a family tea, we pour it out and drink it without anything in it. Just tea.

My Aunt Minnie, at well over seventy, always takes a thermos of tea with her when she goes after her annual deer. Last fall, the menfolk in her family suggested gently that she really should retire from hunting. But she said that she wanted to go along, just for the fresh air. Then while they went trudging off through the hills, Minnie eased herself down on a fallen log to rest her knees and enjoy the autumn woods. Of course it was not just any fallen log — it was right beside what looked to her like a deer trail. She was just putting down her gun and reaching for her thermos when a single twig snapped. "And there he was, the best buck I've ever seen," she said later. "And if I hadn't been sitting there quietly, getting ready for my tea, I'd have missed him."

I am always on the deer's side when it comes to hunting, but I know that Minnie freezes enough meat to last her for months. And I am proud of her — nobody else got anything at all. Only

Minnie, sitting down, at teatime.

I understand the first tea bags, by the way, were made of silk and designed to provide samples of tea for people to try out. I wish they had stayed that way. I do not like my tea flavored with string and paper or cheesecloth. It's perfectly simple to use the leaves, and then you have true tea. The delicate leaves need free motion in the freshly boiled water to infuse their fragrance.

When a mild day comes in fall, I inevitably consider airing things, and Erma discusses the preholiday cleaning with me as we sit at the counter drinking coffee. My tendency is to throw all the tea-colored ruffled curtains in the dump. Not at all, says Erma firmly. She will do them by hand and they will last another season. I mention painting the white woodwork, now grimy and black with prints of small hands. Not at all, she decides, she will wash it and it will go another round. I tell her the washing machine has broken down again, and she gets down on her knees and opens it up and communes with it and extracts a dry quart of diaper lint. It then works. No use spending money, she says. I wouldn't want to add up the money Erma has saved us, but I suppose it would almost pay for a trip to London.

In the early days at Stillmeadow, Jill and I got the mattresses out every fall. Freshens them up, she said. When they were laid in the sun a bevy of cocker puppies bounced on them with cries of joy. It was rather like trampoline practice. We hung the rugs on the picket fence and every puppy tugged at the fringes.

"I'm not sure we are really accomplishing much," Jill said.

We've given up on mattresses and the nine-by-twelve braided rug. But everything easy to carry goes out and gets freshened up in the old-fashioned way. Erma, who helps with this project, agrees with me. The dryer is fine in winter, when sheets freeze before you can put on the clothespins outdoors, but now the wash is hung out in the golden air. We do not iron the sheets either; we let the smell of sun stay with them, along with the whiff of pine.

Around the first week in November, we realize that Christmas is imminent. We begin making lists, worrying over sizes. I am determined to get a small portable electric oven for Connie, whose gas stove blows up every time she turns it on. I know she sits with one hand on the oven door as she roasts something, just to be sure. But how do I know the current in her old apartment house will support this gadget? I read the ads, but they never give the wattage or whatever.

Jill goes around dreamily saying, "I wonder if David and Anne would really be able to use an electric frying pan?"

We have done better since we devised the Christmas chest. This is a pine blanket chest which we emptied of all the old linens and silver stored away there. In it we put things which we suddenly find are *just* what we wish to give for Christmas.

The idea did not originate with us; it is Faith Baldwin's, for she spends all year buying Christmas gifts. She will send a cryptic note in mid August saying, "I found your Xmas gift — did it up."

This gives one a long time to wonder, but is a very sound way to operate.

Planning ahead for Christmas is all very well, but rushing the season is not. November has its own holiday, after all, and it is one of the most beautiful.

For Thanksgiving the house is gay with massed greens in the big copper bowl, with harvest vegetables piled in the old wooden dough tray, with red corn hanging against the mellow pine by the fireplace. Apples and raisins and nuts brim the bowls on the coffee table by the fire; the cheese board is decked forth with pale Swiss, bright Cheddar and creamy Port Salut.

Jill blisters her fingers on the chestnuts for the dressing for the plump turkey, but decides chestnut stuffing is worth it. When the turkey roasts, the savory smell of sage and chestnuts drifts from the kitchen and the onions glazing in honey and catsup add their fragrance.

The children are all at home for the weekend, including Anne, my youngest granddaughter, rosy and sweet as a young apple blossom. She is now over a year old and busily absorbing every detail of this strange and wonderful world. We naturally see signs of very surprising genius in her every gesture, and I am reminded of that doting mama who kept saying "Look at my baby breathe!"

Well, it is pretty wonderful to breathe, at that.

Alice (Muffin) is old enough to set the table and she moves around it with grave dignity, laying out the silverware in perfect rows and tucking a sprig of cedar next to each napkin. This was her own idea and makes the table look very festive.

The onions and mashed potatoes, the pumpkin and mince pies, are traditional. The turnips are beaten to a fluff, dressed with melted butter, salt and pepper. Now the younger members of my family simply loathe turnips and squash, so one year I substituted their favorite peas-with-mushrooms. "Oh, Mama," cried my daughter in anguish, "it has to be turnips for Thanksgiving!" They were all outraged. They said I couldn't go around changing Thanksgiving, for goodness sake.

So I went back to the big bowl of turnips which they do not eat. They were satisfied emotionally anyway.

The children sit quietly while I talk over with God that blessings we have, but I note they lift knife and fork the instant I raise my head. They are, I reflect comfortably, just as hungry now as they were when they were very little, and went out after dinner in bunny suits.

A family holiday, such as this, gives one a chance to estimate the changes in the children. As we pass the plates heaped with the crisply crackling turkey, mellow and delicate under the skin and golden brown on top, the conversation seems like a montage of their lives.

That serious young intern, surely only yesterday he was asking, "Who is the leader of the stars?" The gay young mother, yes, she was the very one who fell off her bicycle and flew through the air a mile a minute. And Connie, as she relates some riotous happenings in her class at Columbia, must be the same little girl that came home from kindergarten and said, "Mama, T. J. kissed me. You know, he's the one with the lavender up-top."

Sometimes one wishes they were little again, yet on the whole I think it is so rewarding to know them as equals that I would not really wish the romper days back. Still, every mother must feel that occasional ache for her child's baby days, and in retrospect even pushing spinach through a sieve seems fun.

After Thanksgiving dinner, the house simmers down to quiet. It seems cozy and natural to hear muted voices from all over, the baby upstairs waking up, Connie and David talking, David's wife tuning the guitar and humming. With all the food around, I reflect comfortably, we won't need to get another sit-down meal — they can raid.

Naturally in a very few hours, there is a kind of stir.

"When are we going to eat?"

"It is almost suppertime?"

"Mind if I eat a little more chestnut stuffing?"

So I say they can help themselves, and before I know it, trays appear with salad, turkey sandwiches, cranberry sauce, hot coffee. And wedges of Wisconsin cheese on the side.

"Are you sure you can't eat anything?" asks Connie.

"Well, just a bite of turkey," I say weakly. So we all overeat quite happily. Someone says, "Perhaps cold is better than hot."

Later on Curt adds another apple log to the fire and we sit toasting our toes against the November chill while the bowl of apples and nuts goes around and one of the family brings out the old corn popper.

Of course, Thanksgiving is far more than the family dinner and the national festival. All people have always had harvest celebrations of one kind or another, so there is nothing distinctive about a feast time after the crops are in. But our Thanksgiving seems very close to our relation with God. It has a deep religious significance not always spoken of but, I think, felt.

I like to slip away for a brief time and sit by the pond on the one bench left out all winter. If it is a warm hazy day, the sun is slanting over the hill with a gentle glow. If it is cold, the wind walks in the woods. I think of everything I have to be thankful for, and it is a long list by the time it is added up. I am thankful for love, and friends, and the family gathering together. For starlight over the old apple orchard. For the chilly sweetness of peepers in April. For my winter birds, so brave, so hungry, and particularly for my little chickadee with the bent wing who bangs away at the suet cake right while I type. He cocks a shining eye at me and seems to say, "Life is really what you make of it, eh?"

I am thankful for music and books. And for the dogs barking at the gate. Well, there are so many things to be thankful for that the list is infinitely long.

And it is good to take time to be thankful, for it is all too easy to let the world's trouble sweep over one in a dark flood and to fall into despair.

I am always sorry when the Thanksgiving weekend is over. After Thanksgiving it will be winter, and I don't feel I had enough sweet corn or garden-ripe tomatoes, or enough summer, or for that matter enough of October's bright-blue weather. I am reminded that I never did order those Christmas cards last August and now it is probably too late.

It snowed yesterday, in a careless sort of way, and afterward the yard looked like a Christmas card sprinkled with bits of sparkle. This may be what brought Christmas cards to my mind. Today the sun came out and the air warmed, and Christmas did not seem to imminent. But it was windy, almost like March, and I had the illusion that there might be snowdrops in the border if I looked. Instead, I looked for bittersweet and found a few berries overlooked by birds and travelers. Bittersweet should be picked earlier, when it is orange and just opening. It darkens to a Chinese red as it stays on the vine. And it should be hung upside down to dry, or it just lies down when you make a bouquet of it.

One year, before our vines had been ruined, I used bittersweet with hemlock for the mantel for the holidays and it was lovely. It is a pity that so many of Nature's special children are killed, for if you pick carefully and pay attention to the vine or bush or tree, it does no harm. People tear off branches of apple blossoms, for instance, leaving a ragged end as a good place for rot. And rip up the bittersweet by the roots. They dig up shrubs too and in return leave eggshells, beer cans and all sorts of trash. A kind of madness comes over some Americans when they are away from home.

The strange thing is that country people will give travelers almost anything, provided the taking does not destroy. It is common for gardeners to pick an armload of zinnias and present them to anyone who stops to admire them. Or to cut apple blossoms where it will not damage the tree, or give away lilacs or roses.

"Ask and it shall be given you" is a good motto, better than "Take what you can pilfer."

Gardeners love to share. We planted some special lilacs some years ago and Jill used to dig up shoots annually to give away. The Borlands never come without a carton of their special treasures. We put in Steve's iris and Alice Blinn's blue hydrangeas and eventually gave some of them away to other gardeners. This sharing makes a garden a friendship affair.

Perhaps the givingest gardener I know is Helen Beals. She is so generous that she will give away her choicest blooms, even if it leaves her garden ragged.

"Come and dig up whatever you want," she says.

The first time she came to call, she brought a bucketful of rare dark Persian lilacs such as we had never seen. In season, she not only brings flowers to her friends but arranges them in a container. She also brings gaiety and warmth and comfort, if you need it.

She seems to sense when I am depressed.

"Come over," she will say, "and I'll put forty-four beans in your cup."

And I start to feel better immediately.

While the children were here, I spent a good deal of time watching Anne practice walking. She goes from the sofa to the chair and then carefully back. When she falls down, she thinks it highly amusing.

So many things strike her as funny. I hope she keeps this sense of humor, for it is the best defense against the stress of life. It is truly the saving grace.

Often when dire events happen, it helps to remember they will be a fine source of amusement later on. For instance, we went to a great deal of the effort one year to put up brandied peaches. We spent a whole hot day at it. Someone, some time, had said the best treatment for brandied peaches was to bury them in the ground for a time. So we did just that. Jill dug a nice hole in the vegetable garden in a row that was empty.

"I wonder whether they should stay six months or six weeks?" she asked.

"I can't see what the ground does for them that the fruit cellar couldn't do," I said. "It's cold and dark there too."

We finally decided to dig up a jar or two for the Christmas holidays. Jill went out and was gone some time. When she came in she looked discouraged.

"Maybe you don't bury peaches except in tropical climates." She took off her mittens. "Ground's frozen like granite," she said, "Maybe we can have brandied peaches on ice cream for Easter dinner."

Winter passed; the ground thawed. I was peeling potatoes one day when Jill came and stood in the kitchen doorway.

"Thought I'd go out and dig up a jar of those peaches." Her voice was casual.

"Fine. We can use them when Steve and Olive come for dinner."

"Fine." She still stood there, and then said, "By the way, did you watch me when I buried them?"

"No. I was hunting for that missing batch of check stubs you wanted."

"I started to put them at the edge of the asparagus bed," she explained, "but I decided not to, I think."

Now I dropped a potato, which Holly bore off in triumph. She loves to snatch potatoes.

"You mean you can't remember *where* you buried them?"

"Now, don't get excited. I know the general area."

"Be careful you don't crack the glass," I called after her.

Then I sneaked to the back-kitchen window and looked out. Jill was wandering here and there, sometimes sticking the spade in, then pulling it out. She had the abstracted air of a water dowser. She was certainly in the general area — she was in the vegetable garden, which is the only place in which you can dig. The rest is merely one stone upon a bigger stone. But the vegetable garden was then about a quarter of an acre or more.

I watched her take up a spadeful by the corn patch, then move toward the raspberry rows. It occurred to me with some horror that when the garden was harrowed, our peaches might be harrowed too. By now, Holly was beside me, resting her paws on the windowsill and peering out earnestly to see what I was looking at. I persuaded her to go away and I went back to the stove.

When Jill came in, I didn't say a word.

"Someday I suppose this will be funny too," she said fiercely. "But do not mention peaches to me for a long, long time."

It was a bitter blow to her, for she was the organized one, the labeler, the filer of papers, the drawer of garden diagrams.

Now the strange fact is, those peaches never turned up. The garden was plowed every year, harrowed, raked, planted. Rocks worked their way through the soil every season, as always. I borrowed spadefuls of good dirt every spring for my violet-transplanting project. But not a shred of glass or a peach pit ever made an appearance.

It was a winter evening some years later when we were popping corn over the open fire and talking of projects for next spring. Jill poured melted better over the popped corn.

"What do *you* think happened to those peaches?" she asked.

"They just went away," I answered. "The Borrowers took them. They must have had a fine party."

Connie and Curt had just introduced me to Mary Norton's book about these mysterious wee people who make off with a single glove or a button or the big spoon of the salad-serving set. Sometimes they take a favorite handkerchief, and sometimes they make off with a bottle opener. Now and then it is a book or a special record. Whatever they need, they take, and you never see it again.

The jars of peaches were their biggest haul, and they had to work for them, for they had to dig, and dig in the exact spot.

"Well, whatever the explanation," Jill said, "the whole thing really was kind of funny." And she laughed.

After that, it was funny, and became one of our favorite stories. We called it the time the peaches went away.

One thing about November at Stillmeadow: the floors are flat again. All summer, when the warm dampness comes in the house, the old wide black-oak boards heave up, and by fall they undulate in every room. They were all right for generations, but when we filled those nice large cracks and made them tight, the floorboards began to rise. Then, when the furnace goes on, the cellar dries out and so do the boards. Gradually and gracefully they relapse into flatness and we can walk about once more without sliding up and down hill.

We are often advised to rip them all out and lay new level floors, or have them split lengthwise and relaid, but to date I have not been able to give up the handmade nails and the broad, beautiful widths of oak. I like to set my feet on the same floor that the house began with, or a reasonable facsimile thereof. Because I like the kinship with yesterday — to belong, in a sense, to the past. So we move warily until the furnace goes into action again.

I suppose you have to be terribly sentimental to be *en rapport* with all that an old house involves. For there are also the windows. Those little bubbly glass panes look like a dream, but of course the windows have no sash weights or modern fittings. To raise a window you brace yourself and heave and then you prop it up with a stick or a book.

We have one new window which we put in for an extra, and that window slides like grease. But I am not fond of that window personally. It is just a window.

The glass is strong and water-clear and the putty is firm. But the one next to it catches the light in a soft, bubbly translucence. And just has more personality for me.

Now at last the storm windows, which I hate, are on. The hooks in the back kitchen wear my storm jacket and raincoat instead of light sweaters. Erma scouts the fence to be sure there are no holes the right size for cockers to squeeze through. Joe rigs up his snowplow and stacks his woodpile high.

My tendency is to make lists. Most of them are questions.

Put on snow tires. When?
Antifreeze in car? Ask Joe.
Heat on in kennel? Or wait?
Still time to paint the well house?

I often get up in the night and add to my list. Somehow the main function of a list is to make me feel well organized. Practically speaking, they aren't much use, as I invariably mislay them. I make careful grocery lists and leave them behind when I go to the village. But it is nice to know that when I get home I'll know what I forgot because the list is under the coffee-maker right where I left it when I unplugged the pot. I put it back on the counter by the door and add to it.

As the season turns toward December, we are settling in. The woodpile high, the freezer filled, heaters ready to be lit in the kennels, snow tires on — we can face the world with a smile.

When the supper dishes are done, I decide against my nightly walk and simply stand at the open door for a while, watching the beaver moon over the dark maples.

The air smells of frost. The house is making the soft breathing sounds very old houses make at night. Embers glow in the fireplace, and Jill is cutting a snow apple in quarters as she happily rereads *The Nine Tailors*. Jonquil is practically in the fire, a little salamander. Holly is in the coolest spot by the batten door.

A good night, I feel, to read the cookbook Alice Blinn gave me and decide on a new recipe for tomorrow.

Twelve

The first big snowfall is worth having
winter for. Comes the morning when Jill
looks up from her buttermilk pancakes
and says, "Look — this is it."

First a few tranquil flakes float down,
then they come faster, and with purpose.
The old grey-stone walls silver over, the
swamp wears a mantle whiter than foam.
The pine trees on the slope begin to cast

feathers of snow from their branches. Inside the house there is a curious luminous look to everything, and outside the sharp etchings of November begin to blur.

Jill finishes her third cup of black steaming coffee and climbs into her winter costume. She doesn't get sewed into it, as they used to sew children into long underwear, but it does seem a part of her from now on: the short fleece-lined coat, the furry boots, the woolen tam and the lamb's wool gloves. She flies to the kennel now to check on the heaters and let everybody out for a run in the white mystery.

I struggle out to the bird feeders, laden with a pail of cracked chick feed, half a pan of sunflower seeds, three slices of crumbled bread, two hunks of creamy suet, and a portion of wild-bird seed. Managing this load is no mean feat, and I seldom have good luck because Holly tries to help me and lunges at me, especially toward the fresh delectable suet. I fend her off with my elbow and slide along on the snow.

The air is so full of birds one could

think them larger snowflakes. My chickadee with the bent wing waits impatiently and says so. Nuthatches and wood-peckers and blue jays and sparrows, including a solitary lark sparrow, a stray starling and a flock of juncos, are all there, hungry.

The pine trees flutter with wings. I feel as if I could fly myself if I just put my mind on it firmly enough.

We have all the kinds of bird feeders that we have room for, and the only one easy to fill is the one made out of an oil can which George Bennett designed and built and gave us. It is a ground feeder; you tilt up half the top and dump, and that is it.

The new green-roofed circular number is my despair. It has four parts and several screw things, and the minute I begin they all fall apart. After I have successfully put it in shape and then attempt to insert the seed in the hole on top, the bottom falls off and all the seeds go down into the snow. Since I can't work the screws well with mittens, I am now quite stiff with cold. But if I put down a single piece of this wretched thing, Holly leaps away with it — it is a fine romp.

The window feeder by my window has to be approached with caution when the dogs are away at the front gate hooting at George's dog. Otherwise I can't get at it, as the level is exactly right for eager paws. It is also a roofed feeder, so you have to spoon the feed in.

The two suet cages are almost higher than I can reach, but by jumping I can often make it and get part of the suet wedged in. Holly of course thinks this is some new kind of game and she whisks around me, barking encouragement.

The small chick feeder on the sugar maple in back is always full of frozen hulls which have to be pried out.

Finally I advance on the supposedly squirrel-proof feeder. It looks like a spaceship and swings suspended from a wire. We got it when we found that we simply could not keep up with the eight large matronly squirrels who were turning up every day. It is true that we discriminate, but they do seem stronger than the tiny neat chickadees and the earnest little brown creepers. Besides, there's always a snack of stale bread or broken crackers set out under the apple tree for them. The problem of filling this feeder without being smacked in the face by it or spilling most of the feed is so baffling that I sometimes give up altogether and wait for Jill or Joe to take over.

But after the birds are fed, I am ready to sit down and think about the joys of our feathered friends. If it continues to snow, the feeders will be empty by dusk, except for the suet cages. And the blue jays do their best by those, tearing out hunks as big as their heads and making off with them.

It all goes to prove, says Jill, that you only get out of anything what you put in. The birds, she adds, are about as much work as the dogs.

Nevertheless, we will drop anything to get the glasses and watch a new guest coming in for the winter. A solitary came in this year, all alone, looking like a sparrow but as if he had been half dipped in white paint. At first I thought he had been, in some way. Dived into a jar or something. But Jill got the book and studied it feverishly and we finally identified him as the lark sparrow. "An accidental," said Jill happily.

At first the other sparrows were terribly rude to him. They elbowed him away, flew at him with harsh words, nipped at him with angry beaks. This went on for some time, yet every day he came back and eased in around the edge of the flock.

A good lesson in perseverance, for in a week he was eating in the middle of the gang, and as he is larger, obviously getting the best of everything. They had accepted him. We have no idea how he came to be here, all alone and in a territory he shouldn't be in anyway, but there he is, and making a very good living for himself.

The nuthatch likes to eat upside down, and I spent some time this week watching a very strong-minded nuthatch trying to arrange it so he could eat from the green feeder which has that roof. He finally made it by curling his toes around the edge of the top circle of the roof and swinging down and grabbing. Now, I thought, any sensible bird would just stand on the floor and eat, but then there are a good many people who won't change their pattern either!

The chickadees may only seem more intelligent, but I think their little heads hold a good deal of wisdom. My little favorite comes to the feeder as I type and is no farther away than a pane of glass.

He sits down, bracing himself by his tail feathers, clings to the bars of the suet cage and rocks his head back and forth. He is actually sitting on his tiny little rear end, and looks absurd and enchanting. When he arrives and when he leaves, he sings so merrily *dee-dee-dee.* It is a sunny note, unlike the harsh dramatic blue-jay voice or the club-committee chatter of sparrows.

Our friends the Stephensons are as ardent bird fans as we are, and they are recent converts, being still city weekenders. Steve will call up in great excitement to say they have spent two hours at the picture window watching indigo buntings. A cardinal calls for a celebration. We can talk endlessly of our respective birds and let anybody else just sit and be ignored. We exchange bird-food knowledge. And Steve in his first mad enthusiasm began putting up nesting houses in January just in case!

Steve and Olive are, by profession, interior decorators, but let us get on the subject of birds and we never mention a color scheme or a decor — we talk birds. Steve reports that recently some of his chickadees have taken to tapping on the window if he is late putting out fresh seed, and yesterday one brave fellow perched on his shoulder and escorted him across the backyard. Before the winter is over, I expect, they will be literally eating out of his hand.

In December the winter sun burns like white fire on the snow. Ice glitters on the cold side of the branches of the sugar maples, melts on the warm side and falls with a soft sound. I do not know why white seems more pure as a color than green or blue, but so it is, and the countryside in winter has a purity we never see in any other season. Under the shell ice at the pond's edge, the water is like polished onyx. When I walk there, I follow rabbit tracks. The prints of small folk make delightful patterns everywhere in the snow, shortly overlaid by the prints of galloping cockers. Holly goes in great leaps and then rolls in the snow, reminding me of the angel wings we used to make when I was a child.

Sometimes after the third blizzard has whooped down, a few people say they have had enough and will certainly go to Florida next year. Next year they will say the same thing. But there is never a mass migration to Florida; only a few people go for a brief time. Most of the valley residents stay put.

"It's good enough for me right here," says my neighbor Willie. "Cold can't bother me."

Since Willie drives eighty miles daily in the course of his work, I was surprised.

"There's no place like Connecticut," says he firmly.

He spent some time describing the wonders of Connecticut to me. He and

Wilma had picked me up on the coldest night we had had, with a biting wind blowing and the thermometer about eight above. We were going to Savin Rock for a seafood dinner, and while the car was warm Wilma and I were quite stiff with cold just getting in and getting out.

"Little cold does you good," said Willie.

The dinner was delicious; the coffee restored some warmth to me.

"May as well drive to the ocean," said Willie afterward.

The ocean was black and the wind was like a sheet of ice. The strip of amusement places was a ghostly, shabby sight. We were the only living beings in sight.

"It's not like this in summer," Willie said.

By the time we got home the wind had died and it was at least less painful to breathe. Some people, I reflected, would stay at home by the fire on such a night, but they would miss a lot. It is the people who give in to winter who have a dull time!

Now along the valley come the Christmas trees piled high in trucks. They used to come in wagons pulled by big farm horses. Now they travel faster but less romantically. Most of them come down from Maine, for Christmas trees are a special business nowadays. The roads are spicy with pine fragrance and the roadside stands have piles of trees beside them. Most of the trucks, however, are bound for the city and do not stop long. Many people hereabouts buy trees grown locally, on our own wooded hills, and some of us cut our own on our own land.

Jill planted a whole slope above the swamp with Christmas trees a number of years ago but we bought our trees just the same. This is a curious fact: if you plant a tree, you are not going to cut it down. You argue that it had better grow another year or two. Then it is doing so well — and is such a fine tree — why not leave it longer?

For a while we tried cutting trees in the woods above the pasture but we cut only where they needed thinning and this meant our Christmas tree was always lopsided.

We backed it against the wall on the scant side.

My husband used to take the three children up the hill, and it took forever to find a tree they could all agree on. The first was too tall; the next too thin; the next was warped. It was as bad as picking a picnic spot, when you lug the hampers for miles and finally collapse and eat where you fall, on an anthill in blazing sun. But at last Frank heaved the ax and, as he said, sort of gnawed down the tree. The cut end looked like a leftover set of false teeth, but the tree came home in style, with the children rendering Christmas carols. Barbara sang a monotone, David followed a tune of his own and Connie had some trouble with the higher notes as they proclaimed:

God rest you mer — ry, gen-tul-mun,
Let nothing you dis — smay . . .

The tree came in smelling of snow and spicy branches.

"To save us all from sinhecame," sang Connie.

And David said, "What's sinhecame?"

After the children were not at home to help drag the tree in, we gave this up and bought a tree someone else had cut and lugged. But we made sure it came from a tree farm, not from the wild land. I hate to think of the forests that have been laid waste down the years by ruthless cutting. It takes years to grow a tall lovely tree but not long to chop it down. It is better to buy a living tree which can be set out after the holidays, but in the city this isn't possible. Even a country yard may not have room for more trees. And children need Christmas trees, and not artificial ones either. The artificial ones have no fragrance, and some of them play tunes, which is dreadful to think of.

For a tree is a symbol of life and a gift of Nature. It should come proudly into the house, smelling of the woods and sap. And after the holidays are over, it should leave pine needles to be swept up for days afterward.

Almost everyone has a love of tradition. I notice that those friends of mine who were raised without benefit of a traditional Christmas are the most dedicated when they have their own homes.

"This angel is *always* going on the top of the tree," said one to me. "It is going to be traditional."

I think it is a fine idea for young people to begin traditions. When they marry and perhaps live in a city too far to go home for Christmas, they can still hang the mistletoe in the doorway, light the bayberry candles, trim a table tree with gold and blue balls. Emotionally, I think most of us have a Currier-and-Ives feeling about Christmas, complete with sleighs, fur robes, prancing horses and Grandfather cutting the tree in his own woodlot. There should be plum pudding steaming on the old iron range. Grandmother is starting the roast beef. This is, in a way, an inherited Christmas memory.

In our family, turkey is only for Thanksgiving, and lamb, of course, is for Easter. But Christmas means roast beef with Yorkshire pudding and currant jelly.

But of course Christmas is primarily a thing of the spirit and can be observed anywhere, in any manner, if the spirit is there. Here in the country, we fortunately have no Santa Clauses on every corner. For one thing, we have no corners. I really think there should be a law prohibiting the flood tide of Santas that bedevil the cities and towns. It makes a mockery of good Saint Nicholas. He should not be seen, even once; he should be the one who comes down the chimney at night, mysterious and wonderful. The hooves of his reindeer paw the snowy roof. His pack just squeezes down the chimney.

What child is ever going to enjoy the delight of this when he has seen ten Santas in shabby costumes in all the stores all day long? Santa does not have to ride in from the North Pole at all — he can step out of the supermarket and go right down Elm Street, and there he is.

In our valley, so far, we have not made a mockery of Santa Claus. We have a giant evergreen in the center of the village, and this is decorated. Since we have no streetlights, we are spared the festoons of colored bulbs. The village store hangs wreaths in the windows, and the farmhouses have candles and wreathed doorways. Not far away is a town that has a competition for Christmas decorations, and this I deplore. It brings out cardboard Santas riding on the roofs, elaborate effects in the yards, some beautiful, some not. But I wish we could keep Christmas simply and with reverence as a spiritual time. Gay and festive it should be, but not a commercial enterprise or a carnival.

At Stillmeadow we use hemlock boughs from the upper woodlot to decorate the old narrow mantels. They are not sprayed with gold or silver. They are just green boughs, for it is the green of evergreen boughs that symbolizes immortality. For the tree, we use the old ornaments, including the lamb that some puppy once ate a portion of, and the shining tinsel, the delicate glass icicles. Then there are the tiny hand-carved birds that Rob and Bebe gave us and the painted unicorn from Faith and the merry Swedish angels from the Stephensons. Sometimes we loop the green branches with a rope of fresh cranberries, glowing like rubies. Best of all are the decorations the grandchildren have made — fat little stars and rather crooked Santas, shaped out of dough and baked in the oven. On top of the tree, as always, goes the same slightly tarnished silver star.

I set the red Christmas candles in the windows, but ever since the barn burned down I set them in saucers for safety. And we no longer have the bayberry candles burning away in the midst of a nice decoration of tinder-quick evergreens. Every year there are disastrous fires from tinsel and tissue paper, candles and pine needles, and it is strange that people never learn about fire hazards except by experience.

Connie has a crèche which she brings out, a tiny virgin and three admiring wise men and a well-fed lamb. I make a table decoration with a flat silver tray banked with cotton, silver and blue balls, sprays of silvery leaves to carry the design higher. Drinking from the silver ice stands my silver glass unicorn; a silver reindeer has just stepped to the snowy shore. I cannot resist popping the little penguin in, though he is not elegant at all. He points a surprised flipper at the unicorn. The whole little scene is edged with ground pine from the back hill.

Something very special happens in December. As the Christmas cards and notes arrive, I step briefly from my own life into the lives of people who are dear to me but far away. And, strangely, I move back in time with old friends. I am glad to know that Charlotte has another grandchild, but I see her as a girl with wind-tossed hair and laughter like golden bells. I am back in the parlor (for we had parlors in my small town), and she is playing by ear on a shiny upright piano. She is always playing "Maple Leaf Rag" because that is what I always ask for. It is good news that Harry has built a new house, but I see him again as a tall, long-legged boy covered with mud and making a touchdown on the football field. Peg is in California; the children are grown up. But I think of the long violet twilights when she walked home with me and then I walked home with her and then she walked home with me and then we both were roundly scolded by our parents for being late to supper.

I cherish too the greetings from new friends and those from friends I have never met except through letters. A good many Honeys were named for my golden Honey, as I wrote about her for fourteen years. And I always get pictures of the other Honeys who are still on this side of the door. Christmas was Honey's favorite time. She loved to sit and listen to the carols, she loved to help unwrap packages and she adored the Christmas cuisine. I often feel her shadowy presence, but especially around Christmastime. Her dark amber eyes and golden velvet muzzle are visible beyond the edge of the firelight, and it is a very comfortable feeling to know she is there overseeing Christmas as she always used to.

Whenever I start wrapping presents, Holly decides to help, and every time I tie a ribbon on a package, I nearly tie a red velvet nose with it. I remember my mother wrapping presents in just this way, only then it was my setter Timmie who used to help. As the season turned toward Christmas, Mama was busy making gifts for everyone who needed them. She had a fierce dedication to Christmas. It was, for her, a giving time. She felt it implied thought for the one you gave a gift to, not just buying something and wrapping it because it was the thing to do.

She was a noticing woman and she could spend all year noticing what some friend did not have and needed. Whenever I feel sad about the overcommercialization of Christmas, which has become such a big business, I think of Mama, happily wrapping the jars of quince preserve that one friend so loved. For the noncooks, she made the most elegant of fruitcakes. For prospective mothers, she made practical layettes, things she called "tubbable." But for me, she spent her saved pennies for a special book of poetry.

For my mother, Christmas was a time to express love and friendship. But then, so was all the rest of the year.

I always think of Father too at Christmastime. He was an erratic giver and an emotional receiver. I always get one gift that is so supremely thoughtful, so very dear, that I almost burst into tears when I open it. It may be a lavender sachet or a bottle of white lilac toilet water from someone who was remembered my love for lilacs — or it may be a camera, which I have yearned for for so long and and never mentioned. But there is always something. Well, Father would open something, and his brilliant lake-blue eyes would just brim over. He would say, cross as a woolly bear, "What's this? What's this?" and then, "It's too expensive. You shouldn't have done it."

Christmas brings all the generations together at our house, and as I look at the grandchildren, rosy as winter apples and merry as puppies, I remember the children elsewhere who are not so fortunate, whose lives are marked by poverty or, worse still, shadowed by war. Now, during the Christmas season, I pray long and earnestly that the babies of today may grow up to find a world released from war. I am told there has never been a time in all of history without war, but early wars were not like war today. The Revolution, for instance, was a bitter and devastating struggle, but it did not consist in blowing up the earth.

Now the science of war has reached the point of no return. The world could be demolished just by mistake if some bomb were to go off. And the careless way we are destroying our resources and polluting our environment is an even greater threat to our survival. *true—?*

But in this season it is well to reassert that the hope of mankind rests in faith. As a man thinketh, so he is. Nothing much happens unless you believe in it, and believing there is hope for the world is a way to move toward it.

"And suddenly there was with the angels a multitude of the heavenly host praising God, and saying, Glory to God in the highest, and on earth peace, good will toward men."

As we light the candles on Christmas Eve, these are staunch words to hold by. I must say that the latest New English Bible puts it in a sorry way: "All at once there was with the angel a great company of the heavenly host, singing the praises of God: Glory to God in highest heaven, and on earth his peace for men on whom his favour rests."

It sounds very pedestrian. But at least the word *peace* is left and isn't *nonaggression pact*. And how many heavens are there if we specify the highest one instead of just Heaven?

And I believe God's blessing is for all men, not qualified as to men on whom his favor rests.

In any case, the substance is generally the same, although I begin to wonder what the next new Bible will have to say! However, I have two copies of the King James Bible which I can hand down to Connie, in case it goes out of print under the impact of modernization. Meanwhile I can enjoy the majesty and poetry of the Bible as I have always known it.

Here at Stillmeadow we have always tried to have a tranquil Christmas Eve with the children gathered around the open fire, and Christmas carols, and marshmallows to toast. But in recent years Stillmeadow has been about as quiet as Grand Central Station at rush hour.

I find it hard to collect myself enough to answer Jill's grandson when he asks, "Does water ever get sour?" And this requires time. One difficulty is that the children seldom arrive until the day before Christmas, and then all at different times. They bring cartons of gifts, all of which are carried up those ladder-steep stairs, wrapped and carried back down (I do not understand this either). At times the traffic is so thick that I go outside the house and around it to get to the kitchen.

But after the babies are settled down "snug in their beds" and the five- and seven-year-olds have pinched all the packages and reluctantly, step by step, gone upstairs, some quiet reigns. The house smells of pine and spice and bayberry candles. The huge candle we first lit years ago still burns in the window, although it is much shorter. We used to warn David not to tip it over; now I warn him not to knock his head on a beam, for he is over six feet tall. He used to be able to get inside the great fireplace and stand up; now he has to bend way down to put a log on the fire.

As I look around the circle, I can hardly believe the children are grown up enough to be married and a new bevy of babies is coming along. I am thankful that the girls' husbands and David's wife, Anne, have only come into the family, not separated it. I think this is rare, and it is wonderful. They are all very verbal and they argue a lot, but it is a close warm unit, this family.

As always, the girls find out that they are giving me duplicate gifts, and this is our favorite family joke. One year was known as my Bach year, another the casserole year, one the pajama year. For weeks they consult and encourage me to say what I want, but since I like almost anything, it isn't much help.

I did make a mistake once as to duplicate gifts. I received three copies of the same book from three different friends. I laid two copies away in the Christmas chest and the following Christmas inadvertently gave back one of them to the friend who had given it to me. I was filled with remorse until the next Christmas, when I got the same copy back from the same friend! I put it away this time with a note: "Under *no* circumstances give this book to Clara."

Anyway, it showed we all liked the same book.

We no longer all go to the church service — the reasons not to are bedded down upstairs. Our babies, if they wake up, want their own mother or father to bring the milk or rock them. Muffin, my own oldest granddaughter, will go so far as lean against me and look up with a most enchanting smile, but she would raise the roof if I picked her up when she had a nightmare (I understand they have nightmares. About what, I can't imagine, since their lives couldn't be more secure or filled with love.)

Christmas morning begins at daybreak with the whispered shushings of the youngest members of the family as they tiptoe down to collect their stockings. They always find that Santa has tucked an orange into the toe as well as a few gingerbread cookies to help them survive until breakfast time. And there is also at least one book or quiet game to pass the interminable hours until the adults are able to wake themselves up.

Grapefruit and hot coffee cake for breakfast, and then on to the pile of presents beneath the Christmas tree. The gifts from the grandchildren are unwrapped with special care, and those from neighbors go straight to the kitchen: cookies, jelly, and lovely pickles from George's sister, Tessie. One of our best Christmas presents ever was a huge kettle of Bebe's soup, brought by the cook herself when she and my cousin Rob drove down from Massachusetts to spend the holiday with us. Rob brought his guitar, and while Bebe flew around the kitchen, he played carols for the children.

Christmas dinner comes late, after the tissue paper is strewn in drifts all over the house. This year I had cream of asparagus soup, followed by real Virginia baked ham, sent from the South, crusty with brown sugar, dark and rich, and cut paper-thin when served. But usually we have roast beef with Yorkshire pudding. Once we had a royal goose. But whatever the main course, we always stuff the cracks with Great-Grandmother's pudding. The recipe is in her faint handwriting, and calls for rolled cracker crumbs instead of flour, which makes the pudding light as well as rich. Plum pudding is often too heavy.

It seems as if nobody will ever eat again, but after an afternoon skating or sledding and hiking with the spaniels, the children will say sadly, "Isn't there *anything* in the house to eat?"

I like Christmas-night supper best of all, myself. Night walks around outside the house like a shadowy fawn, the fire burns bright on the hearth, and the tree glimmers with silver and gold. Galoshes and ski suits and mittens drip in the back kitchen; Teddy is chewing a wooden deer snipped from a low branch; Holly is in the kitchen investigating the possibility of getting a ham bone. Jill undertakes to clear a path across the living room; the children's voices drift down from the bedrooms.

So it is time for supper. Into the earthenware casserole goes a layer of creamed crab or fish, then layers of golden carrots, diced potatoes, half a minced onion. Then buttered crumbs and a deep layer of grated cheese. Into the oven while the cheese melts, the butter sizzles, and cream sauce bubbles.

I make oven toast, a rich crusty gold, and put elderberry jelly in the old majolica leaf-shaped dish.

Everything goes on the table at once, and everything goes.

And after dinner someone reads aloud Dickens's *Christmas Carol* or we play the record of Dylan Thomas's *A Child's Christmas in Wales*. The firelight flickers. The house smells of pine and hemlock.

I realize suddenly that I am very tired. For a moment, I wish it were just over. I wish it were August. And nothing at all going on.

And yet, when the children say, "Thank you for a wonderful Christmas, best we ever had," and one child whispers, "This was *just* all I wanted — how did you know?" and one child curls up to read the

the book you have chosen so carefully, and one says, "We never had such a Christmas," suddenly then all the tiredness ebbs away, and a pure happiness floods in.

At last everyone says goodnight. I hear the familiar sounds in the house: the breaking of a burned log in the open fire, the thud of Holly's paws as she comes in from the kitchen, Teddy's long sight as he settles down for the night. I hear Anne asking for a drink of water and Alice's elfin, flutelike voice saying something. I hear the footsteps coming down those ladder stairs and know Connie is going for fruit juice or milk or something — my grandchildren hate to sleep.

Then Curt appears for a last quiet chat, tall and handsome and looking boyish in his pajamas. The talk is idle, comfortable. Finally everyone is in bed, and I take my nightly look at the icicles hanging from the old well house, the drifts by the picket gate. The ancient white house with its steep roof and low eaves looks like a ship anchored in a still, white sea.

Christmas day is short but the memories

are long. The gifts and food, the candles and the tree, are not all, by any means. As I turn out the last light, I hear a glass ball fall from the tree and plop on the floor, exploding softly. The day has gone like the glass ball — the laughter and excitement are done, but as I sweep up the fragile bits of glass, I hope the memory of the day will remain a shining thing.

The slight sound has roused the dogs and they whisk outside. As I let them back in, I smell the snow. The walk is silver, the picket fence wears pointed caps. Night herself is luminous with the falling snow. A flurry comes in with the dogs and melts on the wide floor-boards. No two snowflakes, I am told, are exactly alike, and this is a mystery. Now the intricate shapes are gone, and only a spot of water remains. It is not very practical to stand in the open door at midnight and let the snow blow in. But it has been my habit for years to close Christmas day just so, sending my prayers out to all the people in the world, those I know well and love greatly and those I shall never see. And as I close the door, I repeat again my

496

Christmas blessing: "God rest you merry, gentlemen."

The time comes when the children go back to the city. The Yule log burns to ash and becomes a thing remembered. The Twelfth Night greens crackle on the hearth and then they too are gone. The Christmas tree ornaments are packed away and put in the attic. The old house settles with a sigh.

It seems very quiet with everyone gone. Jill decides to go to bed early with one of the books she got for Christmas. But I put my storm jacket on and step into boots.

The cockers and Holly are already at the door and rush out ahead of me. They all stop to munch snow and then roll in it. After that, they dash across the yard barking at nothing. I take a few steps feeling the snow crunch pleasantly. When the dogs quiet down, there is no sound at all. Stillmeadow is an island in the winter night but I can see three lights up the hill across Jeremy Swamp Road.

Winter has its own beauty for us who live with it. It is not recommended in travel guides unless for ski addicts, and there are no ski runs hereabouts that are famous, such as there are in Vermont and New Hampshire. Ski fanatics go right on north.

But the winter beauty belongs to us who battle the blizzards, get dug out of snowdrifts, undergo the misery of frozen pipes, the numb hands on the snow shovel. It is for us who buckle on the galoshes, wear two sweaters under storm jackets and watch our breath freeze as we go to the gate.

And we see the bare branches lovely with fallen snow or cased in ice which glitters when the sun comes out reluctantly. We see the meadows with blue shadows across the snow and we hear the brook water running softly under a sheath of ice. We know the beauty of a world dipped in pearl and we listen for the owl, melancholy and rabbit and the rare shape of a deer's hooves on new snow.

We see the delicate beauty of a winter sunset with pale green and lemon in the sky after the sun begins to sink. And we experience the splendor of moonlight on snow. Even on moonless nights the snow itself gives light, delicate and silvery.

And nothing can compare in any land in any climate with the way we feel when the snow melts, the brooks run free and the peepers make their chilly sweet song in the swamp. Without winter, we should not have the special miracle of spring.

Postscript

We were vacationing on Cape Cod in the cottage by the sea. It always reminds me of Byron's "cloudless climes and starry skies." If there were any warnings of disaster, I do not remember them. We were both, we admitted, tired, but we had put in a very busy year and we were justified in being tired. We sat and watched the tide come in and we sat and watched the tide go out. Holly was with us, and she was not tired at all.

She was running the beach all day except when she helped the clammers. When they clammed in deep water, she swam round and round them. If they were in shallow water, she stood up to her nose in the water and pounced whenever they tossed small clams back. Through the field glasses we could see she was waving her tail as best she could although it was underwater.

That night Jill and Holly retired early and I sat up to see the moon lay a gold path across the sea. "And straight was the path of gold for him, and the need of a world of men for me," I thought. But the moon is too feminine. I didn't like Shelley's sad moon climbing with slow steps either, for the moon is not wan and pale or sad. The moon is all things to all men, I thought.

The next morning, after we persuaded Holly to come from the beach and fill the back seat with sand and clam mud, we went across town and to the other side of the Cape to the doctor's to consult him about some minor complaint of mine. I forget what it was.

We had a habit of long standing of going to the doctor together. It began because I am timid about doctors, and Jill went along, and then I began going with her.

So she sat in the waiting room looking past the salt marshes to the shimmering blue water. The gulls went crying over. The sun was like new gold. There was no wind, which is unusual for the Cape. *Cod*

The doctor came out to visit with Jill; by then the waiting room had standing room only.

"Come in. I want to see you," he said, and Jill followed him to the inner office.

I hoped the other people in the room would not mind his taking a few minutes to talk to Jill, for they were old friends. I read the *National Geographic* and a couple of children's books. Time went on, and I thought that even if he had given her a shot for her asthma, she ought to be out. Holly began to bark at the doctor's ancient springer, so I went out and sat in the car with her. Several people came to talk to me, for the Cape is a place for talking.

When Jill came out, she slid behind the wheel silently and started for home.

"What were you talking about so long?" I asked.

"Oh, he wanted to take a blood count," she said. "I have to have shots for two weeks. But there's no use your coming over with me and wasting time. You stay home and get on with your book."

"What's the blood count for?"

"He thinks I have anemia," she said.

So I went on working on my novel. And Holly spent quite a lot of time sitting in the car outside the doctor's office. The weather grew hot, as it can even on the Cape, a good, baking hot. But nights were all moon-gold and salty-piny air. Jill asked me to hunt up an extra blanket.

I remember those two weeks as an interlude. I worked away on my book half a day every day and then we had lunch outdoors and talked idly about not much. We took Holly for rides, finding new hidden roads, coming suddenly at an end at a different beach. If the beach was a lonely one, Holly chased things a while and we picked up polished bits of driftwood or unbroken clam shells for ashtrays.

The day Jill went for her last shot, we planned to go out to dinner. We would have lobster, we said. I spent a full hour that afternoon trying to choose an outfit to wear. Something, I admitted sadly, was wrong with everything I owned.

Jill was late getting back. It was sunset, and the cottages on the point looked as if they were carved from gold.

"I'm going to the hospital tomorrow," she said calmly.

Jill always felt that bad news should be told right out, not deviously worked up to. She said it only made it worse to beat around the bush.

I sat down, saying nothing at all.

"I could do with some coffee," she said casually, starting for the kitchen. In the doorway she turned and said, "The shots didn't work." And added apologetically, "I'm sorry you'll have to get up early. I'm supposed to be there at nine thirty."

"But you can't," I said. "Your pajamas aren't ironed!"

I do not know whether this happens to everyone, but I always have channeled great shocks into as many smaller crises as I can think of. It's a natural defense, like throwing up breastworks against the enemy.

Jill has never been subject to this weakness. She gets right at the enemy. Now she said, "Never mind the pajamas."

"And besides," I said, "you have been wearing out old ones all summer."

"All right," she said, and laughed. "I'll tell them at the hospital all about my pajamas."

"We left the good suitcase at home," I said, "and you forgot your good bedroom slippers. Those calico things you got at the drugstore are *awful.*"

We had some sort of supper, probably liver, for we had been eating liver steadily for two weeks.

"The only thing that worries me," said Jill, "is how you and Holly will manage. If she follows anybody away, call up Millie and Ed. Don't try to chase her

505

yourself. Better get some extra money out of the bank. I'll only be gone a few days for tests and a checkup, so you can let things go until I get back. Just keep on with your book."

She went to bed early, because she said she wanted to feel fresh in the morning. After she had closed her door, I got out the ironing board and ironed all the pajamas she had. I am probably the world's worst ironer, and we only had a small portable iron with us. I kept telling myself that at least I would smooth those pajamas out, but they kept getting extra wrinkles in them and drops of sweat fell on them although I was numb with cold.

We left the Cape three weeks later on a day so beautiful I could hardly bear it.

"This hasn't been much of a vacation for you," said Jill as we crossed the bridge to the mainland. "But we'll come back and begin again, just as soon as I get through with the specialist. Anytime is wonderful at the Cape."

The night before she died, she said, "I wish we'd had time to say good-bye to everyone at the Cape. But we'll go back as soon as I get out of here. I'm sorry I've been such a nuisance."

"I'll be over early in the morning," I said.

Jill does not walk through the gate anymore, tall against the sunlight. I do not see her bending over the garden, or hear her humming as she gathers the vegetables. She was a quiet person, and only hummed or whistled when she was gardening or carpentering. I do not hear her steady footsteps on the old floors. I do not find her down by the pond scything the weeds at the swimming steps. The cockers and Holly no longer leap against her as she crosses the yard; they have given up leaving their choicest marrow bones on her bed. They like to be thanked for such attentions.

Where did the years go? Now there is nobody to remember them except me, for the children remember only certain things but not the whole. All the funny things, the wonderful things, the sorrowful things, that make up a shared life, are left to me, alone.

There is, or was for me, an anesthesia

of grief for a time. And then I woke up one morning and realized that every morning would be just the same. So would every afternoon and every night. A permanent winter season was in my heart. But this wasn't doing anyone any good. I had a greater responsibility than I had ever had, and the sooner I began to grow into it, the better. What it boiled down to, simply, was that I must live so as to justify Jill's faith in me, and making a world out of grief was not it.

I discovered if you take two steps forward and slip back one, you are still a step ahead, which is a cliché but a true one. I also discovered that if I could just survive the worst hours, there would be relief in the next ones. Like everything in this world, grief has a rhythm, and this is a great help to remember when even drawing the next breath seems an impossible task.

Almost always, during the bad times, Erma would appear and make hot coffee and tell me about the neighbors and the village news. Sometimes we went for a ride over the hills and along the river, and this got me over a silly phobia about leaving the house. I hope others do not have this; it is a hard one.

"Get your coat. We're going for a ride," Erma would say firmly, "and don't argue."

I saw the beloved valley, the low, sheltering hills, the Pomperaug purling over its rocky bed. I saw the white farmhouses and red barns and the rich meadows. And I realized that the world was wide and wonderful. I waved at children coming home from the swimming hole. And finally we went to the market, Jill's bailiwick for so many years. I am probably sentimental about our community, but the tact with which I was welcomed would hardly be equaled anywhere. Everyone was just plain glad to see me, but as natural as if I had been in every day.

And so, gradually, I emerged from limbo into life. Fortunately I have faith in God, and often I wonder how anyone can endure the loss of a loved one without faith. It would be unthinkable. My own praying was not always in words, because

I could not find them. But our young minister dropped in frequently. We hear a great deal of criticism of the church these days, and I venture to think the main trouble is that there are not enough ministers like ours.

When Hank Yordan comes he watches me make tea and insists that the water boil hard enough. Then we have three or four cups and he eats quite a few cookies and we talk about everything in the world from the Congo problem to remodeling the parish kitchen. We talk of the books we read and of what happened at the town meeting.

And then he says, "Shall we pray?"

Over the teacups, Hank voices all those words I have not been able to say to God, simply and quietly and with *no* oratory. It might be called a practical praying.

And then I brush Holly's hairs from his dark suit and he swings away, thin, smiling, easy.

"I wish I had your tea-and-cookie minister to drop in and pray with me," wrote a friend who had lost her husband.

The children, Jill's two and my one,

came with their families for weekends as often as they could manage it. This concerned me at first, for they all have full lives, and spare time is not in their vocabulary. They never heard of it. But then I began to realize that perhaps they needed, from me, a reassurance that the family was still a unit. There was, in a way, something to come home to.

And it seemed to me they grew in understanding overnight. Perhaps I hadn't known them before as adults, but now there were moments when they seemed as old as I am. Their children, tumbling around, widened my horizon so that I went ahead into their future in imagination. It's a wonderful thing to dream about the future of a child! It is like day beginning, glowing with sunrise.

As far as immortality is concerned, I think of Emily Dickinson, who wrote after her father's death, "I am glad there is immortality, but would have tested it myself before entrusting him." Some thinkers feel that man invented the idea of immortality as a kind of defense, and invented God because of an irresistible need to have a being to look up to. I cannot agree.

Someone has said we all hope for a cosmic address. I think that most of us do, and if we have faith, that is about all we need to hope for. There are, I would guess, hundreds of different heavens men have dreamed of. There are theories that after death the soul or spirit is absorbed into a sort of general consciousness. There are theories that personality continues to exist.

Much has been written about death, man's mortality being of special interest in this age when it might be universal and all at once for all mankind. The philosopher Henri Bergson said that man is the only animal who knows that he must die, which should add a quality of creativeness to life.

That word *knows,* I would argue with. If Bergson meant man has a general vague perception that the undiscovered country of death lies somewhere ahead, that may be. But I do not think most of us (who are not philosophers) ever realize death until it happens personally to us, putting an irrevocable period at the end of the sentence. We have had plenty of chance to realize it in our era, but we still usually go along pretending there isn't any such finality.

It is only, I think, when the focal point of our lives is gone that we begin to see the shape of death. And we are not prepared. We are no more prepared when the beloved has a long terminal illness than when death takes five minutes in an accident.

And Emily Dickinson summed up the feeling most of us have about what happens after death.

As for me, I believe we never lose those we have loved. I believe in God, or if you wish, an infinite power, for otherwise existence is meaningless, a casual happenstance. I believe in the basic goodness of life, and that love is stronger than hate, although often it does not seem so. I believe that eventually good overcomes evil and that we are put on earth for a purpose which has to do with love and with good. And I believe in faith.

Faith is the evidence of things hoped

for, and the substance of living. With faith, we may face the fact of death and not be defeated.

At least, so I have found it.

Sometimes I go away by myself, up the hill, far enough from Stillmeadow so that I only see the slope of the roof almost lambent with sunset. Holly may come along with me, for she does not disturb the aloneness.

From the upper abandoned orchard the yard is partly visible, dotted comfortably with cockers and cats. If there are guests or children at home, and there usually are, the sound of their voices comes dreamily from the open space where the lawn furniture is.

Somewhere, someone is forever pounding a typewriter; the sound of the typewriter never ceases at Stillmeadow.

There it all is below me, this little world within a world, and I sit down on a warm grey ledge upholstered with feathery lichens and think about it in relation to the rest of the world.

The terrible suffering that man is

undergoing all over the earth is like a tidal wave to overwhelm civilization. If we think of this, what can we find in the whole round turning earth to make any life good?

The intolerance sickens the soul. Race against race, caste against caste — by what dreadful arrogance could I believe myself better than another woman because my skin is pale?

But here in the country we may establish one small territory dedicated to love instead of hate, and possibly that is why we were born. And just possibly when all men have homes, hate will diminish all over the world.

Looking down on Stillmeadow I see the years that have gone, and the mark of them is a good and kindly mark, for the trees have grown, and the lilacs are spreading graciously. When Nature devastates the whole yard full of old and lovely apple trees, she begins new life the next season with young maples, and that year the mallows are as big as full moons.

If I were a wise woman, I should understand many things about life which

I do not now understand. Maybe I would know why there is so much evil walking the highways, why men must suffer, why the governments operate like kaleidoscopes instead of like good blueprints for living, why gentle people must die too soon.

I think about all these things, up in the old orchard with Holly's muzzle soft in my hand. And about the first people who owned Stillmeadow's forty acres more or less. What dreams they had of a fair world with liberty and justice for all.

And suddenly I know. I know there is a dream that will not die, and that Stillmeadow, in a small and quiet way, is an affirmation of that dream.

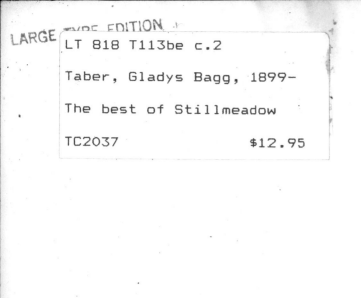

A149